MOVIE
PSYCHOS
AND MADMEN

MOVIE PSYCHOS AND MADMEN

Film Psychopaths From
Jekyll and Hyde to Hannibal Lecter

by John McCarty

A CITADEL PRESS BOOK
PUBLISHED BY CAROL PUBLISHING GROUP

A Citadel Press Book
Published by Carol Publishing Group
Citadel Press is a registered trademark of Carol
Communications, Inc.

Editorial Offices: 600 Madison Avenue, New York, N.Y. 10022
Sales and Distribution Offices: 120 Enterprise Avenue, Secaucus,
N.J. 07094
In Canada: Canadian Manda Group, P.O. Box 920, Station U, Toronto,
Ontario M8Z 5P9
Queries regarding rights and permissions should be addressed to
Carol Publishing Group, 600 Madison Avenue, New York, N.Y. 10022.

Carol Publishing Group books are available at special discounts for
bulk purchases, for sales promotion, fund-raising, or educational
purposes. Special editions can be created to specifications. For
details, contact Special Sales Department, Carol Publishing
Group, 120 Enterprise Avenue, Secaucus, N.J. 07094.

Portions of this book were originally published in *Psychos: Eighty Years
of Mad Movies, Maniacs, and Murderous Deeds* by St. Martin's Press (1986)

Designed by Paul Chevannes

Manufactured in the United States of America
10 9 8 7 6 5 4 3 2 1

Library of Congress Cataloging-in-Publication Data

McCarty, John, 1944–
    Movie Psychos and Madmen: film psychopaths from Jekyll
and Hyde to Hannibal Lecter / by John McCarty.
        p.   cm.
    "A Citadel Press book."
    Includes bibliographical references
    Filmography
    ISBN 0-8065-1392-6
    1. Horror films—History and criticism.   I. Title.
PN1995.9.H6M328   1993
791.43'616—dc20
                                                    92-37552
                                                    CIP

For my wife, Cheryl—
with love and gratitude
for her devotion to the cause

ACKNOWLEDGMENTS

I wish to express my gratitude to the following people and organizations for their many kindnesses and invaluable cooperation in putting together this book on movie psychos:

ABC-TV
Academy of Motion Picture Arts & Sciences
Eric Caidin (Hollywood Book & Poster Company)
CBS-TV
Mary Corliss (Museum of Modern Art/Film Stills Archive)
Walter L. Gay
Bruce G. Hallenbeck
Hammer Films (Roy Skeggs)
Alvin H. Marill (Carol Publishing)
Dave Marshall (Marshall Video Service, Trenton, Michigan)
NBC-TV
Jerry Ohlinger's Movie Material Store
Lori Perkins
Time Warner
Turner Entertainment
Tise Vahimagi (National Film Archive)
Allan J. Wilson (Carol Publishing)

Photo Credits

CONTENTS

Psycho murders abound in Pete Walker's appropriately titled *The Flesh & Blood Show* (1973).

8

FOREWORD

I first became aware of John McCarty when I was flicking through his book *Splatter Movies* and found my name listed in the index. He'd referred to some of the low-budget British horror films I wrote in the seventies.

I was astonished that an American writer knew of these films. They had gone largely unnoticed on double-bills at the time of their original release and, by 1984, when *Splatter Movies* was published, were all but forgotten.

Today, of course, it is inconceivable that any film, no matter how cheap, sleazy, and ineptly made, could ever be forgotten. Thanks to the arrival of video, the growth in popularity of fanzines, and the efforts of film historians like John, even the most unmitigatedly wretched poverty-row shocker has been exhumed from the vaults for the delectation of new generations of admirers.

Around the globe, scream queens, whose names mean nothing even to the film critics of national newspapers, draw crowds of worshippers to fantasy conventions. And an international network of young gore-hounds knows the complete credits of makeup artists and exactly how many seconds are missing from the American video release of *Deep Red*.

Before I reached my teens, I was similarly obsessed with films designed to disturb my sleep, but in Britain in the 1950s I suspected I might be the only one. My friends went to see Westerns. The only clue I had that there might be others out there who shared my ghoulish interests was that one shop in my neighborhood sold a magazine called *Famous Monsters of Filmland*. But I thought that, if I tried to buy it, I might be arrested.

The British Board of Film Censors attempted to curb what it saw as an unhealthy appetite for horror by removing "offensive" scenes regardless of their importance to the plot and, when the entire theme was considered unacceptable, banning the picture altogether. This situation has persisted to the present day.

American readers may be surprised to learn that films up to thirty years old still cannot be shown in Britain. *Blood Feast*, for example, has been prohibited from the time it was made, in 1963; and since tyrannical new legislation was introduced in 1984, the police have been entitled to break into the home of anyone suspected of owning illegal videocassettes and arrest them. A business acquaintance of mine was jailed for eighteen months for distributing *Nightmares in a Damaged Brain*. In many ways, my childhood fears that I would be punished for scaring myself have come to pass.

It may be no accident that in Britain, which now endures what even the BBFC admits to be the most stringent film censorship in the western world, enthusiasm for horror movie culture past and present is at its most vigorous. So-called video nasties may be forbidden, but this does not prevent them being smuggled into the country and passed round a clandestine circuit. This is a dangerous activity—every so often the government authorizes military-style swoops during which ringleaders are rounded up and tapes confiscated—and it engenders an indomitable spirit of insurgence which irresistibly brings to mind the French Resistance.

This may sound a preposterous analogy—until you attend the conventions and talk to the horror movie freedom fighters themselves. These are people who will hold forth into the early hours about the insidiousness and inequity of institutionalized censorship, the moral right of the viewer to see the integral work, and the eternal quest to find a version ten frames longer than anything hitherto located. This is an underground society fostered by unpopular laws.

The average fan is not Joe Public. Joe Public is, after all, at home watching *The Price Is Right*. But nor, it goes without saying, is the average fan the potential psycho from whom the censor would protect us. Far from gloating over the carnage of every straight-to-video slasher, the fan actually discerns between good and bad, and there is fascinating uniformity of opinion on reputable directors and stars. The fan knows more about the artist's career than he knows himself and can leap in a discussion from Lon Chaney (*père et fils*) to Linnea Quigley. British cinema is in a parlous state, with little hope of recovery, but one source of inspiration is that kids today know more about horror movies than I did when I was their age.

The strongest argument in favour of film censorship is that film glamorizes antisocial behavior that impressionable viewers are encouraged to imitate. If there is one type of horror film considered more subversive than all the rest, it is the contemporary psycho thriller.

Once upon a time the madman stalking the shadows with a meat cleaver was a villain to be reviled along with Bill Sikes and Captain Bligh. But little by little, since the release of *Psycho* itself in 1960, the public attitude to the bad guy has changed, and now young audiences are actually cheering even the most deranged and remorseless killer, apparently caring nothing for his interchangeably feckless victims. This

new edition of John's book comes at a time when the psycho has never been more popular.

A fascination with evil is one thing, but how are we to account for the cult-hero status of such monsters as Freddy Krueger and Hannibal the Cannibal? Can we really be straying from the golden pathway and identifying with the beast that represents the dark side of human nature?

Unlike the censor, I don't believe this for an instant. Just as the devil has all the best tunes, the villain has all the best lines. I can personally attest that writing lip-smacking imprecations is the most fun. The hero and heroine are left with all the feeble but necessary clichés ("I thought I heard something," "Stay here," "No, I'm coming with you.") Consequently the most extroverted actors tend to play the psychos, and they give the most enjoyable performances.

Even the current crop of masked, dumb crazies have more impact than the characterless cyphers that fall prey to sharp objects. But still we cannot help but identify with the victim. I well remember the British premiere of *The Texas Chain Saw Massacre*, which, in case anyone is interested, remains my all-time favorite psycho movie. The film was banned in Britain (it still is and so are its two sequels). But its brilliance had been recognized by several respected critics, and a screening at the London Film Festival was permitted.

Most of the picture played to awestruck silence. Then, in the last few minutes, Leatherface falls while chasing the lone survivor and drops his chainsaw, which begins to carve into his own leg. This produced an immediate whoop of delight, a most unseemly reaction from an audience of staid British cinéastes.

This kind of instinctive release proves that, no matter how the cinema may put wicked temptation in our path, all of us who love the movies know right from wrong. I know that this book will encourage everyone who reads it to seek out and study the films that, I earnestly entreat, we will all be permitted to enjoy.

DAVID McGILLIVRAY
London, 1993

Among David McGillivray's screenwriting credits are *House of Whipcord, Frightmare, House of Mortal Sin, Schizo,* and *Terror.*

INTRODUCTION

The idea for this book came to me, appropriately enough, in a dream.

One day in 1984, I recalled a comment my father made to me in 1979 when the Frank Langella *Dracula* was released. "Do you suppose," he asked me wearily, "that those geniuses out in Hollywood will ever think up a *new* monster? I've been looking at Dracula for over forty years!" That night I had my dream. And in the morning I had my answer . . . and my monster: the screen psycho who, surprising as it may seem, has been with us, in varying guises, since the dawn of movies themselves. In my excitement, I dubbed the genre "psychofilm" and determined to explore it in full. The book you now hold in your hand is the result of that exploration.

Writer Colin Wilson has noted that the cinema usually runs thirty years behind literature in tackling new themes and ideas. On the whole, this has been true. But in the area of psychofilm, the cinema can perhaps be excused for running a little late, simply because it was not until after Richard von Krafft-Ebing had written his *Psychopathia Sexualis* and Freud had developed his theory of the unconscious that the medium found an audience. Once it had, the cinema turned to such material with remarkable swiftness. And for a very good reason. Because it consists of photographs that *move*, the cinema has the unique ability to make whatever the camera eye is trained on seem palpably real—even dreams. *And nightmares.*

Before the turn of the century, French magician Georges Méliès had begun making his phantasmagoric "trick films," quickie one-reelers that made audiences believe in even the wildest flights of fancy, culminating in 1911 with his remarkable two-reel *Baron Munchausen's Dream.* D. W. Griffith introduced audiences of 1909 to a naive form of psychoanalysis with *The Restoration,* in which the hero is shocked back to reality after being forced to relive an experience that had earlier traumatized him. A year earlier, Robert Louis Stevenson's *Dr. Jekyll and Mr. Hyde* received the first of its many screen treatments. By the twenties, German expressionism was in full sway, and its vivid depictions of what Freud called the "dark caverns of the human mind" were influencing filmmakers everywhere, particularly a young Englishman named Alfred Hitchcock, who, forty years later, distilled everything he had learned into a film called *Psycho.* It is not without significance that Orson Welles has dubbed this new medium of the twentieth century "a ribbon of dreams." Nor is it a matter simply of exaggeration that Hollywood, which to many stands as a synonym for the movies, has often been called "the dream factory."

The cinema and fantasy have been inexorably linked right from the start. And the screen psycho has been lurking about in the shadows of that fantasy,

11

Friday the 13th Part VIII: Jason Takes Manhattan (1989)

Leatherface: The Texas Chainsaw Massacre III (1990)   *A Nightmare on Elm Street 5: The Dream Child* (1989)

I, Madman (1989)

preying on hapless victims, right from the start too. He (or she) has taken many forms, and they're all here—ranging from the psychopathic child-killer in Fritz Lang's *M*, to the deranged child who murders adults in *The Bad Seed*, to grandiose presidential assassin John Baron in *Suddenly*, to the psychosexual Norman Bates in *Psycho*, to mass murderer John Reginald Christie, the centerpiece of Richard Fleischer's chilling true-crime drama *Ten Rillington Place*. Degrees of madness being what they are, however, I have chosen not to include every "mad doctor" movie ever made—for while many of these flamboyant medical men may indeed be mad, not all of them are crazy, and so they do not fall within the province of the genuine psychofilm.

A final note. It is my belief that film historians and critics can no longer ignore the significant contribution to cinema that is increasingly being made by that relatively recent media development, the made-for-TV movie. Many of these telefilms are so well done that they completely blur the unfair distinction that has been drawn between films made for the small screen and those made for the large. In fact, many American telefilms are released theatrically in Europe and elsewhere to great success. It is therefore no longer reasonable to say that simply because a film such as *Helter Skelter*, the story of the Charles Manson murders, was made for television that it doesn't deserve a place in a book about *movies*. It does, and I've included it—along with a number of other important psychofilms that have been made for television over the years and continue to be made even as you read these words.

1

THE STRANGE CASES OF
DR. JEKYLL AND MR. HYDE

I knew myself, at the first breath of this new life, to be more wicked, tenfold more wicked . . . and the thought, in that moment, braced and delighted me like wine.

—Dr. Henry Jekyll

The publication of Robert Louis Stevenson's novella *The Strange Case of Dr. Jekyll and Mr. Hyde* early in 1886 altered the direction of the modern horror tale. Before it, literature was steeped in the fairy-tale tradition of ghosts, vampires, and other outré manifestations of evil—*monsters*, if you will—that preyed on their opposite number, human beings. But in *Dr. Jekyll and Mr. Hyde*, Stevenson merged man and monster into one. His kindly Dr. Henry Jekyll was no werewolf victim of full-moon madness, but a rational man who concocts a strange brew in order to intentionally release the evil in himself, thereby giving birth to his double, the psychopathic Edward Hyde. True, Jekyll's transformation was also physical and thus in keeping with the established patterns of the genre. But for Stevenson, this was merely a red herring designed to throw the reader off the track, for what he deemed important about his story was that Jekyll and Hyde inhabited the same body, that they were *one*, a fact that he did not reveal until the novella's chilling conclusion. To readers of the time, this came as quite a jolt, for up until then, men and monsters had been thought to be mutually exclusive. Not anymore. The literary psycho had been born.

Although Stevenson began writing *Dr. Jekyll and Mr. Hyde* as a straight horror tale, he burned his first draft at the urging of his wife and on her suggestion refashioned the story into an allegory of contemporary Victorian mores, which he saw as rife with

hypocrisy. Jekyll became a symbol of that society's polished veneer, while Hyde represented its innermost longings and darkest secrets. The story was a very personal one for Stevenson, for, being a lifelong sufferer of tuberculosis (from which he died at age forty-four), he often dreamed of breaking free of the bonds of his sickness and leading a double life—which, in his early years, he did by carrying on a variety of affairs with married women. Because of his illness, he also knew about drugs, which frequently served as his only antidote to the confining nature of his disease. Out of all this emerged *The Strange Case of Dr. Jekyll and Mr. Hyde*, which predated Freud with its shocking theory of the "dual personality."

A literary sensation, Stevenson's novella was quickly purchased for the stage by actor-manager Richard Mansfield, who saw in the dual roles of Jekyll and Hyde the acting challenge of his career. He commissioned playwright Thomas Sullivan to do the adaptation, and the play premiered in Boston in 1887; it was a smash hit. Mansfield later took the play back to England where it proved even more successful. Had he not died suddenly in 1907, Mansfield might have been the first to play the part on-screen as well.[1] As it stands, however, his impact on the various screen versions to follow proved quite significant,

---

1. Edgar Norton, who played the valet Poole to Mansfield's Dr. Jekyll, was the only cast member of the original American produc-

The selfless Dr. Jekyll (John Barrymore) arrives at his clinic for the poor in the prototypical screen version of Robert Louis Stevenson's *Dr. Jekyll and Mr. Hyde* (1920), directed by John Robertson.

The villainous Hyde (John Barrymore) strangles Sir Desmond Carewe (Brandon Hurst), the man who introduced Jekyll to the seamier side of London nightlife.

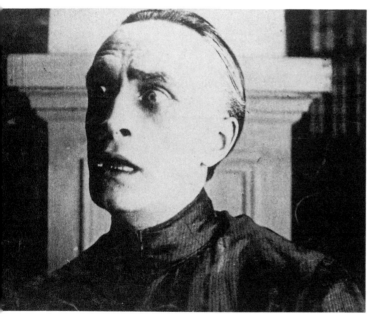

Mr. Warren (Conrad Veidt) feels the evil Mr. O'Connor rising within him in *Der Januskopf* (1920), F. W. Murnau's pirated version of the Stevenson story, prints of which apparently no longer exist.

Miriam Hopkins and Fredric March in a posed shot from Rouben Mamoulian's classic talkie version of *Dr. Jekyll and Mr. Hyde* (1932).

for it was the Mansfield/Sullivan play, not Stevenson's story (and not, as some writers have erroneously concluded, Oscar Wilde's *The Picture of Dorian*

Gray, which was published some years after the play premiered), that served as the model upon which most subsequent film versions have been based.

A lack of strict laws governing the acquisition of film rights to works of another medium prompted early moviemakers to freely adapt virtually any novel

---

tion to crop up in a subsequent Jekyll and Hyde film. He again played Poole to Fredric March's Dr. Jekyll in the 1932 version directed by Rouben Mamoulian.

15

Ivy (Mirian Hopkins) squirms at the touch of her libidinous suitor, the primitive Mr. Hyde (Fredric March), in Rouben Mamoulian's sexy and technically innovative 1932 version of the tale.

or play to the screen that they wanted to. The classics of Shakespeare, Sir Walter Scott, Charles Dickens, as well as more modern writers such as Stevenson, thus became fair game. These early one-reel adaptations consisted mainly of a series of selected scenes, usually the most famous or dramatic, from the original works. The classic literary scene in which the good Dr. Jekyll amazingly transforms into the bestial Mr. Hyde proved ideally suited to the special techniques of the new medium, and so quickie adaptations of *Dr. Jekyll and Mr. Hyde* soon became a staple of the early silent cinema. Between 1908 and 1920, no less than seven such one- and two-reelers were produced by different companies. Indeed, by 1920, the story was so familiar to audiences that it even became the subject of parody in a short film starring comedian and former Keystone Kop Hank Mann.

That same year, however, Stevenson's well-worn tale also received the first of its many feature-length treatments—three of them, in fact, including two produced in America and one in Germany. The two American versions were shot simultaneously on the East Coast in a spirit of angry competitiveness by Adolph Zukor's Paramount-Artcraft and Louis B. Mayer's Pioneer Company, respectively, and were released to theaters within months of each other. The Mayer film, which debuted in July, was a modern version of the story that owed little to the Stevenson original except the requisite transformation scene—which, at the letdown of a conclusion, turns out to have been nothing more than a dream[2] suffered by Dr. Jekyll (Sheldon Lewis) due to exhaustion and overwork. The film was a resounding box-office flop.

---

2. A 1912 one-reeler starring James Cruze, the future director of the 1923 silent-film classic *The Covered Wagon,* used the same ploy.

The murderous Mr. Hyde (Fredric March) fends off the police who have come to arrest him in Jekyll's lab.

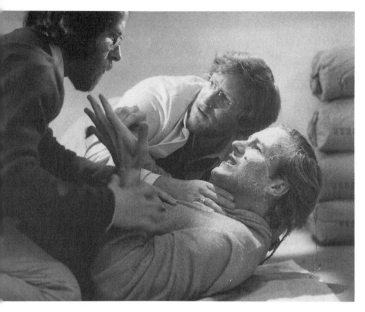

Scientists Bob Balaban and Charles Haid try to converse with William Hurt, who has partially reverted to a primitive state, in Ken Russell's high-tech version of the Jekyll and Hyde story, *Altered States* (1980), based on the novel by Paddy Chayefsky.

William Hurt as Eddie Jessup, the Dr. Jekyll figure in *Altered States*.

Zukor's version, on the other hand, which was released in March, was a huge success, a fact due in no small part to the charisma of its star, John Barrymore.

Freely adapted from the Mansfield-Sullivan play by Clara Beranger, wife of producer William DeMille (brother of Cecil B.) and one of the leading scenarists of her day—a group, incidentally, that seems to have been dominated almost exclusively by women—the Barrymore film remains the archetypal, if not the definitive, screen version of *Dr. Jekyll and Mr. Hyde*. Granted a sizable budget, a polished cast, and a good director, John S. Robertson, who would go on to work with Mary Pickford and other major stars of the day, the film was given lavish treatment. Set squarely in the Victorian milieu described by Stevenson, it boasted some exquisite sets, including a remarkably seedy opium den, and was atmospherically photographed by Roy Overbough. Personally, I have always found John Barrymore's bravura style of silent-screen acting to be excessively hammy, and his Jekyll and Hyde are no exception; he fairly chews up the scenery, particularly when he is playing the distraught Jekyll. The performances of his costars, particularly that of Brandon Hurst as the wily Sir George Carewe, the man of the world who first leads the young Jekyll astray, are relatively restrained and seem quite modern by comparison. There is no question, however, that Barrymore's presence commands the screen—as did Mansfield's the stage. Indeed, there is some likelihood that Barrymore had seen and been influenced by Mansfield's performance, as the late actor was a good friend of the Barrymore family

and had been a frequent visitor to the Barrymore home during John's early years. Mansfield had played both Jekyll and Hyde without the use of makeup, resorting to lighting and pantomime to suggest his transformation. Barrymore likewise insisted upon playing his initial transformation scene without makeup. For subsequent close-ups, however, he did don makeup, including talons and fright wig, to give himself a convincingly grotesque appearance. Movies, after all, are not the stage.

Reviews of the time were unanimous in their praise of Barrymore but not so kind to the film itself. The *New York Times* critic, for example, wrote, "The production, aside from his [Barrymore's] performance, is uninspired. It bears the unmistakable stamp of the motion picture mill." As usual, the truth falls somewhere in between. Overall, Barrymore's performance *is* impressive, especially when he is playing Hyde, and remains so to this day. But the production itself, if not exactly in a class with the work of Griffith, was hardly uninspired, for audiences of the day had certainly seen no *Dr. Jekyll and Mr. Hyde* like this before. Even Barrymore's initial transformation without makeup—which does not hold up so well today—must have rocked them in their seats due to the fervor with which the actor threw himself (quite literally) into the scene.[3]

---

3. A hilarious parody of Barrymore's ferocious mugging and gymnastics in this scene can be seen in Carl Reiner's bittersweet comedy-drama about the early days of Hollywood, *The Comic* (1969), starring Dick Van Dyke.

Dr. Jekyll (Spencer Tracy) recovers from his transformation into Mr. Hyde, a change that was more psychological than physical, in Victor Fleming's critically pasted 1941 version of the Stevenson story.

For the later transformation scenes, director Robertson employed such camera tricks as lap dissolves and double exposures to even more powerful effect. In one of them, Jekyll dreams of a nocturnal visit by Hyde in the form of a giant spider, which crawls up from the foot of his bed, hunkers over him, then melds with his body as he wakes up as Mr. Hyde. Even today, this sequence packs a tremendous punch; one can only imagine the effect it must have had on audiences of the time, who were not as yet inured to moments of such undiluted horror as this.

Though famous for his celebrated profile and virile-hero roles such as Don Juan and Beau Brummel, John Barrymore much preferred roles onstage and on-screen that allowed him to disguise his good looks beneath layers of the most grotesque makeup. The more twisted in body and soul a character was, the more he delighted in playing him. So enamored was

he of his Hyde makeup that he held onto it for many years after, until, in 1927, he shook off the cobwebs and used it once more—not for a film, but to buy a house! Accompanied by his manager and his pet monkey, Barrymore, fully decked out in fangs, talons, and fright wig, went to the plush $60,000 home he had his eye on, but remained inside his limo while the manager negotiated with the real-estate agent. The agent grew so intimidated at the sight of this obviously wealthy but thoroughly grotesque creature in the car (at one point, Barrymore even kissed the monkey on the lips for ghoulish good measure) that he nervously accepted the manager's firm offer of $50,000—a full $10,000 drop in the asking price. When he heard the news and learned that it was Barrymore who was behind the charade, the seller, director King Vidor, accepted the deal with a grudging smile. While not exactly approving of Barry-

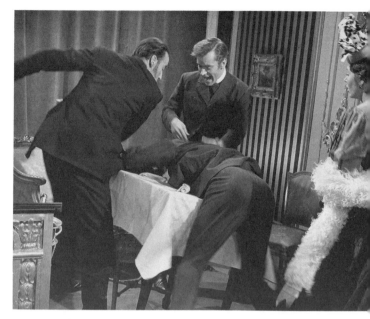

Christopher Lee (left) and Paul Massie (Mr. Hyde) take out a barroom tough (Oliver Reed) in Hammer's *The Two Faces of Dr. Jekyll* (1960), released in the U.S. as *House of Fright*.

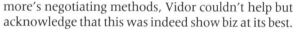

Ivy (Ingrid Bergman) turns to kindly Dr. Jekyll (Spencer Tracy) for protection from Mr. Hyde, not realizing that the two are one. Cast against type, Bergman received the best notices of anyone in the film.

Litauer (David Kossoff) learns the terrible truth about Mr. Hyde from the dying Jekyll (Paul Massie) in *The Two Faces of Dr. Jekyll*, Terence Fisher's interesting reversal of the Jekyll and Hyde theme.

more's negotiating methods, Vidor couldn't help but acknowledge that this was indeed show biz at its best.

The remaining 1920 version of *Dr. Jekyll and Mr. Hyde*, made in Germany, is the most tantalizing because it is the only one of the three that can no longer be seen. Only its script and a few intriguing stills survive. Contemporary reviews of it are also hard to come by, for, to the best of this writer's knowledge, the film was never released in America. This was probably due to legal problems, as the film, titled *Der Januskopf* (The Janus Head), was a pirated adaptation of the Stevenson story to which screen rights had not been purchased. Isolated from the rest of the world and its now-stringent copyright laws in the wake of World War I, German filmmakers frequently made illegal adaptations of works written outside their country. They ran into trouble only when they sought to export them, as was the case with F. W. Murnau's *Nosferatu* (1922), a blatant version of *Dracula*, over which Bram Stoker's widow sued and won. Prints were confiscated and destroyed,

though the film did ultimately survive. *Der Januskopf*, also directed by Murnau, was not so lucky, though its fate was far less dramatic. Due to the combustible nature of early celluloid, its negative and prints prob-

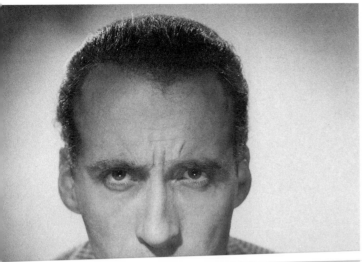

Christopher Lee flirted with this sort of dual personality role himself some years earlier in the low-budget thriller *Alias John Preston* (1955).

Christopher Lee finally donned the role of Mr. Hyde in *I, Monster* (1972), although the character was renamed Mr. Blake.

ably just disintegrated over the years due to carelessness and neglect.

Scripted by Hans Janowitz following his successful and influential *The Cabinet of Dr. Caligari*, cowritten with Carl Mayer and released the year before (see Chapter 4), *Der Januskopf* recounts the psychological misadventures of one Dr. Jeskyll [sic], played by Conrad Veidt. He buys an antique bust of the Roman god Janus, whose two faces represent the opposing natures of man—one side good, the other evil—and quickly falls under the spell of the diabolic half. Assuming the form of the sinister Mr. Hyde, he takes lodging in the slums of Whitechapel in order to conceal the bust and move more freely about his life of pure evil. In the Barrymore version, Hyde rooms in the equally squalid Soho district. Janowitz's use of Whitechapel is aimed at suggesting a parallel between the fictional exploits of Jekyll and Hyde and the real-life exploits of Jack the Ripper, who terrorized London's grimy East End in the autumn of 1888. To accentuate this connection, Hyde is portrayed in the film as a dark, *bearded* figure dressed in a cloak and pulled-down hat, a description that fits contemporary eyewitness accounts of the Ripper's appearance. Janowitz was not the first to note this parallel, of course, for at the time of the Ripper's reign of terror, Mansfield's play was still running at the Lyceum Theatre in London's West End, and a common theory grew up that the Whitechapel murders were, in fact, a reflection of events in the play—that the killer was a genuine Jekyll and Hyde: a reputable doctor by day and a knife-wielding fiend by night. More about this, however, in Chapter 2.

In both the Barrymore and the Murnau films, Hyde tries but fails to woo Jekyll's fiancée.[4] In both films also, Hyde's absolute villainy is illustrated by a scene (taken from Stevenson) in which without provocation he assaults and pummels an innocent child in the street. In *Der Januskopf*, however, this incident escalates when Jekyll hallucinates a dozen Hydes trampling over the bodies of a number of children in his pursuit of him. No matter how treacherous he may be to others, of course, Hyde's true prey remains the soul of Jekyll himself, and at the end of each film the bedeviled doctor is able to save himself only by taking his own life, which he does by downing a capsule of poison.

What is interesting about these two earliest examples of psychofilm are the shadings given the charac-

---

4. Perhaps anticipating possible litigation if his film was released abroad, Murnau changed the names of Jekyll and Hyde on the screen to Mr. Warren and Mr. O'Connor, respectively. He did the same with *Nosferatu*, in which Count Dracula, for example, became Graf Orlock. As has already been noted, however, this ploy did not work in the latter film's case.

Louis Hayward played the hapless offspring of the well-meaning doctor and his villanous alter ego in *The Son of Dr. Jekyll* (1951), here with Doris Lloyd.

ter of Jekyll's alternate self. Barrymore's Hyde is a psychopath with definite criminal tendencies, whose spiderlike countenance recalls the description of Professor Moriarty, the "Napoleon of crime," in Conan Doyle's Sherlock Holmes stories. Barrymore's Hyde makeup, in fact, even foreshadows Gustav Von Seyffertitz's as Moriarty in a Sherlock Holmes film released two years later starring Barrymore himself as the supersleuth. Conrad Veidt's Jekyll, on the other hand, resembling the protagonist in Robert Bloch's short story "The Skull of the Marquis De Sade," falls under the spell of a legendary evil, and his Hyde therefore represents a more mythic example of evil—with a dash thrown in of Jack the Ripper, who, by this time, had become part legend himself. In the first talkie version of the story, however, Hyde took on yet another shading when he became not a criminal or a conjured spirit but a primitive man dressed in walking clothes, a Neanderthal unleashed on the streets of Victorian London.

Revisionist critics have termed Fredric March's apelike Mr. Hyde in the 1932 Rouben Mamoulian film "racist." I find this astounding. To me it says more about these critics' own racist attitudes. From the beginning, director Mamoulian's intentions were quite clear, and his film reflects them completely. He had decided to root the story in the history of mankind itself. "I didn't want Hyde to be a monster," he said. "Hyde is not evil, he is the primitive, the animal in us, whereas Jekyll is a cultured man, representing the intellect. Hyde is the Neanderthal man, and March's makeup was designed as such." To accent this, Mamoulian describes Hyde's first appearance in the film this way: "He's full of animal spirits, full of joy. He's enjoying life. He comes out in the rain, and instead of using an umbrella as an Englishman would, he takes off his hat and enjoys the rain. He's full of *vim*. The struggle or dilemma [in the film] is not between evil and good, it's between the sophisticated, spiritual self in man and his animal, primeval instincts. And Hyde always gives in to his instincts." Once the initially playful Hyde commits murder in order to survive, he evolves yet again, and his character and makeup perceptibly reflect this change.

Screenings of the Mamoulian *Dr. Jekyll and Mr. Hyde* were once hard to come by. I first saw the film at

Hyde (Boris Karloff) once again assumed ape-like characteristics in *Abbott and Costello Meet Dr. Jekyll and Mr. Hyde* (1953).

UCLA in 1969, and I must say that, after years of hearing about its legendary technical virtuosity, I was not disappointed. Ostensibly a remake of the Barrymore silent, it is really a much more vigorous and innovative work, and a whole lot sexier as well. The later Spencer Tracy version strived for a sense of eroticism also, with mixed results, but this film really has the goods. Miriam Hopkins's put-upon harlot, Ivy Parsons—a character whose antecedents are to be found in the Mansfield-Sullivan play and the subsequent Barrymore film where she took the form of Miss Gina (Nita Naldi), a cabaret dancer whom Hyde shacks up with and later discards—is quite an attractive woman indeed; one can fully appreciate the animal lust she arouses in Hyde. Ivy remains Hopkins's best screen performance. Ironically, Mamoulian had to coerce her to take the part. She really wanted the less flashy role of Muriel Carewe (Rose Hobart), Jekyll's traditionally bland fiancée. Mamoulian had to fight for Fredric March as well but for different reasons. Paramount thought of March as little more than a good light comedian—his previous film had been a vehicle called *Laughter*—and insisted that the director use the villainous-looking Irving Pichel instead, who Mamoulian knew could play a convincing Hyde but not the debonair Jekyll. Mamoulian held out, however, and won—as did March, who copped the Oscar as best actor that year for his performance.

Over the years a number of cuts were made in the film for censorship and other reasons, reducing its original running time from ninety-eight minutes to eighty-two. But in 1990, the restored version was finally made available on videocassette and laser disc.

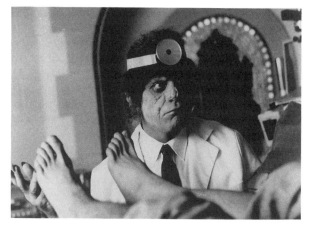

Oliver Reed, as a deranged podiatrist, also played the story for laughs in *Dr. Heckyl and Mr. Hype* (1980).

To my mind, it is the best of all the Jekyll and Hyde films—and its initial transformation scene, which is shown entirely from Jekyll's perspective, culminating in his physical change without the use of lap dissolves or any other apparent cinematic devices, is still a breathtaking piece of cinema. In an interview with Charles Higham and Joel Greenberg for their book *The Celluloid Muse* (Regnery, 1969), Mamoulian described how he and his cameraman, Karl Struss, accomplished it:

> The secret of the transformation of Dr. Jekyll into Mr. Hyde in one continuous shot—without cuts and without rewinding the film backwards in the camera to permit the application of additional makeup—lay in the use of color transparencies which gradually revealed more and more of the actor's makeup. As you know, a red filter will absorb red and reveal all the other colors, and a green filter will do the reverse. Working on that principle, we held graduating color filters one by one before the camera, thus allowing successive portions of March's colored makeup to register on film. It was all rather primitive—the filters were handmade—but it worked.

Mamoulian's innovations in the film were not just confined to the visual, but included the aural as well—this was, after all, the first sound version of the Stevenson story, and it thus required something new in that department also. In the same interview, Mamoulian recounted some of the problems he encountered and the solutions:

> A realistic sound in a magical situation is ruinous, and similarly a realistic sound while Jekyll is being transformed would have pulled you down into the mire of naturalism. So I decided the sound had to be something special. We photographed light frequencies of varying intensity from a candle. I hit a gong and cut the impact off and ran the sound backwards, and to give the sound a pulsing rhythm, I ran up and down a stairway while they recorded my speeded-up heartbeats. When I say my heart was in Jekyll and Hyde, I mean that literally!

The efforts of Mamoulian and his cast, and crew did not go unnoticed. Of their achievement, critic Mordaunt Hall wrote in the January 2, 1932, issue of the *New York Times*, just after the film's premiere, "What with the audibility of the screen and the masterful photography, the new transcription of Stevenson's spine-chilling work emerges a far more tense and shuddering affair than it was as John Barrymore's silent picture. Mr. March's performance is something to arouse admiration."

As I reflect upon the Mamoulian film, it seems unlikely that author Paddy Chayefsky was unaware of it when he came to write his high-tech variation on the Jekyll and Hyde theme, *Altered States*, filmed in 1980 by Ken Russell. In fact, Chayefsky's publisher

Joanne Woodward won an Oscar for her performance as a female Jekyll and Hyde in *The Three Faces of Eve* (1957), which was based on a true story. Here she strikes a pose as Eve Black, the sexier side of the triangle.

Ronald Colman wasn't seeking an Oscar, didn't expect one, but got one anyway (as best actor) when he played another victim of the Jekyll and Hyde syndrome in *A Double Life* (1947), opposite Shelley Winters.

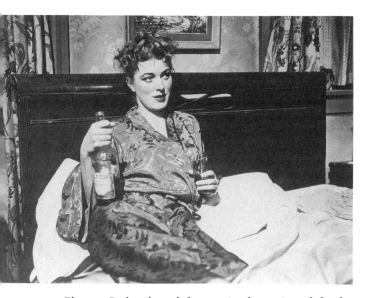

Eleanor Parker hoped for an Academy Award for her portrayal of the loose living *Lizzie* (1957), another victim of multiple personality. But the film and her performance were both eclipsed by the popularity of *The Three Faces of Eve*, released the same year.

even hyped the novel as a "twentieth-century Dr. Jekyll and Mr. Hyde." In the novel and film, a scientist submits to a series of sensory-deprivation experiments in an effort to uncover some ultimate truths about the human mind and its capacity to achieve alternative states of consciousness. Chayefsky based his central character, Dr. Edward Jessup (William Hurt), on the real-life psychoanalyst Dr. John Lilly, who in 1964 underwent a series of similar tests for similar reasons. Stepping into a tank of blood-warm salt water, Lilly closed the top of the tank and floated on the surface in total darkness. To aid him in his pursuits, he had taken a small dose of LSD, obtained under a grant from the National Institute of Mental Health.

"I moved into universes containing beings much larger than myself," wrote Lilly of the experiment. "The first time I entered these spaces, I was swept, pushed, carried, whirled, and in general beat around by processes which I could not understand, processes of immense energy, of fantastic light, and terrifying power. It wasn't bodily death that I feared. It was getting into spaces in which I would lose control and

Amnesiac stage actor John Loder (here with June Duprez)
unwittingly takes his role as *The Brighton Strangler* (1945)
on the road.

from which I would perhaps not be able to come back." Lilly claimed that he had successfully achieved an alternative state of consciousness that was indeed real. Interestingly, Lilly's description somewhat parallels the sequence involving Jekyll's drug-induced experiment in the Mamoulian film, during which the camera, assuming Jekyll's point of view, whirls about the laboratory in a cascading blur of light and shadow.

Like Jekyll, Dr. Jessup (the names even sound similar) not only alters his consciousness but his biology as well, transforming himself into a primitive ape-man who kills to survive when he escapes into the modern world. Connections between the Mamoulian film and *Altered States* do not end here, however, for unlike many other cinematic variations on Stevenson's oft-told tale, each film endeavors to be visually and aurally startling in new ways and employs much technical wizardry to do so. As he gazes into a mirror, Jessup's face begins to metamorphose right before his and our eyes, seemingly without the use of camera trickery, just as Fredric March's had done forty-eight years earlier.[5] There is also a

good deal of similarly themed eroticism in each film, though befitting the current lack of screen censorship, its treatment is obviously more graphic in the R-rated *Altered States*.

When MGM started planning its own version of *Dr. Jekyll and Mr. Hyde* in 1940 as a vehicle for one of its hottest stars, Spencer Tracy, the studio bought the rights to the 1932 Paramount film in order to avoid a competitive rerelease and shelved it for almost forty years. Not until the early seventies did the Mamoulian film again receive theatrical distribution when MGM briefly rereleased it along with two of that studio's own horror classics, *The Mask of Fu Manchu* (1932), with Boris Karloff, and *Mark of the Vampire* (1936), with Bela Lugosi. Curiously, the Tracy *Dr. Jekyll and Mr. Hyde* was not included in the package, no doubt because it had originally been greeted by scathing reviews and had flopped badly at the box office. Tracy remained ashamed of his performance to the end of his life.

In retrospect, it's difficult to understand why the 1941 *Dr. Jekyll and Mr. Hyde* was received so poorly. The longest version of the tale yet filmed, it was also the most lavish and stately, not to mention the most Freudian—perhaps these elements combined are what killed it. In its review of August 13, 1941, the *New York Times* deemed that scriptwriter John Lee Mahin and director Victor Fleming, whose previous film had been *Gone With the Wind*, had created "a Grand Guignol chiller with delusions of grandeur, a

---

5. Dick Smith, the justly celebrated special makeup effects technician who engineered this and other amazing feats of cinematic legerdemain in *Altered States*, cut his teeth on a bona fide version of *Dr. Jekyll and Mr. Hyde* that was videotaped for American television in 1968, starring Jack Palance.

nightmare interpreted by a reader of tea leaves, a mulligan stew hidden under an expensive soufflé. Mr. Tracy's portrait of Hyde is not so much evil incarnate as ham rampant." Harsh words indeed. Too harsh, in fact, for the film simply isn't that bad. And neither is Tracy.

In contrast to John Barrymore and Fredric March, Spencer Tracy played his Hyde with a modicum of makeup. His was a more psychological transformation, and to make both personalities seem convincingly separate and distinct presented quite an acting challenge, one that many, including Tracy, didn't think he was up to. Reportedly, author Somerset Maugham once visited the set during shooting and commented, "Which is he now, Jekyll or Hyde?"

At the height of his fame and popularity, Tracy was also at the height of his alcoholism, and the stress of making *Dr. Jekyll and Mr. Hyde* served to exacerbate it. Often he would disappear for days and have to be tracked down and persuaded to come back to the set. His performance, however, while perhaps not ranking with the best of his career, was certainly polished and professional. One suspects that the hostility with which it was greeted had much to do with critic and audience expectations and his having been cast so firmly against type, a problem that doesn't seem to arise for viewers today.

Also cast against type were Ingrid Bergman, who plays Hyde's harlot victim Ivy Peterson, and Lana Turner, who plays Jekyll's fiancée Beatrix Emery. Originally, Bergman was assigned the role of the fiancée and sexpot Turner was given the part of Ivy. Before shooting began, however, Bergman, who ap-

parently saw in Ivy the same possibilities Miriam Hopkins had to be persuaded of, demanded that she and Turner be allowed to switch. At first reluctant, the studio eventually gave in, and Bergman went on to receive the best reviews of anyone in the film.

Again the emphasis in this *Dr. Jekyll and Mr. Hyde* is on sex, but whereas March's Neanderthal Hyde viewed sex as just one more urge to be instinctively indulged (not unlike the cavemen in 1981's *Quest for Fire*), Tracy's Hyde uses it as a way of releasing himself from the restraints posed by straitlaced Victorian society. Engaged to the hands-off goddess Turner, Jekyll inwardly longs for a roll in the hay with the likes of Ivy—which Hyde allows him to do. Jekyll's inner conflict over sex, which is what the film is about, is nicely (if a bit heavy-handedly) symbolized in the dream sequence in which he sees himself as the master of both women, whipping each, like horses, into a frenzy.

Tracy's Hyde is a somewhat more modern version of the screen psycho in that his physical features and Jekyll's remain quite similar, a nuance Stevenson might well have endorsed. In the first color version of the tale, Hammer Films's *The Two Faces of Dr. Jekyll* (1960), released in the U.S. as *House of Fright,* scriptwriter Wolf Mankowitz intriguingly reworked this theme by making Jekyll into an ugly, bearded, and rather drab gent, whose alternate Hyde is a dashing young libertine and sadist. The film itself is not as innovative or interesting as this unexpected twist, but as with the Tracy film, it is not as bad as critics of the time would have us believe either. In keeping with the Hammer way of doing things, it is nicely mounted

Bela Lugosi (left) is about to become a victim of Boris Karloff (as the psychotic John Grey) in Val Lewton's superb psychofilm, *The Body Snatcher* (1945), also based on a Robert Louis Stevenson story.

and has an excellent period flavor.

Paul Massie's lugubrious Jekyll, whose odd baritone voice sounds as if it were recorded at half speed, unleashes his dual self to get even with his adulterous wife Kitty (Dawn Addams), who is carrying on with his best friend Paul (Christopher Lee). By film's end, the overzealous Hyde (also played by Massie) has laid waste to practically everyone in the cast, including the ardent Kitty, and leaves the repentant Jekyll to hold the bag.

The Two Faces of Dr. Jekyll did not go over well with audiences, who found it (even at eighty-nine minutes) a bit slow moving, but it remains a significant psychofilm, particularly of the Jekyll and Hyde school, for reasons summed up best by director Terence Fisher himself. "I liked the script," he said. "I think Wolf Mankowitz wrote it partly from the point of view that Victorian England was corrupt. But it wasn't fundamentally a deep script. Its strength, I think, was that Wolf Mankowitz realized that evil wasn't a horrible thing crawling about the street. It's very charming and attractive and seductive."

Hammer continued on this path when it filmed its next and even more unusual excursion into Jekyll and Hyde territory, *Dr. Jekyll and Sister Hyde* (1971), written by Brian Clemens, one of the cocreators of television's popular *Avengers* series. In this film, the inventive doctor (Ralph Bates) not only succeeds in changing his personality but his sex as well. The beautiful but evil Sister Hyde (Martine Beswick, who bears a striking resemblance to Bates) resorts to killing a number of street women whose bodies are needed for the serum required to keep Jekyll's experiment afloat, and in so doing she gives rise to the legend of Jack the Ripper. For good measure, *Dr. Jekyll and Sister Hyde* also throws in the anachronism of Burke and Hare, two body snatchers who initially provide Jekyll with the corpses he needs, despite the fact that they actually carried out their historically infamous deeds in Edinburgh, not London, many years before the Stevenson story was written and spring-heeled Jack had felled his first victim.

Christopher Lee, a victim of the villainous Hyde in Hammer's *The Two Faces of Dr. Jekyll,* finally drank the brew himself in 1971 for yet another version of the Stevenson tale. Rather than departing from the original in the unique ways Hammer had done, this version, titled *I, Monster,* went back to basics and remains a fairly faithful adaptation, which was the aim of the enterprise.

"I realized that *Dr. Jekyll and Mr. Hyde* had been done a lot of times," said producer-scriptwriter Milton Subotsky of the film, "but I wanted to do the most definitive version of the book ever. *I, Monster* is the closest ever to the Robert Louis Stevenson story of any version ever made—although I did change the names of the lead characters to Dr. Marlowe and Mr. Blake. The trouble with the picture is that in sticking so closely to the original, we wound up with a film that was rather boring. The Stevenson story has very little action." To give the film some badly needed flair, Subotsky chose to shoot it in 3-D, though it was subsequently released "flat" due to a failure to employ the process properly, a failure Subotsky lays at the feet of the film's inexperienced director, Stephen Weeks.

I, Monster (which has an even shorter running time) is, like *The Two Faces of Dr. Jekyll,* a rather pokey film. But it does have an authentic period flavor; and its acting overall is top-notch. Lee had already flirted with this sort of dual-personality role some years earlier in a low-budget thriller called *Alias John Preston* (1955) for which he received his first major screen credit. In that film he plays a gentle young man who suffers from recurring nightmares in which he sees himself murdering a series of young women. About to be married, he calls on a psychiatrist (Alexander Knox) to cure him of these nocturnal visions only to discover at the film's unexpected conclusion that he has actually been committing these murders all along. Ironically, the earlier *Alias John Preston* is a more interesting and up-to-date psychofilm than *I, Monster,* which again made the good doctor's transformation physical as well as psychological; once more he had to become an ugly-looking brute in order to carry out his ugly deeds.

Over the years, Stevenson's dynamic duo have sired their share of screen sons and daughters and have suffered through a number of purely exploitative reenactments of their familiar legend, such as Andy Milligan's bargain-basement gore film *The Man With Two Heads* (1972). They have been treated comically in the amusing *Abbott and Costello Meet Dr. Jekyll and Mr. Hyde* (1953); the erratically funny *The Nutty Professor* (1963), directed by and starring Jerry Lewis; Hammer's own *The Ugly Duckling* (1959); the woefully unfunny *Jekyll and Hyde . . . Together Again* (1982); and the 1980 Charles B. Griffith romp, *Dr. Heckyl and Mr. Hype,* starring Oliver Reed as a deranged podiatrist. And they have even been the subject of a televised musical starring Kirk Douglas and Susan George in 1973.

In the mid-1980s, David Hemmings played the dual roles in a slick BBC version of the tale adapted by Gerald Savory, the scriptwriter of the BBC's critically acclaimed—and possibly definitive—version of Bram Stoker's *Dracula* (1979), starring Louis Jourdan. The drama aired in the U.S. as a two-parter on the PBS series *Mystery!* In 1989, immortal movie psycho Anthony Perkins took on psychofilm's most durable roles in a kinky version of the tale shot in Hungary under the title *Edge of Sanity.* And in 1990, Michael

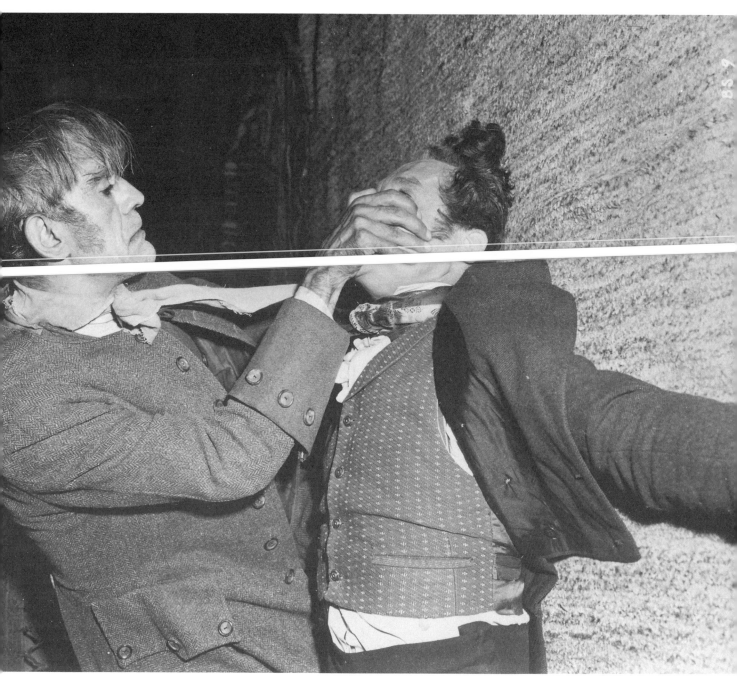

The demented John Gray (Boris Karloff) attempts to "Burke" Dr. MacFarlane (Henry Daniell) in *The Body Snatcher*.

Caine essayed the good doctor and his villainous alter ego in director David Wickes's atmospheric but otherwise undistinguished reworking of the tale, *Jekyll and Hyde*, which had its premiere on American television. Cheryl Ladd played Jekyll's hapless wife, who gives birth to a grotesque "baby Hyde" at the film's laughable conclusion. As of this writing, Wickes's film remains the last attempt at a genuine psychofilm adapted directly (albeit very loosely) from the Stevenson story. The influence of Stevenson's groundbreaking study of dual personality on psychofilm, however, does not end here.

More Double Lives

Psychofilms exploring the phenomenon of split personality in a more realistic context are almost as rare as the phenomenon itself. *Dr. Jekyll and Mr. Hyde* after all was first and foremost an allegory about good and evil in Victorian times and remained so throughout most of its many film incarnations. Nunnally Johnson's *The Three Faces of Eve* and Hugo Haas's *Lizzie,* on the other hand, explore the subject in a more clinical manner.

In both films, the main characters suffer from a total division of personality that is reflected not by any physical change but a purely psychological one rooted in a traumatic incident in their past. In the Johnson film, which is based on a true story, Eve White (Joanne Woodward), as she calls herself, is a mousy young woman afraid of her own shadow. Her alternate, Eve Black, is less inhibited and even a bit of a flirt, and that threatens to destroy Eve's marriage to her uncomprehending husband (David Wayne). Her inner conflict is not so much between good and evil as it is between compassion and self-hate, for Eve Black genuinely detests her alternate self for being so passive and weak-willed. The conflict is finally resolved when Eve's psychiatrist (Lee J. Cobb) discovers yet another personality during therapy and encourages this third face, which combines the gentleness of Eve White with the determination of Eve Black, to assume dominance over the other two. This third, more compassionate personality also reveals the source of Eve's problem, an incident in her youth when she'd been forced to kiss the body of a deceased loved one and had escaped into the personality of Eve Black out of shock and fear.

Lizzie, based on Shirley Jackson's novel *The Bird's Nest,* offered much the same kind of story. Again the title character (Eleanor Parker) suffers a split in personalities due to a deeply rooted psychological conflict, in this case a desire to remain respectable (like Henry Jekyll) while indulging an alternate desire to be promiscuous (like Mr. Hyde). And again a psychiatrist (Richard Boone) resolves the problem by having Lizzie absorb these divergent aspects of her psyche into a stable whole. Curiously, each of these films was released the same year (1957), but only one found favor with audiences and critics—*The Three Faces of Eve,* which earned Joanne Woodward an Oscar as best actress.

Almost twenty years later, Joanne Woodward switched roles when she played Sally Field's therapist in *Sybil* (1976), the true story of a young woman who undergoes not three changes of personality but *sixteen.* *Sybil* emerged as a shocking study in multiple personality—more shocking in that it was made for television—for a number of reasons, not the least of

Boris Karloff finds himself up to his old murderous tricks after twenty years of remission in *The Haunted Strangler* (1958).

which was the unexpectedly powerful performance of its star, whom audiences were more accustomed to seeing on the home screen in such frothy title roles as those in *The Flying Nun* and *Gidget.* Sally Field's fragmented Sybil was a far cry from these roles, and her performance came as a revelation—as did the disquieting cause of Sybil's malady, that as a child she had been sexually abused by her unhinged mother, who mutilated the little girl's sexual organs to keep her on the "straight and narrow." Revealed in flashback, this scene is presented by director Daniel Petrie in quite graphic terms and has a profoundly disturbing effect, made even more disturbing (and frightening) by the knowledge that the incident actually took place. Deservedly, Sally Field won an Emmy for her harrowing portrayal(s).

As we've seen, multiple-personality roles have often served actors and actresses well come award time because of the unique opportunity they give them to strut their stuff. John Barrymore pulled out all the stops as Jekyll and Hyde and might very well have won an Oscar for his performance had there been such a thing back in 1920; twelve years later, Fredric March did. Eleanor Parker hoped to win an Oscar for *Lizzie,* but when the film bombed at the box office, her hopes were dashed. Ronald Colman, on the other hand, wasn't seeking an Oscar, didn't expect one, but got one anyway (as best actor) when he played yet another victim of the Jekyll and Hyde syndrome in *A Double Life* (1947).

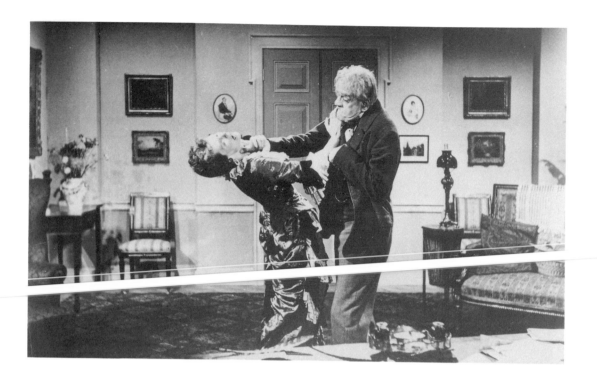

In this film, Colman stars as a more conventional screen psycho, a Shakespearean actor named Anthony John who has been treading the boards so long as Othello that he finally cracks under the strain and begins to believe that he really is Othello, a belief that is enhanced when he falls for blond bombshell Shelley Winters, a genuinely unfaithful Desdemona whom he ultimately strangles for her infidelity. Out of grief and remorse, he then dons his makeup for a final bow as the murderous Moor and actually commits suicide onstage at the conclusion of the performance.

In *The Brighton Strangler* (1945), John Loder suffers a similar psychological upheaval when he is knocked unconscious during the Nazi blitz of a London theater where he is starring in a play about a strangler. Awakening with amnesia, he heads for Victoria Station and coincidentally hears someone make a comment that is an exact repeat of a line in the play. The remark stirs the memory that he's a killer, and he buys a ticket to Brighton where he sets out to enact his part in the play for real. With both films, one can't help but ask, of course, how much of the murderer already existed in each character prior to his dramatic change in personality.

This same question does not arise, however, in *The Haunted Strangler* (1958), which starred Boris Karloff not as an actor but as a Victorian writer who becomes obsessed by a twenty-year-old murder case involving a man who was convicted of strangling a series of women and summarily executed. As Karloff sifts through the evidence, he grows convinced that an innocent man was sent to the gallows and that the real "Haymarket Strangler" is still at large. His theory proves correct when he takes on the personality of the strangler and starts killing. At the film's not-so-surprising conclusion, it is revealed that the respectable Karloff was the real strangler all along—a sort of Jekyll and Hyde in remission.

Throughout his career, Karloff played all manner of Jekyll-and-Hyde-type roles—including the good doctor and his villainous alter ego themselves in the 1953 Abbott and Costello comedy mentioned earlier. But arguably his finest performance in this vein was in the 1945 Val Lewton film, *The Body Snatcher,* also based on a story by Robert Louis Stevenson. In the film, Karloff plays John Gray, by day a respectable cabdriver in nineteenth-century Edinburgh and by night a grave robber and murderer who supplies corpses to a medical school run by the esteemed Dr. MacFarlane (Henry Daniell).

Gray enters the film when he delivers a young woman and her crippled daughter to MacFarlane's medical school for examination. On the surface, Gray appears to be both gentle and kind as evidenced by the sympathetic manner with which he treats the

Stacy Keach plays a lunatic who takes the asylum in William Peter Blatty's compelling (and quite funny) *The Ninth Configuration* (1980).

child, whom he allows to pet his horse. But when MacFarlane's housekeeper answers the door, we sense from her reaction to him that Gray is not all that he appears to be. This is substantiated later when we see him enter a cemetery at night (a sequence that begins with a marvelously subtle dissolve from the formaldehyde vat in MacFarlane's basement to the graveyard gate creaking open, tying both locations together) to exhume the body of a recently deceased youth, whose terrier is guarding the boy's grave, and brutally clubs the noisy dog to death with his shovel.

Gray, it emerges, is a psychopathic mass of contradictions. He robs graves and murders for profit without conscience. Yet he is also gentle with children and surrounds himself with animals, including his horse, whom he has named Friend, and a cat that he calls Brother. Even after he murders Joseph (Bela Lugosi), MacFarlane's blackmailing handyman, he pauses, straddling the corpse, to stroke his frightened cat. Gray wears no real face at all, just a series of psychotic masks, each of which is quite recognizably human.

One of the most profitable thrillers Val Lewton ever made and a big hit with most critics as well, *The Body Snatcher* was nevertheless tossed off as a B movie by Hollywood and thus ignored at Oscar time. At the

very least, Boris Karloff should have gotten a nomination, for his John Gray remains one of the subtlest and scariest dual-personality villains in the entire history of psychofilm.

In all of the Jekyll-and-Hyde-themed psychofilms discussed so far, the aberrant face of the duo has appeared either human or at least humanoid. In Oliver Stone's *The Hand* (1981), however, the main character's alternate self assumes an entirely different shape. Michael Caine stars as a successful cartoonist who loses his drawing hand in a freak car accident. Filled with frustration and bitterness over the incident, he dreams of being reconnected to his lost member and eventually comes to believe that the hand is actually alive and crawling its way back to him. Soon after, people start turning up strangled. Not until the film's last scene, however, do we know for sure that it has not been any marauding beast with five fingers that has been evening Caine's score against humanity, but the demented Caine himself, whose Jekyll half simply cannot vent the anger he feels over the cruel blow fate has dealt him. To do so, he arouses what is certainly one of the most unusual Mr. Hydes that psychofilm has given us yet.

2

"YOURS TRULY, JACK THE RIPPER"

I'm not a butcher
I'm not a Yid,
Nor yet a foreign skipper,
But I'm your own lighthearted friend,
Yours truly, Jack the Ripper.

—from a verse supposedly
written by the Ripper

In his 1959 book *The Identity of Jack the Ripper*, Donald McCormick writes that deprived of his grim nickname, in all probability the crimes the Ripper committed would have long ago been forgotten. Certainly in the one hundred-plus years that have gone by since the Ripper prowled the alleys of Whitechapel, his monstrous reputation in the annals of crime has been considerably challenged by a whole parade of even more spectacular fiends. And yet because of the bogeymanlike nature of his self-applied name and the fact that the Ripper murders have never officially been solved, Jack still fascinates us. At the same time that such fictional characters as Frankenstein's monster and Dracula have become almost like real people to us through cinematic and literary overkill, this true-life killer of the London fog has been transformed through similar media license into a supernatural being, an unreal phantom wrought by the imaginations of such writers as Mary Belloc-Lowndes.

My interest in the Ripper dates back to my teens when I was drawn by all the advertising hoopla on radio and television to see a "shocking new film" called *Jack the Ripper* (1958). The film was actually a rather tame low-budget British import that flamboyant Boston film distributor Joseph E. Levine had purchased cheaply for his growing Embassy Pictures, then spent millions to advertise and turn into a major media event. Earlier that year, Levine had done the same thing with a cheap Italian spear-and-sandal epic called *Hercules*, which he'd recut, dubbed into English, then promoted into a huge box-office success, even making a brief celebrity out of its obscure star, muscleman Steve Reeves.

Produced, directed, and photographed by the slick British B-movie team of Robert S. Baker and Monty Berman, *Jack the Ripper* was a decidedly more polished affair than *Hercules*. Nevertheless, prior to its tumultuous release in America, promoter Levine did change one thing. He replaced the film's existing musical score by British big-band musician Stanley Black with a jazzier one by American composers Jimmy McHugh and Pete Rugulo. Never having heard the Black score, I can't compare the two, but the McHugh-Rugulo score is a viscerally exciting piece of music that did much to enhance the film as well as to identify it; released as a sound-track album, it became a hit.

Scripted by Jimmy Sangster, who had worked as assistant director on an earlier Ripper film called *Room to Let* (1950), *Jack the Ripper* played fast and loose with the facts of the case. In it, a visiting American (Lee Patterson) helps a Scotland Yard inspector (Eddie Byrne) solve the mystery of the elusive harlot-killer by tracking him to his lair at a local hospital. The Ripper (Ewen Solon), a deranged sur-

Bucks Row, Whitechapel, the site of the Ripper's first murder victim, as it looked in 1975.

geon who has been systematically eliminating whores in order to find the one he wants, a girl named Mary Clarke who had driven his son to suicide, is trapped beneath a descending elevator and crushed to death. Though the film was in black and white, this last sequence was shot in color so that the Ripper's blood gushed a bright red. Prints now circulating on television, however, do not include this sequence in color.

One of the reasons why this otherwise mediocre film struck me at the time as being so powerful was its evocative atmosphere, a characteristic of most other Ripper films as well. The idea of a caped killer striking unseen at night out of the swirling London fog was a disturbing one even for fiction, but the fact that it actually happened—and that the killer went uncaught—proved even more disturbing and intriguing. The mystery of the Ripper's true identity captured my imagination immediately, and I began reading everything I could on the subject. I just had to know who he (or she) was. As part of that quest, I even took the Jack the Ripper tour while on a visit to England in 1975. The tour, a walking expedition of the Ripper's Whitechapel haunts, an area now considerably changed as the result of the Blitz and urban renewal,

"Mary Clarke?" asks the Ripper of his intended victim. From *Jack the Ripper* (1960).

34

was both a chilling and fascinating experience—like stepping inside a Ripper film—but it ultimately proved unsatisfying insofar as discovering the Ripper's identity was concerned.

The Lodger

For the benefit of those who are not familiar with the grisly history of the Ripper, or Saucy Jack, as he was also called, he murdered and hideously mutilated—seemingly at random—five down-on-their-luck prostitutes in London's East End slum of Whitechapel between August 31 and November 9, 1888. With the death of the final victim, Mary Kelly, the murders ceased as abruptly as they had begun, and the murderer himself ~~—————————— into obscurity and legend.~~ In the wake of the Ripper's reign of terror, which gripped all London and not just Whitechapel, accusing fingers were pointed everywhere. One of the more popular myths to grow up surrounding the case was perpetuated by a number of the city's landlords, who insisted that the mysterious fiend had once been a lodger in their rooming houses but had moved on before they could get the goods on

him. In 1911, mystery writer Mary Belloc-Lowndes used this rumor, which she had personally overheard, as the basis for her enduring Jack the Ripper novel *The Lodger*.

In the book, a strange young man takes a room with a family named Bunting. Hearing him come and go at odd hours and pace about his room late at night, they soon begin to suspect that he is the man all Scotland Yard is looking for, a killer nicknamed the Avenger on account of the calling cards he leaves beside the bodies of his victims. The Buntings soon begin to fear for the safety of their daughter Daisy, who has taken quite a fancy to the reclusive young man, but as Daisy's steady beau is also a detective, all turns out well in the nick of time.

A ~~————————— gripping~~ account of the widespread fear that even in 1911 was still fresh in Londoners' minds, *The Lodger* was a critical failure but eventually grew into a huge hit with the public. Not surprisingly, it was scooped up for the movies and in 1926 became a hit film directed by a young British filmmaker and true-crime buff named Alfred Hitchcock.

At this early point in his career, Hitchcock desperately needed a hit. His first two feature films, *The*

The suspicious lodger (Ivor Novello) asks Mrs. Jackson (Marie Ault) if she has any rooms available. From Alfred Hitchcock's *The Lodger* (1927).

One of the expressionistic title designs created in post-production to enhance the release print of Alfred Hitchcock's *The Lodger*. From a frame blow-up.

Pleasure Garden (1925) and *The Mountain Eagle* (1925), both made in Germany, remained unreleased because their distributor considered their Germanic style too arty and confusing for English tastes. While in Germany, Hitchcock had seen F. W. Murnau at work on *The Last Laugh* (1924) and had been so impressed by the director's expressionist style of rendering thought and emotion purely through images and montage that he remained influenced by Murnau to the end of his days.[1]

Problems quickly arose for Hitchcock, however, when matinee idol Ivor Novello was signed for the title role. Delighted at first by the presence of the star, whose popularity would do much to assure the film's box-office success, he became chagrined when Novello, feeling that his public wouldn't accept him as a murderer, demanded that the film's ending be changed. Having no clout, Hitchcock could do little but accept. Ironically, although Novello's ultimate innocence went against the director's wishes, the switch remains consistent with the theme of the innocent man who is judged guilty of a crime he didn't commit that is to be found in many of Hitchcock's subsequent thrillers. In most other areas, however, the film remains a fairly faithful adaptation of the book.

Hitchcock's initial difficulty with Novello eventually proved the least of his worries, however, for when *The Lodger* was finally completed, it too was deemed unreleasable by the distributor. It was felt that while Hitchcock's two previous movies may have been unduly influenced by the German expressionists, his latest was a downright expressionist art film that no one would spend a tuppence to see. Not agreeing with the distributor, but feeling the financial squeeze of having three Hitchcock films sitting on the shelf gathering dust rather than the necessary return on their investment, producer Michael Balcon turned to a young film cutter (and former zoologist) named Ivor Montagu for help. Montagu screened the film and was knocked out by its shivery atmosphere and many innovative narrative techniques; such as the now-famous sequence in which the lodger is seen pacing back and forth in his room through a transparent floor. Nevertheless, Montagu saw an opportunity to improve the film by reediting it, in his words, "toward, not away from, its exceptional qualities." Ungrudgingly, Hitchcock went along with Montagu's suggestions.

"As finished in its first-cut version, *The Lodger* was cluttered with titles," Montagu said some years later.

> They were mostly unnecessary, but according to the fashion for a silent feature at that time, numbering in the region of three hundred and fifty to five hundred. I got *The Lodger*'s titles down to eighty. We then persuaded American poster artist Ted McKnight Kauffer to draw us some sinister title backgrounds and reshot some scenes where it seemed the intended effect had not quite come off. My contribution was in the nature of that which a gallery director makes to a painting in suggesting how it should be framed, where hung, and in what light. The changes renewed Balcon's confidence. The press show ate up the picture, so did the trade show, and later the public. *The Lodger* opened the door to Hitchcock's two delayed predecessors waiting in the wings, and from then on Hitch was unstoppable.

Interestingly, Montagu maintains that the "arty touches" Hitchcock included in the film that the distributor had been so against were the director's way of calling the press's attention to himself. Despite Hitchcock's many later pronouncements that he made pictures only for the public, Montagu insists that Hitchcock really made them for the press and that he had confided as much. "This, he explained, was the reason for 'the Hitchcock touches'—novel shots that the critics would pick out and comment on," Montagu states. "As well as the trademark he later made his own of a momentary flash appearance in every film he directed. If you made yourself publicly known as a director—and this you could only do by getting mention in the press in connection with your directing—this would be the only way you became free to do what you wanted. If your name were known to the public, you would not be the prisoner of where you happened to be working. We

---

1. To see clearly just how influenced Hitchcock was by Murnau, check out Murnau's superb 1927 Hollywood film, *Sunrise*, a film whose overall staging and editing—particularly during an early scene in which George O'Brien wrestles with his conscience as he plans to murder his wife, Janet Gaynor, while she gradually comes to realize his intentions—look like the work of Hitchcock himself.

Ivor Novello takes once more to the foggy streets of London for the 1932 remake of *The Lodger*, released in the U.S. in 1935 as *The Phantom Fiend*. Elizabeth Allan is the lady in distress.

all knew him well enough to know that while the fame and money of success might be to him a pleasant side effect, it was not his primary motive. He lived to make pictures. To make them better was his use for freedom."

The Lodger does not strive to be an authentic account of the Ripper's crimes. Rather, it is a vivid depiction of the fear that pervaded the city of London at the time and reached into the hearts of all its citizens—a situation not unlike what happened in Boston in the early sixties at the height of the infamous Strangler case and in Los Angeles following the Tate-LaBianca murders of 1969 (see Chapter 7).

Reflecting a greater psychological truth, Mary Belloc-Lowndes had simply progressed Stevenson's Jekyll and Hyde concept its logical next step forward by making her fictional protagonist a monster who needs no physical transformation in order to carry out his psychotic deeds. Thus she gave birth to the twentieth-century literary psycho. Indeed, while the authentic Ripper may have been a nineteenth-century killer, his crimes, on the surface, seem much more common to our own age, which has seen a considerable rise over the years in the phenomenon of the random-attack, serial-murder type of killer.

Because of its changed ending, Hitchcock's *Lodger*

Laird Cregar, one of the screen's premiere psychos, as Mr. Slade, a.k.a. Jack the Ripper, in John Brahm's superb *The Lodger* (1944).

reflects little of this, of course. Though a psychofilm, there is no psycho in it. While everything may point to the lodger's being the on-the-loose Avenger, he turns out to be an avenger of a very different stripe, having taken rooms near the crime scene in order to track the murderer on his own for having killed his sister.

The Lodger proved such a successful vehicle for Novello that when the talkies arrived, he decided to have a go at it again. By this time (1935), however, Hitchcock had gone on to bigger things, and so he secured a different director, Maurice Elvey, to remake it for him, which Elvey did virtually shot for shot. Again Novello played the mysterious lodger who is wrongly accused of being the Avenger and is saved at the last minute from the hounding mob when the real killer, who bears a striking resembl~~~~~~~~~~~~~~~~~~~~~ In this version, Elizabeth Allan played Daisy, the Buntings' infatuated daughter, and a newcomer named Jack Hawkins played the detective beau who is ultimately left in the lurch. Released to huge success in Britain as *The Lodger,* the film was retitled *The Phantom Fiend* for the U.S. and earned even better reviews than the Hitchcock version that preceded it. "For sheer, cold-blooded, suspenseful, and spine-chilling melodrama," said the *New York Times* in its April 22 review, "nothing like it has been seen since the German picture *M* was shown here about a year ago."

The venerable Belloc-Lowndes tale again reached the screen nine years later. However, reviewers were less kind even though this version—for my money, the best of all of them—followed her original premise to its logical conclusion and was given the A-1 Hollywood treatment. For this version of *The Lodger* (1944), screenwriter Barré Lyndon and director John Brahm, a German émigré who was also strongly influenced by the expressionist tradition, discarded the name Avenger and finally called the killer by his proper name, Jack the Ripper. Merle Oberon played the imperiled daughter Kitty, a music-hall artiste, while George Sanders played her detective boyfriend. Heavyset Laird Cregar played the lodger, who this time around does indeed turn out to be the Ripper. Of the film, however, the *New York Times* reviewer wrote, "If *The Lodger* was designed to chill the spine—then something is wrong with the picture." In particular, he singled out Cregar's performance as being quite overdrawn, noting that the actor himself had been sitting in the audience near him during the screening and "obviously was not prepared for the ripples of laughter which greeted his more ominous movements on the screen."

As with Spencer Tracy's *Dr. Jekyll and Mr. Hyde,* which also initially received scathing reviews, time has been kind to this version of *The Lodger* and to

Jack Palance starred as the lodger/ripper in yet another adaptation of Mrs. Belloc Lowndes's famous story, *Man in the Attic* (1954). Showing concern is Constance Smith.

John Carradine lookalike Valentine Dyall (as the mysterious Dr. Fell) menaces Christine Silver in *Room to Let* (1950).

Freudian psychologist Dr. Pritchard (Eric Porter) used hypnosis and drugs on young Anna (Angharad Rees) to get at the root cause of her aberration in Hammer's *Hands of the Ripper* (1971).

Cregar's performance, which is anything *but* laughable. As the Ripper, he is genuinely frightening. When Kitty reaches out to him in friendship, one sees in his eyes and hears in his placid voice a conscious desire to be delivered from his madness even as he clings to that madness and subconsciously urges it on.

Trapped by the police at the conclusion of the film, he reacts like the hunted and dangerous animal he has become, a psychotic creature whose eyes no longer reflect any human will or understanding. Though only in his late twenties, Cregar died suddenly a few years later from a massive heart attack suffered while

Jack the Ripper (David Warner) uses H. G. Wells's time machine to flee from 19th century London to modern-day San Francisco in Nicholas Meyer's fanciful *Time After Time* (1979).

David Warner as Jack the Ripper and Mary Steenburgen as his potential victim in *Time After Time*.

Tod Slaughter (center) as Spring-heeled Jack in *Curse of the Wraydons* (1946), a barnstorming rendition of the Ripper theme.

undergoing a severe crash diet he'd determined to put himself through in order to get more romantic-lead roles. Thus ended the career of one of psychofilm's most realistic and convincing screen crazies.

In 1954, established screen villain Jack Palance was typecast once more when he too played the notorious Ripper in yet another—though as of this writing final[2]—big-screen adaptation of *The Lodger* called *Man in the Attic,* directed by Hugo Fregonese. Based by writer Robert Presnell, Jr., on the Barré Lyndon screenplay for the 1944 film, it is a rather tepid affair, however, with little to recommend it except for Leo Tover's nicely atmospheric black-and-white photography—which is still nowhere near as impressive as Lucien Ballard's brilliant work for the 1944 version—and Palance's all-stops-out performance. Of the film and Palance, one critic noted, "As the gaunt, soft-spoken fiend, carving out a bloody course he attributes to matricide, Mr. Palance is well nigh perfect. As for Mrs. Lowndes, though it seems doubtful, may her poor betrayed spirit rest in peace."

Mary Belloc-Lowndes was not the only writer to exploit the theme of the rooming-house Ripper. British mystery writer Margery Allingham, a contemporary rival of Agatha Christie's, did so too in a late-forties BBC radio play she called *Room to Let.* The play was quickly purchased for filming by an aggressive

young company called Hammer Films and released domestically in 1950 under its parent banner Exclusive Films. Adapting popular radio and television plays for the big screen was not an unusual policy for Hammer at this time, and its profitability led to Hammer's becoming one of Britain's most successful independent production companies by the late fifties.

2. Charles Gray appeared as the Ripper in a television version of *The Lodger* videotaped for a late-night series of thrillers on the ABC network in the early seventies.

Ostensibly, *Room to Let* is *The Lodger* all over again with just a few more wrinkles added. Set in 1904 and told in flashback, it recounts how a plucky reporter named Curly Minter (Jimmy Hanley) stumbles upon the identity of the Ripper, a mysterious medical man named Dr. Fell (played by John Carradine look-alike Valentine Dyall), who has taken rooms in a lodging house run by a crippled widow and her daughter Molly (played by Christine Silver and Constance Smith, respectively). Interestingly, actress Smith must have enjoyed her bouts with the Ripper because she played a similar role four years later in *Man in the Attic*.

Not released theatrically in the U.S. to the best of my knowledge, *Room to Let* does turn up in syndication on American television from time to time. Overall it is a tidy but unobtrusive little thriller. Its real claim to fame, however, lay mostly in what its makers went on to achieve in psychofilm history. In the wake of the success of Hitchcock's *Psycho* (1960), Hammer, by then a world-renowned company, produced a whole slew of psychofilms in the Hitchcock mold, many of them written (quite well too) by Jimmy Sangster, *Room to Let*'s assistant director, and produced by Anthony Hinds, who was responsible for the same chores on *Room to Let*. More about this, however, in Chapter 5.

Hammer's interest in the Ripper did not begin and end with *Room to Let*. As has already been mentioned, the fiend made an oblique appearance in the company's *Dr. Jekyll and Sister Hyde*. In Hammer's *Hands of the Ripper* (1971), however, he plays a prime role—or, rather, his daughter does.

Written by L. W. Davidson from a story by Edward Spencer Shew and directed in Hammer's colorfully gothic tradition by Hungarian-born Peter Sasdy, *Hands of the Ripper* remains one of the company's gems—at least in its theatrically released form. The television version has virtually been destroyed by some arbitrary cuts (mostly violence) as well as the insertion of a number of ridiculous flash-forwards in which a psychiatrist pads out the plot by explaining (as if we were idiots) what the characters are up to.

Traumatized when she sees her Ripper father knife her mother, kiss her corpse, then perish in their flaming house, young Anna (Angharad Rees) grows up to develop a bad case of Ripperitis herself whenever she is shown any affection. She falls under the care of a Freudian psychologist, Dr. Pritchard (Eric Porter in a superb performance), and the two become linked in an unhealthy symbiotic relationship (with undercurrents of romance) similar to what happens in Hitchcock's *Spellbound* (1945) and *Marnie* (1964). At the film's moving conclusion in a cathedral, Pritchard, who has been mortally wounded by the otherwise sweet and placid Anna during one of her

"Jill the Ripper" attacks "Jill the Victim" in *Knife for the Ladies* (1973).

Ripper seizures, urges the confused girl to come to him, which she does by jumping from one of the cathedral balconies. The pair dies in each other's arms—the only real way out of the whole mess for both of them.

Variations on a Ripper Theme

Pandora's Box (1929), while not a movie about the Ripper, nevertheless used him, as have many films before and since, as a sort of deadly symbol. Its main character, Lulu (Louise Brooks), is an amoral young woman who has a devastating effect on the lives of all the men (and women) with whom she becomes involved. Murder, suicide, and scandal surround Lulu, who is finally arrested for shooting her husband. Released for lack of evidence, she flees to London where her fortunes take a turn for the worse and she becomes a prostitute. She picks up her first customer on Christmas Eve, tries to work the same old charm on him, but is dealt a nasty retribution for her past and present sins when he turns out to be none other than Jack the Ripper. After he murders her, he disappears into the night.

Another German film, Paul Leni's *Waxworks* (1924), also used the Ripper as a symbol, not of

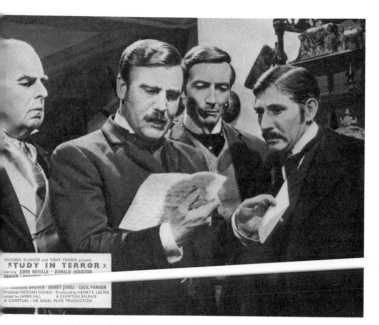

Sherlock Holmes vs. Jack the Ripper in *A Study in Terror* (1966). From left to right: Robert Morley (as Mycroft Holmes), Donald Houston (as Dr. Watson), John Neville (as Sherlock), and Frank Finlay (as Inspector Lestrade).

retribution this time but of tyranny. In it, a penniless poet (played by future Hollywood director William Dieterle) is hired by a carnival showman to write a series of stories about the figures appearing in the showman's waxworks. One of the figures, Jack the Ripper (Werner Krauss), apparently comes to life and mercilessly stalks the writer and his girlfriend, the showman's daughter. The episode, however, turns out to be nothing more than a nightmare suffered by the anxious young man. Nevertheless, Leni and scriptwriter Henrik Galeen's use of the historical Ripper as a representation of the arbitrary threat to personal freedom and happiness that can stalk anyone at any time was quite clear and, considering what ultimately happened in Germany, quite prescient indeed.

Also using the Ripper as a symbol—in this case of society's moral decline and escalating world violence—was *Time After Time* (1979), in which, prior to writing his famous novel *The Time Machine*, H. G. Wells (Malcolm McDowell) actually invents one. But before he can test it out for himself, Jack the Ripper (David Warner) steals it to elude capture by Scotland Yard and is propelled forward in time to San Francisco circa the late seventies, where he finds society's wall-to-wall sex and violence very much to his twisted tastes. Wells follows in the hope of bringing him to justice and saving the future from his ravaging influence and succeeds by rigging his machine so that the again-fleeing Ripper is trapped forever in the fourth dimension, thus providing the answer as to why he was never caught.

Not all variations on the Ripper theme are as thoughtful as these three films. *Curse of the Wraydons* (1946), based on a hoary British stage melodrama called *Springheeled Jack, the Terror of London,* posed the Ripper (Tod Slaughter) as a mad inventor and former spy for Napoleon who seeks revenge on his brother's family by means of a diabolical machine, thus giving rise to the legend of Vanishing Jack. Jess Franco's splattery (and incoherent) *Jack the Ripper* (1976) offered Klaus Kinski as a somber necrophiliac who carves up _____ _____ that he can have sex with them, then dumps their bodies in the Thames. Equally shoddy was *Black the Ripper,* which was made during the "blaxploitation" phase of American filmmaking of the early seventies. Finally, in 1973, ubiquitous Jack (or in this case, Jill), following Horace Greeley's famous advice, donned spurs and went west to wield yet another *Knife for the Ladies.*

Considering all the merging of Ripper fact with fiction that has gone on over the years, it seemed inevitable that someday some enterprising filmmaker would decide to wed the two permanently by pairing fiction's greatest supersleuth, Sherlock Holmes, with the real-life fiend in an ultimate battle to the death. In fact, this has happened on-screen at least *three* times, the first time in a polished 1966 British film called *A Study in Terror,* the second in a 1971 Spanish hodge-podge titled *Jack el Destripador des Londres,* and finally in the definitive *Murder by Decree* of 1979.

Of the three, the Spanish film starring Paul Naschy and directed by José Luis Madrid is the only one that is so inane and downright laughable that it takes a deserving place alongside the previously mentioned Kinski fiasco and *Black the Ripper* as among the worst Ripper films in psychofilm history. In it, London Chief Inspector Sir Charles Warren hires Holmes to bring an end to the Ripper's terrible career, which by this time has claimed *thirty-nine* victims! Combining elements of the real Ripper story (and very few of them indeed) with details from Conan Doyle's *Sign of the Four,* the film even has Holmes dress up in drag in a final effort to seduce the harlot killer out in the open. Again the Ripper turns out to be a Jekyll-and-Hyde-type doctor.

A Study in Terror is nearer the mark in that it not only maintains an accurate body count but even uses the victims' real names, though for some reason it does get them out of sequence. Its screenplay (by Donald and Derek Ford) places the responsibility for the Ripper murders squarely on the doorstep of

43

Sherlock Holmes (John Neville) comes under the knife himself in his search for the elusive and deadly Ripper. From *A Study in Terror*.

Peter O'Toole as the deranged 14th Earl of Gurney (Jack the Ripper?) in *The Ruling Class* (1972). Seen here with James Villiers.

royalty, a theme (and theory) later explored more fully in *Murder by Decree*. As in the 1958 *Jack the Ripper*, prostitutes are being systematically eliminated by an elusive madman. This time, however, the killer is not a vengeful doctor but rather the elite Lord Carfax (John Fraser), who has been murdering his way through Whitechapel in an effort to trace a fictional prostitute named Angela Osborne (Adrienne Corri) for having married and supposedly dragged his brother to ruin, thus endangering the family name. Sherlock Holmes (wittily played by John Neville) solves the case in due course, but both the evidence and Lord Carfax are consumed in a fire, and so the Ripper's identity remains officially unmasked. Only Holmes and the ever-faithful Dr. Watson (Donald Houston) know the truth, but they both consider it too potentially explosive to reveal.

Based on a Holmes short story called "Fog" written by Adrian Conan Doyle, the son of Holmes's creator, who also served as one of the film's financial backers, *A Study in Terror* is much more successful as a Holmes pastiche than it is as a Ripper film. Nevertheless, the fictional solution it poses to the crimes is an interesting one that has found a great deal of favor among Ripper buffs over the years. Indeed, even at the time of the murders, there was some suspicion that royalty or at least a member of the upper class may have been involved. Most who claimed to have caught a glimpse of the Ripper did, in fact, consistently describe him as looking like a gentleman or a "toff." For many of these people and for some social reformers (such as George Bernard Shaw, for instance), the Ripper thus became a symbol of all that was wrong and rotten about the British class system, a system that allowed the elite to prey on the lower classes without any fear of reprisal—which is why, they say, the Ripper was never caught or, at least, never charged. This idea was later ferociously satirized in *The Ruling Class* (1972), in which Peter O'Toole stars as the schizoid fourteenth Earl of Gurney, a gentle flake who believes that he is Jesus Christ until his avaricious relatives convince him otherwise. "Your name is Jack!" they insistently shout at him in an effort to make him come to his senses and assume his royal role. And so Jack he becomes—Jack the Ripper, that is. Imagining himself adrift in Whitechapel, he comes upon a whore and cuts her down, only to realize that it is his wife whom he has just slain in their living room. No matter. He gets his seat in the House of Lords anyway, a spot that now allows him to indulge his violent appetites more freely in an even more powerful arena: *politics*.

The *Real* Jack the Ripper?

Politics and the Ripper converge completely in the ultimate Jack the Ripper film, *Murder by Decree*. This one does indeed present a solution, based to a large extent on material unearthed for a riveting television docudrama produced for the BBC in 1973 and later sold to American television, where it turns up infrequently due to a commercially unwieldy six-hour length.

A London policeman discovers the body of one of the Ripper's victims in the BBC's riveting six-part 1970s docu-drama *Jack the Ripper*.

Watt (Frank Windsor) and Barlow (Alan Stratford-Johns) examine their chart of victims and clues in an effort to ferret out the truth behind the legendary crimes. From the BBC's *Jack the Ripper*.

Jack the Ripper, or *The Ripper File* as it is also known, represented a unique collaboration between the BBC's documentary and dramatic-features units in an effort to separate fact from fiction in the Ripper case and come to a satisfying conclusion once and for all. Three researchers under the guidance of documentary producer Paul Bonner spent months combing archives and private papers to come up with the evidence, much of which had never been made public before. To reveal that evidence in as dramatic a way as possible to the audience, it was decided to use characters in Britain's most popular television detective series, *Barlow at Large,* as a vehicle. "The only way of reaching the truth in this tangled case," said Bonner, "was to take all the factual evidence from the nineteenth century and recreate it word for word from the original court transcripts and police reports. Then we have it argued through by two people who are known to the public as two of their best policemen." The scripts were coauthored by *Barlow* creator Elwyn Jones and documentary writer John Lloyd.

Reopening the case as a matter of professional curiosity, Detective Chief Superintendent Barlow (Alan Stratford-Johns) and Detective Superintendent Watt (Frank Windsor) sift through massive piles of evidence, clues, and red herrings in each episode, cross-examining each other on their findings, and in the final episode titled "The Highest in the Land," presenting their astonishing conclusion: that the murders were the result of a political cover-up.

Although there were five victims, Barlow and Watt believe that the last, Mary Kelly, was the one the Ripper was really looking for. The other four lives had been snuffed out in such a horrendous manner simply to make the killings appear to be the work of a madman bent on destroying the whores of Whitechapel. That the Ripper's final and most frenzied orgy of slaughter (Kelly) marked the end of his career seemed consistent with the madman theory, a theory that claimed that, as there seemed to be no worse way in which a human body could be mistreated and mutilated, the Ripper had finally sated himself and retired or committed suicide. A perfectly reasonable theory, it was lent credence when the

Sherlock Holmes (Christopher Plummer) pursued the legendary Ripper again in Bob Clark's *Murder by Decree* (1979), the best of all Jack the Ripper films.

body of a real suicide victim, Montague John Druitt, the down-and-out son of a surgeon, was found floating in the Thames, having been there for about a month since the Ripper killings had ceased. Druitt could never be convicted, but he remained over the years the number one perfectly reasonable suspect. Until now.

Barlow and Watt discover that many investigators over the years had attempted to involve the grandson of Queen Victoria, the Duke of Clarence, in the Jack the Ripper murders. The fact that he and Druitt looked very much alike helped to fan the flames of this speculation. In their "highest in the land" theory, Barlow and Watt follow this same line, implicating the Duke as well, but not in the role of murderer. Through independent investigations, both detectives simultaneously learn that as a young man of twenty, Clarence took up residence in Cleveland Street, an artists' ghetto near Whitechapel, and there met a girl of the lower classes named Ann Elizabeth Crook with whom he fell in love. She became pregnant and they were married in a ceremony kept secret because Clarence didn't want Crook to discover his true identity and because Crook was a Catholic. Learning of the marriage and determining it to be a threat to the established Protestant government should it become public knowledge during those politically troubled times, some high government officials secretly express their displeasure, and soon after, Annie Crook is run down by a carriage driven by a man named Netley, the Duke's private coachman. Sent to a hospital in Fulham on the orders of Sir William Gull, the royal physician, she remained confined there till her death. With Annie Crook out of the way, there was one more problem, however: finding and silencing the friend of Crook's who had acted as witness to the marriage ceremony. That girl, Barlow and Watt discover to their astonishment, is none other than Mary Kelly. From this and more incredible data, they conclude that the job of silencing her (and anyone she may have spoken to about the affair), which was made to look like the work of a madman, was undertaken by the hireling Netley and the surgically skilled Sir William Gull.

Anarchist police inspector David Hemmings falls victim to one of the co-conspirators (Peter Jonfield) in the Ripper murders in *Murder by Decree*.

As one might expect, the BBC drama created quite a stir. Seeking a broader audience for this material, the BBC agreed to bankroll a feature film on the subject of the Ripper that Canadian director Bob Clark had long wanted to make. Once again it was decided that the most dramatic way of presenting the material would be through the eyes of a fictional detective investigating the case, but one who was more well-known than Barlow and Watt. Sherlock Holmes became the obvious choice. Because this was to be an Anglo-Canadian coproduction, a British writer, John Hopkins, was signed to do the script based on Jones and Lloyd's *Ripper File*. Initially titled *Sherlock Holmes Meets Saucy Jack*, which seemed to have a comic connotation, it was later changed to the more thematically pointed *Murder by Decree*.

Holmes (Christopher Plummer) is brought in on the case the night of the Ripper's double murder of Elizabeth Stride and Catherine Eddowes, his third and fourth victims, when a Whitechapel committee for public safety hires him to solve the crimes that the police seem unable or unwilling to solve. With the help of his trusty aide Dr. Watson (played by James Mason,[3] who was a tad too old for the part but is magnificent in it nonetheless), Holmes's investigations lead him to the conclusion that the responsibility for the Ripper murders may go as high as the throne. He traces Mary Kelly (Susan Clark), who, terrified for her safety and in hiding, breaks down and reveals some details of the Annie Crook affair to him

prior to her being kidnapped and his being knocked unconscious. Recovering, Holmes locates the pathetic Annie (Genevieve Bujold) in a mental hospital, and, to his mortification, she confirms his suspicions shortly before her death.

"Jack the Ripper is not the whole point behind the plot, but who is trying to hinder Holmes's investigations," says director Clark. "Radicals and socialists are helping him, monarchist organizations are trying to stop him, and a couple of secret societies [particularly the Freemasons] are involved. It is more an adventure/intrigue than horror. The horror story evolves into a *Chinatown* or Watergate situation." Indeed it does. Learning that Annie Crook and the Duke of Clarence had a child, Holmes confronts the prime minister (John Gielgud) with evidence of the whole sordid affair and indignantly announces to him and his underlings that he will keep quiet about it only so long as the child remains safe and no more blood is spilled. Later, in his rooms at Baker Street, he picks up his violin and, reflecting on the tragedy of all

---

3. Fiercely loyal to his queen and country, Watson finds it difficult to believe that the government could ever be involved for political motives in so underhanded and scurrilous an affair as the Whitechapel slayings. In interviews, actor Mason claimed that he patterned his performance as an inherently decent, politically naive man after former president Gerald Ford. On another curious note, actor Frank Finlay, who plays Inspector Lestrade in the film, played the same role in *A Study in Terror* (1966).

James Spader as a modern-day Jack the Ripper in *Jack's Back* (1988).

that's happened, movingly reprises the haunting Scottish dirge that had been played at Catherine Eddowes's funeral.

One suspects that everyone's heart was really in this film as the script, the acting, the direction, the photography are all of an exceptionally high order. Certainly director Clark, whose career has since taken a downward spiral (albeit a financially successful one) with films such as *Porky's* (1981), has yet to match his work here. Though a modest box-office success, *Murder by Decree* astonishingly did not get overall good reviews at the time of its release—perhaps because most critics felt compelled to lump it into the same category as most other thrillers and horror films. Clearly, *Murder by Decree* is more than that. It is a psychofilm with political overtones. And while its Jack the Ripper may lack the traditional qualities we have come to expect from previous Ripper films and from their Jekyll and Hyde antecedents, he does bear more than enough in common with some of the crazies in the chapters to follow.

On the centennial of the Ripper's reign of terror,

British writer-director David Wickes reopened the legendary case once more and finally solved it (according to him, if no one else) in the lavish American-British coproduction *Jack the Ripper* (1988), which aired as a two-part, four-hour miniseries on American television. Michael Caine starred as Frederick Abberline, the chief detective on the case, who finally nails the Ripper but keeps his identity secret from the public out of deference to the high-born killer's family. Wickes too poses the theory that Sir William Gull (referred to by name this time around) was the Whitechapel fiend, but he does away with *Murder by Decree*'s political motivations for the crimes. He simply suggests that the overworked and obsessive Gull had suffered a severe breakdown and committed the murders while in a fugue state—an uninspired conclusion at best. And director Rowdy Herrington commemorated the Ripper's centennial with equal lack of inspiration in *Jack's Back* (1988), in which the fiend's crimes are reenacted on the streets of Los Angeles by a modern-day copycat (James Spader).

3

DELUSIONS OF GRANDEUR: MASTER FIENDS, ASSASSINS, AND OTHER CRAZIES

There are *no* midgets in the United States Air Force!

—Gen. Lawrence Dell (Burt Lancaster)
in *Twilight's Last Gleaming* (1977)

If one accepts the solution posed by *Murder by Decree,* the Ripper murders were motivated by a desire to maintain the political status quo. Whatever their motivation, however, the murders themselves were obviously insane acts perpetrated by men who were clearly unbalanced. Certainly *Murder by Decree* portrays them that way. Gull (called Sir Thomas Spivey in the film), the actual fiend who commits the bloody deeds, has eyes like a shark, and the grisly zeal with which he disembowels the still conscious Mary Kelly in order to wrench from her the hiding place of Annie Crook's baby is a frightening sight to behold. Obviously, the act of murder holds a special appeal for this man, although what that appeal may be is never defined in the film. One can only guess. This is not the case with the psychos to be encountered next.

In *Order of Assassins* (Panther, 1972), author Colin Wilson describes assassins this way:

> They are in-betweeners, too clever and dominant for the place society has to offer them, but not clever—or perhaps stable—enough to compel society to accept them on their own terms. When such men become killers, they are "assassins" rather than ordinary murderers. They know they are unlike other men, they experience drives and tensions that alienate them from the rest of society, they possess the courage to satisfy these drives in defiance of society. The assassin always walks alone. [For him], murder is not

only an ultimate purpose, but also a means of self-fulfillment.

In varying ways, this description fits not only presidential assassin John Baron (Frank Sinatra) in *Suddenly,* but also Captain Wolf Larsen (Edward G. Robinson) in *The Sea Wolf* (1941), Cody Jarrett (James Cagney) in *White Heat* (1949), Prof. Henry Jarrod (Vincent Price) in *House of Wax* (1953), Lawrence Dell (Burt Lancaster) in *Twilight's Last Gleaming,* and even Stanley Kubrick's symbolic caricature Dr. Strangelove (Peter Sellers). These are psychos who suffer from extreme delusions of grandeur, men who will stop at nothing—not murder, or even *mass* murder—to assert their frustrated wills. And to watch these frightening creatures evolve on-screen, we must once more go back to the early days of the movies.

Dr. Mabuse, the King of Crime

In the wake of World War I, German society suffered an economic and cultural nervous breakdown. Inflation soared out of sight, crime became rampant, and weirdness in personal behavior and in the arts was *très chic.* Christopher Isherwood's fictional *Berlin Stories,* later dramatized as *I Am a Camera*

50

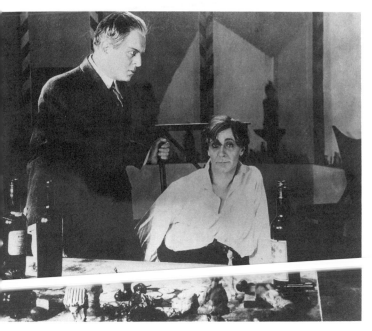

Master fiend Dr. Mabuse (Rudolf Klein-Rogge) bends another victim to his malignant will in Fritz Lang's *Dr. Mabuse, Der Spieler* (1922).

Count Zaroff (Leslie Banks) reveals his darker side to Eve Trowbridge (Fay Wray) and big game hunter Bob Rainsford (Joel McCrea) in *The Most Dangerous Game* (1932).

Terrence Granville (Charles Starrett) brings the sword of Genghis Khan to master fiend Dr. Fu Manchu (Boris Karloff) and his daughter Fah Lo See (Myrna Loy) in *The Mask of Fu Manchu* (1932).

and musicalized as *Cabaret,* paints a vivid picture of the decadent conditions of the period, eventually allowing the likes of Adolf Hitler, history's greatest master fiend, to assume power and bend the country, not to mention much of the world, to his malignant will. Not surprisingly, German films of the time were looked upon by audiences as a kind of release valve, and so escapist fare such as fantasies and romantic adventures and costume epics flooded the cinemas. Artists being what they are, they couldn't help but reflect the German state of mind in their work, and so the tortured visuals of a new artistic movement called expressionism began finding their way onstage, in painting, and into the movies as well. In the vanguard of the cinema's movement in this direction was the Austrian-born director Fritz Lang.

A former student of architecture, Lang turned to the movies in 1917 as a writer. By 1919, he had succeeded in moving into the more influential director's chair where he quickly became one of the leading screen fantasists of his day. His body of work during the silent-film era ranged from multipart action movies such as *Die Spinnen* (1919, 1920), a *Raiders of the Lost Ark*–type adventure about a secret organization bent on discovering an ancient Incan treasure with magical powers to enslave the world, to *Die Nibelungen* (1924), a spectacular two-part saga of

Shipwrecked intellectual Humphrey Van Weyden (Alexander Knox) learns that the brutal Captain Larsen (Edward G. Robinson), a disciple of the philosopher Nietzsche, is more of a monster than he thought in *The Sea Wolf* (1941).

the lives of Germany's legendary lovers, Siegfried and Kriemhilde, to the still-amazing science-fiction tale of urban life in the year 2000, *Metropolis* (1927). Without exaggerating, he was the George Lucas[1] and Steven Spielberg of his day, for many of Lang's films proved extremely popular not just with German audiences but with filmgoers all over the world.

Unlike American audiences, however, German moviegoers enjoyed—and often preferred—films whose length required attendance over several evenings in order to take in the entire work. And so it was

not uncommon for producers and directors to construct their films to be released in separate parts. Many of Lang's epic fantasies, such as *Die Spinnen* and

1. Lucas's *Star Wars* saga draws inspiration from many sources, not the least being Fritz Lang. The marshy haunt of Yoda in *The Empire Strikes Back* (1980), as well as Yoda himself, are clearly reminiscent of the enchanted forest in Lang's *Siegfried* (part one of *Die Nibelungen*) and the omniscient, though wicked, dwarf Alberich who dwells there.

Master fiend John Barrymore works his charms on Carmel Myers in *Svengali* (1931).

Die Nibelungen, were released in just such a manner, often under individual titles rather than simply being billed as "Part I" or "Part II." Such films were not so much serials—though the popularity of serials may have inspired them—as what today is known as miniseries, that is, a single film broken up into several episodes. When released in America, these episodes were often combined and the overall film truncated to a more commercial ninety minutes or less, a paring down that usually rendered it incomprehensible. Such was the case with *Dr. Mabuse der Spieler* (1922),

Lang's epic psychofilm in which he first introduced his Hitlerian master fiend Dr. Mabuse (Rudolf Klein-Rogge) to audiences.

In his otherwise splendid book on Lang (*The Cinema of Fritz Lang,* Barnes, 1969), Paul M. Jensen takes the director to task for humanizing Mabuse, thereby clipping his wings as a symbol of evil and turning him into little more than an unbalanced master criminal. But to my mind, this is precisely Lang's point. While the director may have intended his film to reflect the decadent times in which it is set

53

and wished Mabuse to serve as a sort of coordinating influence over those times, Mabuse is not principally a symbol. He is a man, one of those in-betweeners Colin Wilson writes about, a dominant outsider who attempts to crush society because he can't fit into it.

Using counterfeit bank notes of his own manufacture, Mabuse manipulates the economy and causes inflation to soar. Through hypnotism, he bends weaker souls to his will and forces his enemies to commit suicide. Others he destroys through sexual scandal. The film's title tells all. He is Dr. Mabuse, *der Spieler*—"the gambler," who uses people for chips and achieves self-fulfillment only through destruction. The fact that his archenemy Von Wenck (Bernhard Goetzke) bests him in the end and gets him committed to an insane asylum does not mean that Mabuse has suddenly gone mad. He *is* mad and has been all along. And has gotten much of society to join him.

Lang's portrait of Mabuse as the kind of criminal who alters the shape of society to serve his own twisted needs removes him from his literary counterparts Professor Moriarty and Dr. Fu Manchu, characters on whom Norbert Jacques, the author of the original Mabuse novel (*Dr. Mabuse, Man of Mystery*), clearly based his fiend. Moriarty and Fu Manchu may have had their grandiose dreams, but they never succeeded in imposing them on society overall. Mabuse does. At least for a time.

Released in two parts, *Dr. Mabuse der Spieler* and *Inferno,* as the two halves were called, proved an enormous box-office success in Germany and the rest of Europe. In America, though, the two films were combined, cut to ninety minutes, and retitled *Dr. Mabuse: The Fatal Passion* (a good title by the way) for a brief and unsuccessful run. And so Mabuse never became the cultural icon in America that he remains in Europe even to this day.

Ten years after the release of the first Mabuse movie, Lang returned to the subject with *Das Testament der Dr. Mabuse* (1932), the film that sealed his fate in then-Nazified Germany and forced him to flee to France and ultimately America to continue his career. Lang's original Mabuse film was not based on Hitler, as the Führer had not yet risen to power. But it eerily foreshadowed his rise. In *Das Testament,* however, Lang chose to make the parallel obvious, even to the extent of having his master criminal mouth some of Hitler's more well-known Nazi slogans. After screening the work, Goebbels, Hitler's propaganda minister, invited Lang to his office and told him that he was going to ban the film. This was not Lang's first encounter with Nazi officialdom (see chapter 4), and so he knew something was up. An admirer of the director, who enjoyed a reputation as one of Germany's greatest filmmakers, Goebbels attempted to

Ruthless Captain Stone (Richard Dix, right) gives his third officer (Russell Wade) a lesson in power in a scene cut from *The Ghost Ship* (1943).

sugar the pill by offering Lang the opportunity to head up Germany's movie industry, which was soon to begin devoting its energies to the making of propaganda films. Seeing the handwriting on the wall, Lang said he'd think it over, then later that night fled to France, leaving behind all of his belongings, his considerable wealth, and even his wife, Thea Von Harbou, the novelist-screenwriter (and former wife of Dr. Mabuse himself, Rudolf Klein-Rogge), who had already committed herself to Nazism. The two divorced shortly thereafter, and Lang didn't return to Germany for almost thirty years. Drawing the circle closed, he then made another, updated Mabuse adventure called *The 1,000 Eyes of Dr. Mabuse* (1960), which typically enjoyed great success in Europe but failed in America due to an atrociously dubbed sound track (this print occasionally turns up on American television). *The 1,000 Eyes of Dr. Mabuse* turned out to be Lang's final theatrical film. He died in 1976.

The Master Fiends

Unlike Dr. Mabuse, who chose to topple an existing society because he couldn't be part of it, a number of other screen master fiends have elected to remove themselves totally from society in order to set up their

One of the screen's most perverse psychopathic loners, Dr. Moreau (Charles Laughton), uses his island hideaway to conduct bizarre experiments on animals in *Island of Lost Souls* (1933). He is shown here with his most successful creation, Kathleen Burke as the Panther Woman.

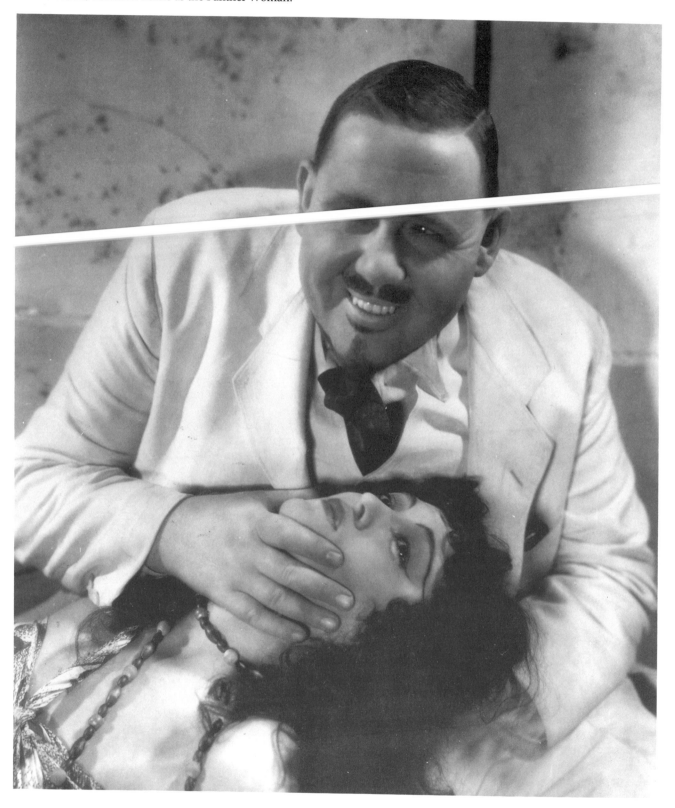

own. Surrounding themselves with misfits such as themselves, but ones with considerably weaker wills, they then mold this society to reflect and satisfy their own warped desires. No less crazy than Dr. Mabuse, but a lot less ambitious, they either make their victims come to them or feed savagely off their own kind. Two prime examples of this type are Count Zaroff in *The Most Dangerous Game* (1932) and Wolf Larsen in *The Sea Wolf*.

The first (and best) screen version of Richard Connell's oft-filmed tale, *The Most Dangerous Game* was produced by Merian C. Cooper and directed by Ernest B. Schoedsack (and Irving Pichel), who shot the film back-to-back with their more celebrated production of *King Kong* (1933), using many of *Kong*'s cast and crew members as well as its sets. When the ship he is traveling on strikes a reef and explodes, big-game hunter Bob Rainsford (Joel McCrea) survives by swimming to a seemingly uninhabited island nearby. Once ashore, he comes upon a huge castle owned by the mysterious Count Zaroff (Leslie Banks), a hunter who expresses much delight at Rainsford's sudden appearance. With the help of one of Zaroff's other shipwrecked "guests," Eve Trowbridge (Fay Wray), Rainsford soon discovers the truth about his benefactor—that he is quite mad and that he himself caused the shipwrecks by altering the marking lights in the channel so as to lure hapless survivors to his island. Exploring Zaroff's secret trophy room, Rainsford and Eve soon find out why, for the walls are adorned with human heads. Zaroff is a hunter alright, but one who, out of boredom with hunting animals, has secluded himself away from the disapproving eyes of society so that he can rejuvenate his interest in the sport by now hunting the most dangerous and challenging game of all: man himself. Rainsford, of course, proves the ideal opponent.

With Eve as the prize ("One does not kill the female animal"), Zaroff gives the weaponless Rainsford a head start, and the remainder of the film is taken up by one long, exciting, and violent stalk during which Rainsford succeeds in killing off two of Zaroff's pursuing hounds, a number of bearers, and finally Zaroff himself, who, mortally wounded, is torn apart by his remaining hounds as Rainsford and Eve escape in a motor launch.

What makes *The Most Dangerous Game* not just a good, high-tension horror-adventure film but a significant psychofilm as well is the character of Zaroff himself. As portrayed by Leslie Banks, he is no eye-rolling, drooling maniac whose insanity can be spotted a mile off, but is on the surface a refined and rather cultured man whose psychotic inner nature takes Eve and Rainsford some time to spot. During his darker moods, he tends to rub a scar on his forehead that he got while hunting a buffalo, but while this

Lionel Atwill as the mad sculptor in *The Mystery of the Wax Museum* (1933), later remade as *House of Wax*. Allen Vincent is his assistant.

may *suggest* an explanation for his dementia, it is really only a red herring, for Zaroff's psychosis goes much deeper than that. He, like Mabuse, is a man with drives and tensions that alienate him from the rest of society. When he reveals them, his words take on a potent logic and conviction. After all, this is *his* world about which he is speaking, and within its distorted boundaries, it is the rest of the world, not Zaroff, that is insane.

"My father was a very rich man, with a quarter of a million acres in the Crimea, and an ardent sportsman," he tells Rainsford. "When I was only stirrup high, he gave me my first gun. My life has been one glorious hunt. It would be impossible for me to tell you how many animals I have killed. I escaped with most of my fortune. Naturally, I continued to hunt all over the world. One night, as I lay in my tent with this—this head of mine, a terrible thought crept like a snake into my brain: Hunting was beginning to bore me. When I lost my love of hunting, I lost my love of life, of love." As an antidote, he decided to seek a greater challenge. "Here on my island, I hunt the *most* dangerous game," he explains, adding later, "Only after the kill does man know the true ecstasy of love." In this, of course, he is in part referring to Eve, the intended prize. But only in part, for to Zaroff killing is a purpose, and as such it serves as his means of self-fulfillment. Rainsford thinks he's nuts, of course,

Professor Henry Jarrod (Vincent Price), the mad sculptor with delusions of grandeur who feels he has been touched by God, discusses his art with financial backer Sidney Wallace (Paul Cavanagh) as his assistant Igor (Charles Bronson) look on. From *House of Wax* (1953).

but the irony is that in the rational world, Rainsford too fulfills himself, and makes a living, by killing for *sport* as well. In a sense, it is only the nature of their prey that separates the two men. But by how much? Killing, after all, is killing. Chillingly, Zaroff himself poses this very question to Rainsford, who at the time can provide no adequate response.

Like Mabuse, Zaroff also foreshadows the Hitlerian master fiend, a detail not lost on Hollywood, which, in most subsequent (and inferior) screen versions of the Connell tale, painted him in just such a light. In up-and-coming director Robert Wise's *A Game of Death* (1945), a virtual remake of the 1932 film that even uses stock footage from it, Zaroff's name was changed to the more Teutonic-sounding Krieger (Edgar Barrier) in order to suggest some past Nazi affiliation as the possible reason for his murderous dementia. In British director Roy Boulting's *Run for the Sun* (1956), the Zaroff character (played by Trevor Howard) was finally transformed into an outright Nazi war criminal whose South American hiding place is stumbled upon by Richard Widmark and Jane Greer. His subsequent stalking of the two when they try to escape from his clutches is done therefore not so much for sport as it is to keep them from revealing his whereabouts to the world. *Bloodlust* (1961), a low-budget exploitation film aimed at the drive-in crowd, used the once-fascinating character

of Zaroff, here called Dr. Balleau (Wilton Graff), to even lesser purpose.

Adapted to the screen a number of times, but never better than in 1941, *The Sea Wolf,* based on Jack London's classic novel, has much in common with *The Most Dangerous Game* in that its central character, Wolf Larsen (Edward G. Robinson), is a misfit who has chosen to set up his own society so that he can mold it to reflect his twisted view of life—in this case, a seal-hunting terror ship called the *Ghost,* whose roughneck crew Larsen rules mercilessly with a sadistic, iron hand. Into this floating hell stumbles Humphrey Van Weyden (Alexander Knox), a soft-spoken intellectual who has been shipwrecked. Refusing to put Van Weyden ashore, Larsen makes him his cabin boy for the rest of the voyage. Thinking the captain to be ~~an illiterate~~ ... ~~mindless brute,~~ Van Weyden is stunned to find his cabin filled with books by the philosopher Nietzsche, whose strong-arm avowal of the survival of the fittest the psycho Larsen has embraced to justify his actions. Though an exciting adventure film, it is during the movie's quieter moments, when Larsen and Van Weyden—like Zaroff and Rainsford—take to arguing their opposing points of view, that *The Sea Wolf* really comes alive. As with Zaroff, what makes Larsen so scary is that he fully believes in himself and can argue his twisted convictions in such a seemingly rational and convincing manner. It is Van Weyden who makes no sense in Larsen's distorted world, and his psychosis is never really all that visible until he translates it into deeds.

As good as these conversations are, however, there aren't enough of them. Unlike the book, which made Van Weyden the protagonist, the film introduces another major character to share the spotlight—a rebellious young crew member, played by Warner Bros.' then-rising new star John Garfield, who spurs the beleaguered crew to mutiny. Still, for most of its length, Michael Curtiz's *The Sea Wolf* is a compelling psychofilm that derives much of its power from an exceptionally well-written screenplay (by Robert Rossen) that doesn't pander to the audience or skirt the book's philosophical issues, and from Edward G. Robinson's superb performance as the screen's definitive Wolf Larsen.[2]

Two years after the release of *The Sea Wolf,* Val Lewton, Hollywood's legendary producer of low-budget but high-quality B movies, turned out *The Ghost Ship* (1943) for RKO. Though not directly based on *The Sea Wolf,* it has more than a little in common with the London story in that its central character is a

2. Barry Sullivan and Chuck Connors also played the Nietzschean sea captain in two minor versions of the Jack London tale, both called *Wolf Larsen* and released in 1958 and 1975, respectively.

The disguised sculptor Henry Jarrod (Vincent Price) menaces his ultimate Marie Antionette (Phyllis Kirk). From *House of Wax* (1953).

psychopathic skipper, Captain Stone (Richard Dix), whose philosophy is that "men are worthless cattle, and a few men are given authority to drive them." Meaning, of course, himself. Taking a liking to his new third officer, Tom Merriam (Russell Wade), Stone slowly begins to reveal himself much as Wolf Larsen does with Humphrey Van Weyden.

Though proclaimed by those few who have seen it as one of Lewton's finest productions, *The Ghost Ship* is now a "lost" film. Due to a lawsuit brought against Lewton and RKO by two obscure writers who claimed that Lewton had plagiarized one of their scripts, *The Ghost Ship* was pulled from release. It was permanently shelved when Lewton and RKO lost the case. Some television prints do exist, but they are seldom shown.

Lewton, of course, was not above borrowing material from other sources, but those sources were usually classic works of literature that he then used, possibly for time or budgetary reasons—and definitely for artistic ones—as springboards for his own scripts. A good example of this is his superb *I Walked With a Zombie* (1943), a very loose adaptation of *Jane Eyre* set in Haiti. Curiously, *The Sea Wolf* is seldom mentioned in connection with *The Ghost Ship*, but that was clearly its model.

Of all the screen psychopathic loners who have set up societies unto themselves, perhaps the most perverse is Charles Laughton's Dr. Moreau in Erle C. Kenton's *Island of Lost Souls* (1933), a very free adaptation of H. G. Wells's famous antivivisectionist novel *The Island of Dr. Moreau*. In an effort to demonstrate and speed up the evolutionary process, Dr. Moreau, who has been drummed out of his native England because of his cruel experiments on animals, sets up shop on a remote South Sea island and, through surgery and other techniques, creates a subservient race of lumbering "humanimals" who helplessly look upon him as their wrathful "God." Moreau's professed goal may be science, but as played by Laughton, he is really a fiend who gets his jollies by inflicting pain—the humanimals call his workshop the House of Pain and live in fear of being recalled there for one of the crazed doctor's frequent modification jobs. Interestingly, like all the other master fiends we've encountered, Moreau also foreshadows the upcoming horror of the Nazis, who, less than a decade later, would be conducting similar unholy experiments in the name of science not on animals but on human beings.

Moreau's perception of himself as a superman, as one who has been "touched by God"—in the words of Prof. Henry Jarrod (Vincent Price), the mad sculptor with artistic delusions of grandeur in *House of Wax*

(1953)—is the core belief of the genuine screen *master* fiend. Beside him, all those hokey mad doctors, mad scientists, and mad whatevers in other movies pale because, unlike him, they are typically motivated by little more than greed, a desire for revenge, or some other melodramatic contrivance. In the best psycho-films, it is the self-absorbed character of the master fiend, not the film's action, plot, or even its hero, that always serves as the focus of both his and our attention.

A good case in point is the Hammer series of six Frankenstein films made between 1957 and 1973

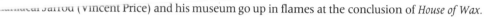
maniacal Jarrod (Vincent Price) and his museum go up in flames at the conclusion of *House of Wax*.

starring Peter Cushing. Unlike most other Frankenstein movies—indeed most other mad-doctor movies—it is the character of Frankenstein that dominates these films. It is he who is the monster, a bona fide psycho like Mabuse and all those others before him who consider themselves to be superior beings surrounded by ants. Not all of these films are equally good, of course—the first two, *Curse of Frankenstein* (1957) and *The Revenge of Frankenstein* (1958), are probably the best, followed in descending order of quality by *Frankenstein Must Be Destroyed!* (1969) and *Frankenstein and the Monster From Hell* (1973), which concluded the series. But Cushing is equally good in all of them because he actually lets his character develop rather than stand still. As the series progresses, his Frankenstein evolves from a callous, ambitious youth to an effete snob to a sadist and murderer to a doddering but still perverse old man—reminiscent of de Sade in his final years—who continues to press on with his experiments even though he no longer seems to care if they succeed or not, because like Moreau he has simply become hooked over the years on his capacity for cruelty. As he performs his final brain transplant, drops the discarded brain into a bowl on the floor, then steps absentmindedly into it, it becomes clear that this is one Dr. Frankenstein who decidedly belongs in an insane asylum—which is precisely where the series leaves him.

The Assassins

In his autobiography *Each Man in His Time* (Farrar, Strauss & Giroux, 1974), director Raoul Walsh remarked that if you asked James Cagney what he considered his greatest picture, the actor would probably answer *White Heat* (1949). Film buffs might agree, but not Cagney, who, at the time of the film's release, had some pretty harsh things to say about it.

Walsh's *White Heat* marked Cagney's return to Warner Bros. after many years of going it alone with his own production company, an enterprise that didn't prove too successful either with the critics or the public. He'd never been overly fond of the gangster roles that had made him famous and considered his comeback part of Cody Jarrett to be just "a cheapie one-two-three-four kind of thing." Nevertheless, he threw himself into the role with a fervor that astonished everyone, and the film became his biggest success in years. After its release, however, Cagney could only comment with frustration, "It's what people want me to do. Someday, though, I'd like to make another movie that kids could go to see."

Because of Cagney's white-hot central performance as the mom-fixated Cody Jarrett, however,

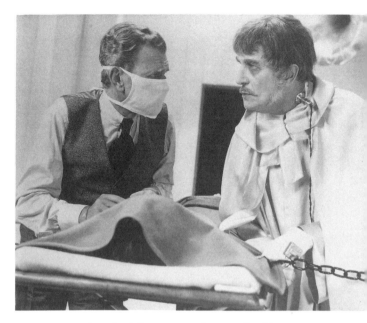

Vincent Price played a different type of master fiend bent on revenge in *The Abominable Dr. Phibes* (1971). Joseph Cotten is the guy in the doctor's mask.

White Heat goes right to the top of its class as not just a superb crime thriller but a riveting psychofilm as well. Cagney's Cody is not just your average tough-guy gangster; he's a psychopath whose dreams of making it to "the top of the world" take on an apocalyptic meaning by the end of the film. Cody knows that his old-fashioned desperado methods don't stand him a chance in the new postwar world of ultrasophisticated detection devices that allow the police to track his every move—and in which undercover cops now act with the cunning, efficient, and cool duplicity of the cleverest superspies. But he presses on anyway because winning out over the law isn't his real aim. For despite his seeming outdatedness, Cody is quite a contemporary killer in that he foreshadows the modern terrorist, or political assassin, who doesn't really care if he's caught or even if he dies so long as he makes a name for himself.

During a railroad heist at the beginning of the film, Jarrett cold-bloodedly kills the train's two engineers because they overhear his name and can therefore identify him. At this point, despite his Mabuse-like image of himself, Jarrett is still acting the part of the traditional gangster. By the end of the film, however, his psychosis progresses to the point where such concerns no longer matter to him.

To throw the police off his trail, Jarrett confesses to a robbery committed in another state at the same time as the railroad job and lands two years in prison.

Beginning with *The Curse of Frankenstein* (1957) and *The Revenge of Frankenstein* (1958) and ending with *Frankenstein and the Monster From Hell* (1974), Peter Cushing's

Promethean doctor evolved from a callous, ambitious youth to a doddering, perverse old man who has become hooked on his own capacity for cruelty.

Knowing Jarrett's guilty of killing the two railroad men (among others) and intent on convicting him, undercover cop Hank Fallon (Edmond O'Brien) is placed in the same cell with instructions to get close to Jarrett and help him break out. Posing as Vic Pardo, a convicted felon, Fallon carries out his assignment with such unscrupulous CIA-like efficiency that it is ultimately the dangerous but pathetically sick Jarrett who gains our sympathy. Having lost his mother (and only confidant) and allowed Fallon to assume her role, Cody discovers Fallon's duplicity, and that sends him around the bend. For the repugnant Fallon, it is not enough to have successfully carried out his assignment, however; it is he who enlists to shoot Jarrett down. Wounded, Cody triumphantly shouts, "Made it, Ma! Top of the world!" as he suicidally pumps bullets into the petroleum tanks atop which he has been trapped and is subsequently blown into eternity—a classic cinematic moment that also stands as an unsettling metaphor of the derangement of our nuclear age and its frightening potential to enable some future name-seeking Cody Jarrett to go out someday in a real "blaze of glory." And take most of us with him.

If the psychopathic Cody had served in the war rather than pursuing his criminal career at home, he might have found his true calling and become a professional hit man like Frank Sinatra's John Baron in *Suddenly* (1954). As it is, both men still have a lot in

Escaped convict Cody Jarrett (James Cagney) enjoys a quiet evening with his wife (Virginia Mayo) and "pal" Hank Fallon (Edmond O'Brien) in *White Heat* (1949).

common, for Baron, like Jarrett, has delusions of grandeur too. Baron's goal is to kill the president, and although he is being handsomely paid for the job (by whom we never learn) and announces his plans to slip safely into obscurity once it is over, it becomes clear at the film's conclusion, when all hell is breaking loose around him and he is fast losing his chance to escape, that Baron is not a man motivated by money. He is a psycho whose chief desire is to achieve notoriety by committing the crime of magnicide. Outwardly, Baron sneers at Booth and all those other president killers who failed to get away, but inwardly he knows he's just like them. Oh, sure, he'd *like* to get away. But that would simply be a bonus. The deed itself is what really matters to him, for Baron is that kind of warped individual for whom the American dream has taken on a new meaning—celebrity—and if a boy can't achieve that dream by growing up to *be* president, then growing up to be the man who shoots him is clearly second best.

Suddenly was Frank Sinatra's first film after getting the Best Supporting Actor Oscar for his memorable comeback performance as Maggio in *From Here to Eternity* (1953). In the wake of the assassination of John F. Kennedy, however, the film was taken out of circulation for close to twenty years. Some say it was at the instigation of Sinatra himself, who, having been a close friend of the dead president's, bought the rights to it and his other film with an assassination theme, *The Manchurian Candidate* (1962), to keep them from being shown and perhaps inspiring other crazies to similar misdeeds.

The title for *Suddenly* is taken from the sleepy California town where icy Sinatra and his two henchmen (Christopher Dark and Paul Frees) lay over to await the president's arrival for a secret changeover in trains. They install themselves in a private home overlooking the train station and hold the town sheriff (Sterling Hayden), his girlfriend (Nancy Gates), and her family at gunpoint while waiting for the appointed hour. Hayden and the others finally realize that their only option is to take action against the thugs themselves, and they do, using whatever means are available, including electrocution with the family television set.

Suddenly holds up remarkably well due to director Lewis Allen's having siphoned every ounce of suspense available from Richard Sale's taut and credible screenplay—all *too* credible, in fact, as Americans would find out to their horror less than a decade later. The performances are uniformly good too, though there is no doubt as to who is the film's star. And to his credit, Sinatra's performance is a chilling tour de force.

Many critics have taken *Suddenly* to task for not filling in more details about the political reasons behind Baron's assassination attempt. It's true that because Baron admits someone hired him to kill the president, we can't help but wonder who they are and why they want it done, but the fact that *Suddenly* never deals with this issue is not really a failure of the film, for the "politics of assassination" is not its point. The film's aim is to provide insight into the character of John Baron, whose motives clearly have nothing whatsoever to do with politics. In John Frankenheimer's *The Manchurian Candidate,* however, both the "politics of assassination" and the assassin himself are brought sharply into focus.

Candidate's assassin, army officer Raymond Shaw (Laurence Harvey), is really a pawn in a much larger and ultimately much madder game. Returning home from Korea with a Medal of Honor, he is touted as a

"Made it, Ma! Top o' the world!" James Cagney as Cody Jarrett goes out in a blaze of glory in Raoul Walsh's *White Heat.*

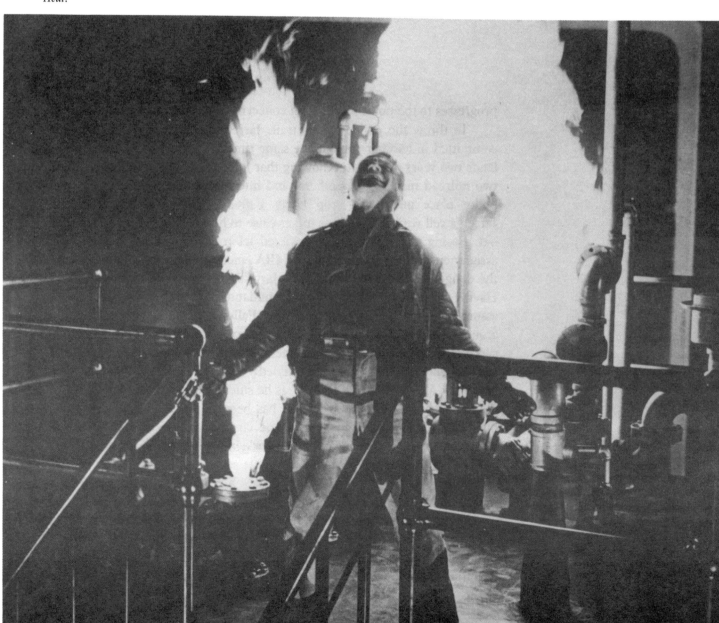

Assassin John Baron (Frank Sinatra) holds small-town sheriff Sterling Hayden and his girlfriend (Nancy Gates) hostage while awaiting the arrival of the train bearing the President of the United States. From *Suddenly* (1954).

Angela Lansbury costarred as the scheming mother from Hell who will stop at nothing to realize her Machiavellian dreams—including destroying her own son, Raymond (Laurence Harvey)—in *The Manchurian Candidate* (1962).

Bennett Marco (Frank Sinatra) attempts to deprogram Raymond (Laurence Harvey) in John Frankenheimer's *The Manchurian Candidate.*

war hero even by his fellow platoon members, who uniformly and sincerely refer to him as the kindest, bravest, most wonderful human being they have ever met, even though they *know* that Shaw is a cold and insensitive loner. The truth is that they have been brainwashed by the Communist Chinese into believing that Shaw is a hero. Shaw has also been brainwashed. He has been programmed to kill his party's presidential nominee during the upcoming convention at Madison Square Garden so that the vice-presidential nominee (Shaw's stepfather), a flag-waving, seemingly anticommunist, McCarthyite senator (James Gregory), who is secretly a puppet of the Reds, can take the dead man's place. The mastermind behind the whole insidious plot is Shaw's unscrupulous mother (Angela Lansbury).

When two less-successful victims of the brainwashing experiment, Bennett Marco (Frank Sinatra) and Corporal Melvin (James Edwards), begin having similar troubled nightmares and start comparing notes, Marco manages to piece the puzzle together and tries to persuade Shaw that he has been duped.

Shaw slips away, however, and heads for the convention where, at the appointed time, he unexpectedly shoots his mother and stepfather instead. Then, just as Marco locates him, the luckless young man mutters, "Oh, God, Ben." And turns the gun on himself. "Poor Raymond . . . poor friendless, friendless Raymond," Marco mourns at the film's moving conclusion. "He was wearing his medal when he died."

Raymond Shaw is not an overt psycho like John Baron and Cody Jarrett, but he shares with them a deep psychological craving to be looked up to, which is why the Communists' brainwashing experiment works so well on him yet fails on the more stable Marco and Corporal Melvin. Through their mind-altering techniques, the Communists successfully instill in Raymond a feeling of self-worth, a feeling that he is loved by his fellow platoon members for having saved their lives. And they send him home thinking that he is a hero. In return—even though he doesn't consciously know it—all he has to do is kill for them. And he *does* kill—not for them, as it turns out, but for himself. Raymond's Communist manipulators have

The deranged General Dell (Burt Lancaster) takes over a nuclear silo so that he can take on the U.S. government in Robert Aldrich's *Twilight's Last Gleaming* (1977).

Director Stanley Kubrick (right) lines up a shot of Sterling Hayden (as the demented General Ripper) and Peter Sellers (as Group Captain Lionel Mandrake) for his nightmare comedy, *Dr. Strangelove* (1963).

understood his type all too well, yet ultimately not well enough, for upon learning the truth of his deception, Raymond elects to make his medal real.

Suddenly and *The Manchurian Candidate*, like *Murder by Decree*, are psychofilms that offer an unsettling message for our time. In the last, a small group of power brokers within government uses the idea of a psycho on the loose to achieve political gain. In the Sinatra films, two equally power-hungry groups, again for political motives, resort to using the real thing—although in *Candidate*'s case, the ticking time bomb that is Raymond Shaw finally explodes in their faces. The disturbing thing about all this, of course, is that as the world increasingly makes use of such men, the more the world begins to look and act just like them. Such a situation not only has homicidal implications, but suicidal ones as well.

In Robert Aldrich's powerful and disturbing *Twilight's Last Gleaming*, all lines of ethical, not to mention sane, behavior in such a world have become so blurred that it finally takes a madman to point them out. The madman in question is Lawrence Dell (Burt Lancaster), a railroaded air force general who has escaped from a military prison and commandeered a nuclear silo with the express purpose of triggering a nuclear exchange with the Russians if the president (Charles Durning) refuses to make public the minutes of a secret national-security meeting, which was held by a former administration during the early years of

the Vietnam War. The minutes, which outrage even the president when he reads them, outline the commitment of the United States government to a strategy of limited warfare throughout the world in order to convince the Russians to stay within their own sphere of influence. What this bombshell boils down to, the shocked president announces to his advisers, is that the Vietnam War was nothing more than a "public relations gimmick" aimed at showing the Russians that America means business. To make matters worse, one of the president's own advisers (Joseph Cotten), who had attended the long-ago meeting, informs him that the reason the strategy was adopted was because the Russians have a similar one—and that such a policy is necessary in this cold war world in order to avoid any possibility of a face-to-face confrontation between the two superpowers that could result in a nuclear holocaust.[3]

The president takes a survey of his advisers, most of whom feel that the explosive minutes are too politically damaging to reveal to the American public at this time—especially at the point of a gun. And so they opt for a military solution to the dilemma posed by the messianic general—ironically, they try to nuke him with a mini-atomic bomb. When this fails, how-

---

3. Director Aldrich and screenwriters Ronald M. Cohen and Edward Huebsch derived this material not from Walter Wager's *Viper Three*, the novel on which their film is based, but from a 1957 book called *Nuclear Weapons and Foreign Policy* in which author Henry Kissinger outlined and endorsed just such a strategy.

The screen's ultimate master fiend: Peter Sellers as *Dr. Strangelove*.

ever, and the outraged Dell almost lets loose his Titan missiles, the president agrees to his demands. He instructs his secretary of defense (Melvyn Douglas) to reveal the document to the public should anything happen to him and reluctantly agrees to accompany

Dell and his surviving accomplice (Paul Winfield) as hostage in their flight to freedom. At the film's devastating conclusion, however, all three of them are shot down, and the document is never revealed.

Apart from its potent political message—and make no mistake about it, *Twilight's Last Gleaming* is a *very* political film—what makes the movie so fascinating is the character of General Dell. Because the policy he wants exposed is so morally repugnant, he seems like a hero, and we can't help but side with him. And yet the subtle fact is that Dell is really a mirror of that same insane policy. He denounces the government for committing murder in order to prove a point to the Russians. And yet he is willing to murder millions with a nuclear warhead in order to prove *his* point. He also denounces the government for at first choosing a military solution to the dilemma he poses. And yet his solution to the dilemma the government poses is to threaten military might if it doesn't reveal the truth. Like the superpower he is challenging, he believes that the only way to deal with such strength is to become a superpower himself.

Director Aldrich felt that he failed to make Dell's madness obvious. "My hope was that you gradually came to understand that Lancaster is crazy," he said at the time of the film's release. "But I don't think we did it." I disagree. I think the point is eminently clear, and all the more powerful because it is stated so subtly. What Dell has in common with so many of the psychos in this chapter is that on the surface he seems so rational. But then again, so does the security council's strategy of limited war as a way of averting all-out war. Only if you look beneath the surface do you see that each is quite deranged. Nowhere is this more evident than the scene in which Dell's terrorist buddy jokingly suggests that the air force might be hiding midget snipers in the tanks outside to shoot them when they come out with the president. With deep indignation, Dell proudly responds, "There are *no* midgets in the United States Air Force!" Not only does this line fully reveal the confused nature of Dell's alliances, but it symbolizes why both he and his morally upright commander in chief must die in the end. For when real power is at stake, the rules of the game are pretty rigid.

Though released thirteen years before *Twilight's Last Gleaming*, Stanley Kubrick's *Dr. Strangelove, or How I Learned to Stop Worrying and Love the Bomb* (1964) seems the perfect capper to it, for not only is it just as difficult to tell the good guys from the bad in *Strangelove*, but virtually everyone in the film is *obviously* deranged. Gen. Buck Turgidson (George C. Scott) is a blustery paranoid who equates megadeath with getting one's hair mussed; Gen. Jack D. Ripper (Sterling Hayden) is a sexual crazy who blames the Russians for poisoning the water and thus causing his sudden impotence; and the title character is practically a composite of every madman we've encountered in this chapter. In the face of such powerful and all-pervasive lunacy, of course, the evenhanded president (Peter Sellers), like *Twilight's* Durning, stands no chance at all.

Kubrick began his cautionary tale of cold war madness as a serious dramatic film,[4] but he soon switched to comedy when, in his words, he found that "in trying to put meat on the bones and to imagine the scenes more fully, one had to keep leaving things out which were either absurd or paradoxical in order to keep it from being funny; and these things seemed to be close to the heart of the scenes in question." The end result was a nightmarish cartoon whose scariest feature—more than a quarter century after the film's release—is that it still seems remarkably contemporary. The specter of its concerns, like the ghost of Jacob Marley, just will not go away.

After the deranged Ripper commits a SAC squadron to a bombing mission in Russia, the president and his staff hustle to recall the planes or shoot them down in order to avert World War III. Complications arise when the Russian ambassador (Peter Bull) admits to the existence of a Russian-made doomsday machine, a device that is automatically set to reduce the world's surface to rubble if but one bomb explodes inside the Soviet Union. Faced with such a calamitous possibility, the president turns for advice to the wheelchair-bound Dr. Strangelove, an ex-Nazi scientist with a dark plan for survival. Strangelove, whose name betrays the nature of his twisted desires, actually relishes such a possibility because it will mean that, in order to survive, the world will have to be reconstructed according to his dictates, which include indiscriminate mating in underground mine shafts in order to keep the species alive. His is the ultimate delusion of grandeur, the most frightening aspect of which is that its fulfillment now seems the only viable alternative.

As the last plane gets through and drops its bomb, setting off the doomsday machine, Strangelove rises suddenly from his wheelchair and, exulting on behalf of Mabuse, Zaroff, and all those other screen misfits who have preceded him, shouts, *"Mein Führer! I can walk!"* Through Strangelove, the demented spirit of each has finally emerged triumphant.

4. The film was loosely based on an antinuclear novel called *Red Alert* by Peter George, who also collaborated with Kubrick and Terry Southern on the screenplay. Some years later, George, convinced that nuclear war was fast becoming inevitable, committed suicide out of despair that his cautionary book had had so little effect.

4

THE FORERUNNERS OF NORMAN BATES

I am always forced to move along the streets, and always someone is behind
me. It is I. I sometimes feel I am myself behind me, and yet I cannot escape.

—Franz Becker (Peter Lorre)
in Fritz Lang's *M* (1931)

As deceptively sane as many of the psychos in our previous chapter may have appeared, there was little chance of mistaking them for "that nice boy next door." Count Zaroff, for example, may have seemed a very cultured gentleman, and was, but at heart he was also a maniac who eventually tipped his hand because of his sinister behavior. This is not the case, however, with our next category of screen psychos: a group of Jekyll and Hydes whose madness proves even more terrifying because it is masked by a seeming innocence. On the surface, these fellows seem quite average, not misfits at all, and quite likable. But they are killers all the same, driven to acts of violence by compulsions they don't understand. And of which they are sometimes not even aware.

The Murderer Is Among Us

Executives at Germany's Decla-Bioscop studios first offered their unusual production of *The Cabinet of Dr. Caligari* (1919) to rising young director Fritz Lang. The script by Carl Mayer and Hans Janowitz told the story of a traveling fair whose main attraction is a sinister hypnotist named Caligari (Werner Krauss) and the zombielike medium Cesare (Conrad Veidt) he commands. One of the onlookers, Francis (Friedrich Feher), soon grows suspicious when vari-

ous murders start taking place around town and eventually traces them to Caligari, who has been using the somnambulistic Cesare as his instrument of death. In reprisal, Caligari sends Cesare out to kidnap Francis's girlfriend Jane (Lil Dagover), but the plot fails, and Caligari is subsequently unmasked as the power-mad director of an asylum who has been using his hypnotic skills on inmate Cesare to commit murder. When Cesare is killed, Caligari goes mad and is put in a straitjacket.

Lang liked the script and agreed to do the film, but first suggested that a framing device be added to give the story, in his view, greater punch. In the framing story, we are introduced to Francis sitting on a bench talking to a friend to whom he proceeds to tell in flashback the terrifying story of Caligari. At the conclusion of the flashback, Francis is revealed as a patient in an asylum and his story a figment of his disordered mind. Mayer and Janowitz were furious with this change because it altered their script completely, but the producers liked it and that's the way the film was shot. Lang had to bow out, however, due to pressure to complete his multipart *Die Spinnen*, and *Caligari* was directed by Robert Wiene.

What's interesting about Lang's framing device is that without it, *Caligari* is little more than a variation on the Frankenstein legend, with Caligari enacting the role of the mad scientist and Cesare that of his

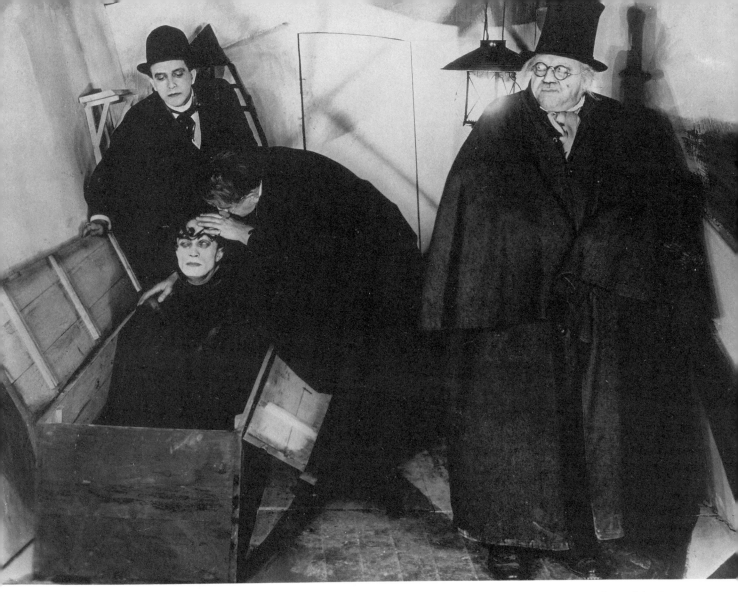

Although the maniac on the loose appears to be the somnambulistic Cesare (Conrad Veidt), seated in box, who kills at the behest of Dr. Caligari (Werner Drauss), right, the real psycho is Francis (Friedrich Feher), far left, a mentally disturbed young man who is imagining the whole story.

From *The Cabinet of Dr. Caligari* (1919), acclaimed for its imaginative sets, which were designed from necessity to keep production costs down. Note where the set stops just above Caligari's hat.

creation. Indeed, as historian William K. Everson aptly points out in his indispensable *Classics of the Horror Film* (Citadel, 1974), director James Whale was clearly influenced by this aspect of *Caligari* when he came to make *Frankenstein* for Universal in 1931.

With the framing device, though, *Caligari* becomes a psychofilm and its main character, Francis, a clear forerunner of the screen's ultimate Jekyll and Hyde, Norman Bates (Anthony Perkins), in that he is a genuinely sincere, likable, and unassuming young man whom one would never suspect of being a lunatic. And yet he is—a fact that is revealed in an ironic or "twist" ending that also foreshadows the unexpected revelation of Norman Bates's madness in the later Hitchcock film. Both Francis and Norman are examples of that scariest of all psychos: the one who lurks invisibly within our midst.

One could, I suppose, consider Lang's framing

Psychopathic child killer Franz Becker (Peter Lorre) lulls little Elsie into a false sense of security of Fritz Lang's masterful *M* (1931).

device to be little more than a gimmick—which is exactly what Mayer and Janowitz considered it to be and why they objected to it—were it not for the fact that the emphasis it gives the movie is so much in keeping with what Lang would do later in his own films on the subject of the criminal psychopath. Thus, the focus of the story is shifted away from Caligari as a master fiend to center on the Jekyll-and-Hyde personality of Francis, who actually believes that the story he is telling is true. The trouble with the framing device is that it doesn't go far enough. We never really know if the crimes Francis has been attributing to the imaginary Caligari were actually committed by Francis—or if they were even committed at all. The nature of Francis's illness is never fully explored; one is left with the impression that he suffers mostly from a well-advanced case of paranoia.

Lang's masterful *M* is much nearer the mark in that

Trapped, the pathetic but terrifying Becker (Peter Lorre) feels hysteria rising within him. From *M* (1931), which director Fritz Lang made, he said, to warn mothers to take better care of their children.

it openly states what *Caligari*, in its divisive form, merely suggests. *M*'s pudgy, baby-faced child killer, Franz Becker, is a sexual psychopath whose cherubic appearance[1] not only makes this hideous truth hard to believe but impossible to perceive. In keeping with this theme, Lang intended to call his film *The Murderer Is Among Us* and announced it as such in the trade papers prior to going into production. Because of the title, however, he was immediately denied floor space by the studio's chief executive, a staunch Nazi, who had determined that the film was an attack on the party. Lang persuaded him that the script was not political but rather a psychological thriller loosely based on the career of mass murderer Peter Kürten,[2]

---

1. Curiously, although Peter Lorre's Becker is much younger, he physically matches the description of Norman Bates in Robert Bloch's novel *Psycho*. For the film version, Hitchcock not only made the character younger but slimmed him down as well.

2. Very loosely, in fact. The only real point of similarity is that Kürten, like Becker, was a sexual psychopath whose unassuming manner and physical appearance belied his monstrous urges. Also, he didn't prey just on children. Unlike the outcast Becker, Kürten was not a loner but held a respected position within the community, a fact that made the revelation of his crimes all the more shocking. Sentenced to the guillotine, the condemned Kürten asked of the prison psychiatrist, "After my head has been chopped off, will I still be able to hear, at least for a moment, the sound of my own blood gushing from the stump of my neck? That would be the pleasure to end all pleasures."

Mentally unbalanced Mark Lamphere (Michael Redgrave), having imagined he killed his first wife, thinks he is repeating history which his second (Joan Bennett) in Fritz Lang's *Secret Beyond the Door* (1948).

who had recently been executed for killing eight people in the city of Düsseldorf between 1929 and 1930, a reign of terror that had given rise to his being nicknamed the Vampire of Düsseldorf. As mass murder seemed a much more palatable topic than politics, the assuaged studio chief gave Lang the go-ahead, and *M,* as the title was shortened to, went quickly into production.

Scripted by Lang and his wife Thea Von Harbou, *M* is about a compulsive killer whose crimes are so heinous that even the city's underworld elements conspire to track him down and bring him to justice. Fingered by a street vendor who sold him a balloon to give to his latest victim, a little girl named Elsie, Becker is chalked on the back with the initial *M* so that he can easily be followed. When he catches on to the fact that he is literally a marked man, he flees into an empty office building to hide out. Meanwhile, the criminals move in and capture him. Unsuccessful in their own efforts to catch Becker, the police, under the direction of Inspector Lohmann (Otto Wernicke), learn of the killer's entrapment from an informant and arrive just in time to save him from the wrathful justice of the criminals' kangaroo court.

Apart from its many technical innovations such as Lang's imaginative use of sound (*M* was his first talkie), the film draws its power from a number of quarters. Anticipating the realistic post–World War II docudramas of producer Louis de Rochemont, it is an exciting police procedural that gives audiences a real insight into the drudgery of day-to-day police work as Lohmann and his investigators doggedly pursue their needle in a haystack, only to be frustrated time after time. It also paints a vivid portrait of Berlin's seedy underworld—actual criminals were used as advisers and even as extras on the film. But the main reason *M* endures as a gripping psychofilm is Peter Lorre's electrifying performance as Franz Becker.

A student of psychology, Lorre had planned for a medical career. But when the stage bug bit, he opted for a theatrical career instead. He nevertheless maintained a lifelong interest in his studies and used his knowledge to provide his screen psychos with a greater depth of character than is customarily evidenced in such roles. This was certainly true of his multilayered performance as Franz Becker in *M,* the film that marked his screen debut and which success catapulted him to stardom. Lorre's Becker is a terrify-

The Lipstick Killer (John Drew Barrymore) menaces Mrs. Kyne (Rhonda Fleming), the philandering wife of the news magnate who has made the killer's capture a contest for promotion within his organization. From Fritz Lang's *While the City Sleeps* (1956).

ing figure because he cannot help himself. He's driven to kill by some monstrous inner voice that will not be silenced until its demands have been met. Afterward, Becker wakes up as if from a deep sleep and only then does he begin to suspect what's happened. "The specters are always pursuing me unless I do it," he tells the kangaroo court as he pathetically begs for his life. "And afterward, standing before a poster, I read what I have done. Have I done this? But I don't know anything about it. I loathe it. I must loathe it. Must!" Lorre's delivery of this speech is one of the screen's great exercises in unbridled hysteria, the most frightening aspect of which is that it is aimed at himself. Becker is trying to convince *himself* that he hates his crimes as society does. And yet there is that other self—that someone who is behind him—that will not allow him to do so and, in fact, will compel him to commit even more crimes unless both Franz Beckers are irrevocably silenced. Becker is as much victim as victimizer and as such, a damned character indeed. The brilliance of Lorre's performance is that he makes us hate Becker's illness, not the man himself.

M is a grim film—not at all graphic, but grim nevertheless. Lang made it, he said, "to warn mothers about neglecting their children." But there is clearly more to his preoccupation with the dual personality and its impact on society than this, for he returned to the theme[3]—albeit less successfully—twice more in his career, with *Secret Beyond the Door* (1948) and *While the City Sleeps* (1956), both made in Hollywood.

Secret Beyond the Door is a romantic melodrama in the tradition of *Jane Eyre* and *Rebecca,* though in this case the Edward Rochester–Max de Winter character—played by Michael Redgrave—not only appears mentally unbalanced but is. Celia (Joan Bennett), a young businesswoman, meets widower Mark Lamphere (Redgrave) while on vacation and after a whirlwind courtship marries him and moves into his brooding old house—a place with a history of murder tied to its various rooms. Mark is quick to talk about the secrets behind the doors of all the rooms but the one that belonged to his dead wife. Eventually, Celia comes to suspect that Mark may have killed his wife, a suspicion that the tormented Mark later confirms. The real murderer turns out to be Mark's sister, who'd been jealous of the first Mrs. Lamphere's usurpation of her dominant role in Mark's life. This knowledge, however, doesn't cure Mark, who does have a predisposition toward violence and eventually tries to strangle Celia with a scarf. Celia manages to save herself, though, by playing amateur psychoanalyst and curing Mark of his murderous tendencies on the spot. Even Lang came to despise this ending, which he later denounced as "ridiculous. No such man is cured so fast. Or even stopped!"

Though just as Hollywoodized and melodramatic,

3. One of Lang's unrealized projects was to be a thinly veiled adaptation of *Dr. Jekyll and Mr. Hyde* that he'd hoped to make for MGM in 1935. Called *The Man Behind You*—a title that certainly betrays its ties to *M*—it was to be about a self-sacrificing doctor named *Jyde* who gets involved in an illicit romance with a stage actress that ultimately leads to murder.

David Wayne as the child killer in Joseph Losey's unsuccessful 1951 remake of *M*.

Basil Rathbone as a modern-day Bluebeard—with his latest wife and next victim (Ann Harding). From *Love From a Stranger* (1937).

John Hodiak assumed the Rathbone role and Sylvia Sidney that of his wife victim in the 1947 version of *Love From a Stranger*.

While the City Sleeps, is a much more interesting example of the Langian psychofilm because of its strong echoes of *M*. Again the film is loosely based on a real-life psycho—Chicago mass murderer William Heirens. Like Franz Becker, the seventeen-year-old Heirens was commanded to kill by a demonic inner voice over which he was powerless. In 1946, he killed three people (two women and an eight-year-old girl), whose bodies he hideously mutilated. He was caught because he made no attempt to conceal his identity, left the murder scenes littered with his fingerprints, and even scrawled the words "For God's sake, catch me before I kill more" in lipstick over the bed of his final victim. He was sentenced to life in prison.

In *While the City Sleeps,* psychosexual mama's boy Robert Manners (John Drew Barrymore) writes "Ask Mother" in lipstick at the scene of one of his crimes and is thereafter dubbed "the lipstick killer" in the press. The difference between Manners and Heirens (or Manners and Becker for that matter) is that he gives himself away not so much because he wants to be caught[4] as because he wants publicity, for Manners shares not a few of Dr. Mabuse's delusions of grandeur. He sees himself as a master criminal, which leads to his downfall when a newsman (Dana Andrews) taunts him in the media to lure him into the open.

Again Lang's story is constructed around a triangle. On the one side, there is Manners, the hunted criminal; on the other, the police who are trying to track him down. The third side of the triangle this time is represented not by the underworld but by the media—the ambitious top reporters of a major news organization whose scheming owner (Vincent Price) has turned the unmasking of the killer into a race for an important position within the company. Although not out for the job himself—at least not consciously—reporter Andrews brings the killer to justice by using his girlfriend (Sally Forrest) as bait.

Though not admired by the critics, *While the City Sleeps* was director Lang's choice as one of his best American films—probably because of its close ties to *M*, which he considered his best overall work and which he had been urged over the years to remake in an American setting. He had always declined, however, because he felt that *M*—particularly its underworld motif—was representative of a particular time and place and that too much of it would have to be altered in transposing it to America. When *M*'s original producer, Seymour Nebenzal, did come to make an American version in 1951 set in San Francisco (directed by Joseph Losey), he found Lang's misgivings to be valid. The film, which starred David Wayne as the child killer, was a box-office disaster that suffered at the hands of the MPAA, Hollywood's self-censoring body, which ordered severe cuts prior to release because Losey had tried to sway as much from Lang's original conception as possible. Because

---

4. By whistling a self-identifying tune (Grieg's "In the Hall of the Mountain King") as he snares his victims in public, Franz Becker too seems to be expressing a subconscious desire to be caught.

of the unsavory nature of *M*'s theme, which defied a number of MPAA tenets, the production had been given Code blessing only because it was to be a remake of an acknowledged classic that the director was presumably to re-create shot for shot. He didn't. Ironically, the resulting film contained too many of the wrong ingredients from the original to seem believably American (Lang was right about the underworld motif), yet not enough that was new to make it stand on its own. Losey himself then aggravated the situation by claiming that his remake was superior to the original in every way, a judgment not shared by the critics, who, in comparing the two films, gave Lang, in his words, "the best reviews of my life."

It should be noted, of course, that *While the City Sleeps* is not the classic that *M* is, either. But as Lang was not out to remake his earlier film, only to recall it in different terms, this is ~~serious criticism of~~ ~~its overall merit~~. Actually, the film is a superior melodrama whose theme is ambition and the extreme lengths people will go to, particularly in America, to achieve it. Even a sicko such as Robert Manners, who keeps on killing as much out of a desire to maintain his notoriety as to satisfy his murderous impulses.

The Smiler With a Knife

Another reason why psychos like Franz Becker and Robert Manners seem to pass unnoticed by society until it is too late is that such men are essentially loners who keep pretty much to themselves and allow few people to really get to know them. The only person who even seems familiar with Becker is his landlady, who sees him only on occasion. The equally friendless Manners, on the other hand, lives with his mother, who is so busy doting on him that she not only fails to detect his illness but has probably contributed to it. There is another type of boy-next-door psycho, however. No less sick, he manages to cloak his madness not by keeping away from other people but by charming the pants off them. He is the smiler with a knife.

In 1935, Welsh actor-playwright Emlyn Williams pondered how such a situation could occur. How could supposedly normal people accept such a fiend into their midst, interact with him almost daily, and yet never see him for what he really is? The result was his famous (and twice-filmed) play *Night Must Fall*, the story of an ingratiating Welsh waiter named Danny, who insinuates himself into the home of a wealthy dowager and her niece so that he can steal the old woman's money. He needs the money to skip the country, for Danny is not the innocent charmer he

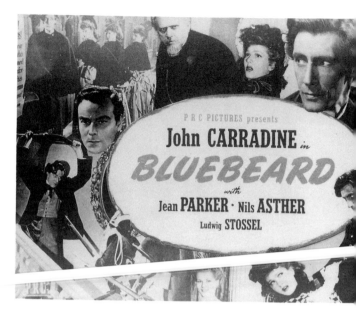

John Carradine played the historical lady killer in Edgar G. Ulmer's less-than-factual *Bluebeard* (1944).

Richard Burton donned the role of *Bluebeard* in 1972. His victim here is Virna Lisi.

appears. He is a psychosexual killer with a fondness for chopping ladies' heads off (the head of his latest victim he keeps in a hatbox in his room), and he knows that the cops are fast closing in. At the conclusion of the play, he kills the old lady but is unmasked by the niece, a shy girl named Olivia who is romanti-

Danny (Robert Montgomery) reveals his fear of the dark when he insists on more light. Mrs. Bramson (Dame May Whitty) is completely taken in by his charming ways, but her niece, Olivia (Rosalind Russell), is beginning to suspect the truth about him. From *Night Must Fall* (1937).

cally drawn to him and to whom he eventually breaks down and confesses during a ferocious storm.

Though *Night Must Fall* is largely fiction, Williams drew his inspiration from an actual case about a murderer who also charmed his victim to death. He modeled Danny after Patrick Mahon, a thirty-three-year-old married man, whose neighbors thought him a good husband and father until he was hanged in 1924 for killing and dismembering his mistress, whose body parts he had stuffed in a hatbox and other containers, which he concealed in an abandoned coast-guard hut. Like Danny, Mahon had a fear of thunderstorms, whose violent noise had a visible effect on him. Mahon killed his victim during such a storm, and when another occurred during his trial, he all but broke down and confessed on the witness stand. In addition to writing the play, Williams created the role of Danny on the London and Broadway stages, thereby making the character his own in more ways than one.

Curiously, at the same time that Williams was writing *Night Must Fall*, a friend, actor-playwright Frank Vosper, was writing a similar play about an equally engaging killer, a modern-day Bluebeard, in which Vosper also planned to star. The two works would eventually reach the stage within weeks of each other, then accompany one another like a pair of matching bookends for a number of years to come. Like *Night Must Fall*, Vosper's *Love From a Stranger*, which he based on an Agatha Christie short story, would be filmed twice, although neither actor would re-create his stage role on-screen. Robert Montgomery and Albert Finney would play Danny in 1937 and 1964, respectively, whereas Basil Rathbone would assume the role of Vosper's Bluebeard in 1937 and John Hodiak in 1947. Coincidentally, the first film

Danny (Robert Montgomery) disposes of the body of his latest victim—all but the head, that is, which he keeps in a hat box. From *Night Must Fall*.

Made in the wake of *Psycho*, the 1964 version of *Night Must Fall* was much less restrained than the earlier Montgomery film and actually showed Danny (Albert Finney) committing his bloody misdeeds.

versions of each play would receive their premiere engagements in New York exactly eleven days apart.

Of the two, of course, *Night Must Fall* is the one that has endured the longest. The play itself remains a staple of high-school drama groups and community theaters everywhere, and both film versions still turn up frequently on television. *Love From a Stranger,* on the other hand, is seldom performed today, and its first screen incarnation with Rathbone is almost totally forgotten.

One of the reasons for this, perhaps, is that the plot of Vosper's play—an innocent girl marries a charming swindler and only gradually becomes aware of his murderous designs on her—has since been done to death with little variation. Williams's plot is no longer

Preacher Harry Powell (Robert Mitchum) demands that John (Billy Chapin) tell him where the money is hidden as the frightened and bewildered Pearl (Sally Jane Bruce) looks on. From *The Night of the Hunter* (1955).

unique either, but it is surprising just how few psychofilms over the years have reprised the character of Danny. Suave wife-killers seem to come and go, but charming Danny with his boyish grin, sociable manner, and that ax behind his back stands relatively alone. Even Anthony Perkins's Norman Bates, while he shares much of Danny's boyish affability, is still very much a loner who knows not what he does. Danny *does* know, and yet he still manages to fool elderly Mrs. Bramson and Olivia into liking and trusting him.

The role of Danny is not an easy one for an actor, for it requires absolute credibility in the part if the story is to work at all. The audience too must share in Mrs. Bramson and Olivia's acceptance of him if the revelation of his true nature is to have the required punch. The role therefore presents an actor with a rare opportunity to deliver a real ~~tour de force per-~~ ~~f...~~ ~~...screen~~ versions were lucky in this regard, for Robert Montgomery and Albert Finney are equally charismatic and persuasive in the part. My particular preference, however, is for Montgomery, who took the role of Danny because he was tired of being typecast as a debonair playboy and wanted to change his screen image completely. Although the film now seems overly restrained and slow-moving when compared to the blood-and-thunder psychofilms of today, Montgomery's Danny of 1937 has weathered the years quite well. His accent is more Irish than Welsh, but otherwise he's perfect. His performance in Richard Thorpe's film earned him a Best Actor Oscar nomination, but he lost to Spencer Tracy for *Captains Courageous.* Nevertheless, the change of pace accomplished precisely what Montgomery wanted it to; he became an important star and eventually the director of his own films.

Albert Finney is equally impressive, though a bit more rakish, as Danny in the 1964 remake by Karel Reisz. His performance is also more flamboyant and energetic—as is the film itself, which has been criticized for showing Danny committing his misdeeds, whereas the Montgomery film kept them "tastefully" off-screen. One must keep in mind, however, that the Reisz film followed in the wake of Hitchcock's *Psycho,* which had shocked audiences around the world—thereby irrevocably altering their expectations of similar screen fare from then on—with its brutal depiction of murder as a decidedly tasteless and ugly business. Had this new *Night Must Fall* been modeled precisely after the original, it would have appeared an anachronism—or worse, a dinosaur. Even Emlyn Williams concedes that while his play may have been quite chilling for its time, it is much less so today. Perhaps in anticipation of this, he kept his eye out over the years for a more contemporary subject that would ignite a similar spark in his imagination. The

result was his 1967 book *Beyond Belief* (Random House), a chilling—and anything *but* subtle—account of England's sensational Moors Murders case of the year before. The book, which is written in a prose style reminiscent of Danny's colloquial patter in *Night Must Fall,* recounts the horrific events that led to the capture of mass murderers Ian Brady and Myra Hindley, two sadistic thrill killers who tape-recorded the cries of their victims as they tortured and murdered them and later took snapshots of each other as they disposed of the bodies on the moors. The case received worldwide attention when the tapes were played to a stunned courtroom during the pair's trial. Both were sentenced to life in prison without parole. Announced for filming several times, *Beyond Belief* has yet to make it to the screen, however.

For ~~many...one of the~~ screen's most terrifying smilers with a knife is Robert Mitchum's crazed preacher Harry Powell in Charles Laughton's superb *The Night of the Hunter* (1955), based on the novel by Davis Grubb. Published in 1953, Grubb's picaresque thriller shot immediately to the top of the best-seller list, where it stayed for sixteen weeks. The story of a knife-wielding preacher who relentlessly stalks two orphans (whose mother he has killed) in order to get his hands on a cache of stolen loot in their possession, *The Night of the Hunter* was brought to the attention of Laughton by his business associate, producer Paul Gregory, who thought the book would be an ideal subject for Laughton's film directorial debut. Although he was active as an important stage actor and director, Laughton found that his film career had sagged considerably over the years, and he had been reduced to accepting roles in such vehicles as *Abbott and Costello Meet Captain Kidd* (1952). To help Laughton regain some of his former prestige in the industry, Gregory felt that he should move away from film acting, for which he was no longer in great demand, into film directing, where he might again reestablish himself as a major creative talent. *The Night of the Hunter,* a proven commercial property, seemed an ideal place to start, and so Laughton and Gregory quickly purchased the rights and secured a deal with United Artists to distribute the film. James Agee was hired to write the screenplay, but when he turned in a draft that was five times the length of a normal script and seemed to completely lose track of the original story, he was dismissed and Laughton adapted the novel himself. Agee got exclusive screen credit for his work, though.

Robert Mitchum was Laughton's only choice to play the con man–preacher whose warring inner demons are symbolized by the words *love* and *hate,* which he has inscribed on the knuckles of his right and left hands. Shelley Winters was selected to play the sexually frustrated widow Willa Harper, whose husband Ben (Peter Graves) had briefly shared a prison cell with Powell before being hanged for bank robbery and murder. Prior to being captured, Harper had secreted the stolen $10,000 with his son John (Billy Chapin), who then stashed it in his sister Pearl's (Sally Jane Bruce) doll. When Powell is released, he heads for the town where the Harpers live, establishes himself in the community as a paragon of virtue, and marries the lonely but naive Willa to get at the cash—which she knows nothing about. Revolted by her aroused passions, which he deems unclean, Powell subsequently cuts her throat, dumps her body in the river, and tells his neighbors that she ran off and left him with the children. The townsfolk, of course, believe him. John knows better, however, and escapes with Pearl down the river, with Powell in relentless pursuit. The desperate youngsters are finally taken in by a kindly farm woman (Lillian Gish), a sort of Mother Courage figure with a houseful of orphans, who manages to scare Powell off with a shotgun and see him brought to justice.

To prepare for the film, which he wanted to exude an atmosphere of early rural Americana, Laughton went to the Museum of Modern Art and screened its collection of silent films by D. W. Griffith, an undisputed master at creating such atmosphere. Laughton

The madman-preacher (Robert Mitchum) consummates his marriage to Willa (Shelley Winters) with a knife in actor Charles Laughton's magnificent directorial debut and swan song, *The Night of the Hunter*.

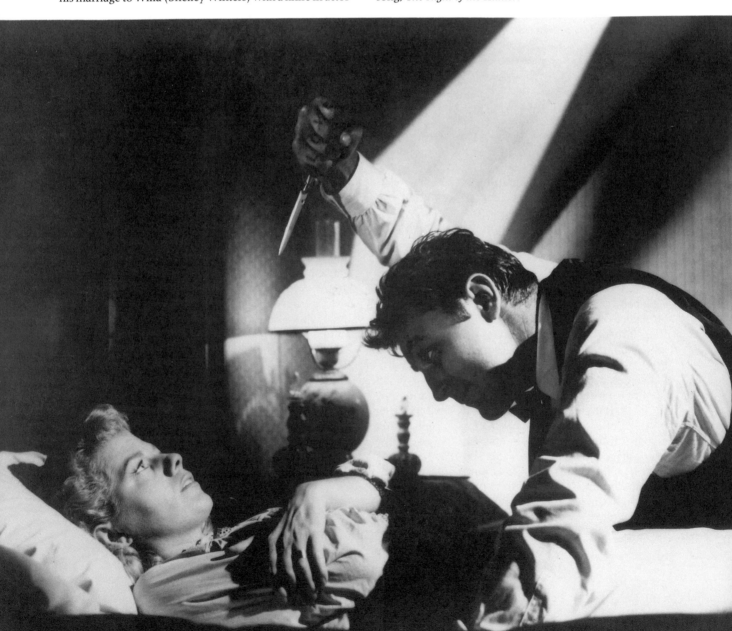

Robert Evans (center) played a psycho cowboy opposite Hugh O'Brian and Dolores Michaels in *The Fiend Who Walked the West* (1958), a remake of the classic gangster film *Kiss of Death*.

must have had some of the German silents in mind also, for the film bears many traces of expressionism as well, particularly in its interior scenes. The result was a pictorially striking but decidedly unusual combination of picaresque adventure, fairy tale, and psychological thriller that apparently proved too unusual for audiences of the time, who stayed away from it in droves. Subsequently, Laughton made an attempt to bring Norman Mailer's recent best-seller *The Naked and the Dead* to the screen, but when he failed to secure financing due to his no-hit track record (the film was eventually made in 1958 by Raoul Walsh), he gave up and went back to acting. He died in 1962.

Howard Hawks once advised that a director should strive for his film to have a few good scenes linked by no bad ones. Using this as a yardstick, Laughton's achievement is a triumph, for *The Night of the Hunter* is devoid of any bad scenes and has so many good—indeed, *magnificent*—ones that they continue to linger in the memory even to this day. Some examples: the tense wedding night when the deranged preacher suppresses his bride's natural ardor by converting her into a Holy Roller; the perverse murder scene, which is played out by the deranged Powell as if he were making love; the riverboat captain's (James Gleason) nightmarish discovery of Willa's body tied to an automobile at the bottom of the river; John and Pearl's moonlight escape down the river as seen from above by the creatures of the night. Very few first-time film directors have displayed such a natural gift for the medium as Laughton does here, which makes it even more of a shame that he never got the chance to direct again. *The Night of the Hunter* may have been a box-office flop that also eluded some critics at the time, but, after all, so was Orson Welles's equally smashing debut film *Citizen Kane* (1941). Both are now generally considered to be classics of the American cinema. As Laughton's cameraman, Stanley Cortez (who also worked with Welles), pointed out later, "I used to go to Charles's house every Sunday for six weeks before we started and explain my camera equipment to him piece by piece. But soon the instructor became the student. Not in terms of knowing about the camera but in terms of what he had to say, his *ideas* for the camera."

Laughton's success with his actors was no less dramatic, particularly with Robert Mitchum, whose frequently listless performances in such blockbusters as *The Winds of War* disguise what a fine actor he can be given the proper guidance. With Laughton, he got it, and his performance as Harry Powell stands out as one of the highlights of his career—perhaps *the* highlight. Very few actors can believably pull off the quicksilver changes in mood and personality that are characteristic of the true madman. Mitchum is one of them (Jack Nicholson is another), and in *The Night of the Hunter* he does so time and time again. When he gently coaxes Pearl to come to him so that he can take away her doll, then screams at her that she's a "foul, disgusting little wretch" when she obeys John's instructions to stay where she is, scaring the wits out of both her and the audience, Mitchum is astonishingly convincing. And his frustrated cry of sheer animal rage when the boat the children are fleeing in slips inches from his grasp as he wades into the river after it is one of those isolated moments in psychofilm when the viewer can't help but experience a cold breeze from hell run up his spine. To quote from the *New York Times* review of the film, "The locale is crushingly real, the atmosphere of the 'sticks' is intense, and Robert Mitchum plays the murderous monster with an icy unctuousness that gives you the chills. There is more than malevolence and menace in his character. There is a strong trace of Freudian aberration, fanaticism, and iniquity."

83

5

THE HITCHCOCKIAN PSYCHO

We all go a little mad sometimes.

—Norman Bates (Anthony Perkins)
in *Psycho* (1960)

The archetypal Hitchcockian hero has often been described as an ordinary man who gets caught up in an extraordinary situation. This description also fits the Hitchcockian psycho, for he too is an inherently ordinary type who suddenly finds himself up to his ears in an equally extraordinary situation—his own madness.

By contrast, the traditional Hitchcock villain generally is a rather suave and glamorous sort. James Mason's silky-smooth superspy Philip Vandamm in *North by Northwest* (1959) and William Devane's soft-spoken jewel thief Adamson in *Family Plot* (1976) come readily to mind. But the Hitchcockian psycho does not belong in such company, for he is inwardly a rather drab fellow whose polished veneer, if he has one (Robert Walker's murder-swapping mama's boy Bruno Anthony in *Strangers on a Train* in 1951, for example), is only superficial.

The first view we get of Uncle Charlie (Joseph Cotten), the Merry Widow murderer in *Shadow of a Doubt* (1943), is of him lying in bed in his seedy hotel room—scarcely the domain of a successful master criminal. As the police tighten their net, he flees to the sleepy California town where he grew up. To his adoring niece (Teresa Wright) and her neighbors, Uncle Charley seems the ultimate in sophistication because, unlike them, he has been around. But through the efforts of the police, the niece finally comes to see her uncle for what he really is—a slayer of vulnerable old women, who is driven to kill not by any glamorous psychosis with a fancy-sounding name but by a head injury incurred when he was a youth. In other words, dangerous Uncle Charley is just a small-town boy gone bad.

College-boy thrill killers Brandon (John Dall) and Philip (Farley Granger) in *Rope* (1948) are linear descendants of Uncle Charley. Patterned after real-life killers Leopold and Loeb, they are motivated to commit murder by a spurious belief that they are superior intellects whose brilliance places them above the law. But their outraged college professor (James Stewart) reveals them for what they truly are—callow youths who have simply been educated beyond their intelligence.

Seen within this context, the quote from *Psycho* that headlines this chapter takes on an added significance. For what it seems to be telling us is that while a vast gulf may separate us from the likes of a Philip Vandamm or an Adamson, given the right set of circumstances any one of us could be a Bruno Anthony or an Uncle Charlie. A Brandon or a Philip. Or even a Norman Bates.

84

Master psychofilmmaker Sir Alfred Hitchcock.

Psycho

Alfred Hitchcock's vastly influential *Psycho* (1960) had its source in Robert Bloch's novel of the same name published by Simon and Schuster in 1959, but its genesis on film goes back to the mid-1950s when Hitchcock was offered the screen rights to another book called *Les Diaboliques* by French suspense writers Pierre Boileau and Thomas Narcejac, two Hitchcock enthusiasts who felt their book would have strong appeal for the director. Hitchcock declined, but Boileau and Narcejac persisted and wrote a later book *D'Entres les Morts,* which he filmed in 1958 as *Vertigo.* However, *Les Diaboliques* didn't lie dormant. It was superbly filmed in 1955 by French suspense director H.-G. Clouzot, whose earlier film, the equally stunning *The Wages of Fear* (1953), was based on a book that had also been turned down by Hitchcock. For obvious reasons, Clouzot quickly became dubbed "the French Hitchcock." He died in 1977.

Les Diaboliques deals with two women (Vera Clouzot and Simone Signoret) who conspire to murder the former's overbearing husband (Paul Meurisse) only to have their victim seemingly return from the grave to haunt them. In an unexpected twist, the murder plot turns out to have been a hoax perpetrated by lovers Meurisse and Signoret to induce Ms. Clouzot into suffering a fatal heart attack so that Meurisse can inherit her money.

One can see from this skeletal outline why both the novel and the film of *Les Diaboliques* had such an influence on Hitchcock as well as why he declined to film it himself. The novel's oppressive air of Grand Guignol gloom, its chilling surprise ending, and its horrific bathroom murder (of Ms. Clouzot) would all be recalled in *Psycho.* But as *Les Diaboliques* was more of a murder mystery than a straight suspense story, Hitchcock opted to wait for a more appropriate (to him) vehicle in which to include these same elements. Bloch's novel *Psycho,* which came across Hitchcock's desk shortly after its unheralded publication, struck him as ideal. By slightly refashioning the book's structure,[1] he was able to mold it into a suspense film yet still retain its surprise ending. For a

Dangerous Uncle Charlie (Joseph Cotten) reveals his true self to his adoring niece Charlie (Teresa Wright) in Hitchcock's *Shadow of a Doubt* (1943).

number of reasons, he also chose to shoot the film in stark black and white. Because of this, *Psycho* not only looks a lot like *Les Diaboliques* but also vividly recalls the expressionist psychofilms of the silent-film era.

As we've seen, *Psycho* was certainly not the first film ever made about a sexual psychopath. But it remains for me the scariest, because it served at the time as a sort of warning bell for what society was to experience during its next decades at the hands of Richard Speck, Albert DeSalvo, Dean Corll, John Wayne Gacy, and a host of other less well-known but equally monstrous psychos. A voracious reader of true-crime stories since his youth, Hitchcock very early on perceived the dark side of the human psyche, feared it, but was also drawn to it. Sadomasochism, kleptomania, sadism, and voyeurism were all grist for Hitchcock's mill throughout his long career. He always approached these subjects with a moral viewpoint, though. His parents were devout Catholics, and he was brought up in a stern Jesuit environment.

---

1. Bloch introduces Norman Bates on page one and unfolds the novel chiefly through his eyes. Hitchcock (and screenwriter Joseph Stefano) introduces the character some thirty minutes into the film, however, so as to lure the audience into following and identifying with Marian Crane (Janet Leigh), whose death in the Bates Motel shower comes as an unexpected shock. The apparent death of star Kim Novak halfway through *Vertigo* foreshadowed this twist, but in that film, of course, Novak doesn't really die. Leigh, whom audiences of the time considered to be the star of *Psycho,* does die, and her demise came as such a jolt that the audience was thrown completely off balance thereafter.

Jimmy Stewart confronts thrill-killers Farley Granger (left) and John Dall in *Rope* (1948), Hitchcock's experimental psychofilm based on the real-life Leopold and Loeb murder case.

This undoubtedly left its mark, for Hitchcock's work, psychofilm or otherwise, has always dealt with such moral concerns as guilt and confession. In his early films such as *The 39 Steps* (1935), where an innocent man is wrongly accused of murder and must clear himself, to his middle-period films such as *Saboteur* (1942), in which an innocent man is wrongly accused of espionage and must clear himself, he approached these themes in tongue-in-cheek fashion. But as the century wore one, as wars, political assassinations, and other forms of violence followed, his films grew more serious (the late François Truffaut said more mature). And every so often in these later films, Hitchcock's camera, which was frequently a stand-in for the director himself, would soar to a great height (the celebrated "God's-eye view" shot) to show the audience just how small and sometimes petty the characters' problems and obsessions were when looked at in the overall scheme of things. His film *The Birds* (1963), in fact, was made to address this

very point. Whenever the birds attacked, it was usually following some act of pretense, pettiness, or neurosis of one of the characters. Fittingly, they attacked from above.

That's the key to Hitchcock. He sought all his life to give order to the chaos that surrounded him, from the preparation of a gourmet meal, to human relationships, to the creation of his films, which he planned out meticulously shot by shot, seldom wavering from that plan once he got on the set. This desire to impose order on all things posed a dilemma, however, for it made Hitchcock particularly attuned to all the things in life that existed to threaten or resist that order, be they jealousy, sexual aberration, murder, or a "difficult" actor. As a result, Hitchcock possessed a highly developed sense of the anxieties of life, feelings that he exorcised over and over again in his films by passing them on to audiences all over the world. The irony is that those audiences, if not the critics, loved him for it.

Psycho Bruno Antony (Robert Walker) plants the seeds of murder in the mind of Guy Haines (Farley Granger) in Hitchcock's *Strangers on a Train* (1951).

Paul Meurisse feigns death in H.G. Clouzot's *Les Diaboliques* (1955), the film that inspired Hitchcock's *Psycho*.

With *Psycho*, though, Hitchcock's viewpoint seemed to change. He came to see that his quest for perfect order was fruitless, and this is what made many of his later films, as entertaining as they still are, so deeply disturbing. At the end of *Psycho*, a glib psychiatrist (Simon Oakland) attempts to offer a rational explanation for Norman Bates's apparently irrational acts. His explanation is meant to give the audience a sense of order regained, so that it can start breathing a little easier again. And yet, the overpowering image Hitchcock leaves us with is not of order but chaos: the insane Norman sitting all alone in his cell, his mad eyes staring out at us from the screen. "Why, I wouldn't even harm a fly," he says in his mother's voice. But Hitchcock knows better, and he has tried to make us know better too. And that knowledge makes the psychiatrist's pat reassurances seem feeble indeed.

This growing feeling of Hitchcock's that we are all at the mercy of a world now gone completely mad (like Norman Bates) and that chance alone determines our safety was echoed even more strongly in *Frenzy* (1972), Hitchcock's last psychofilm. Here, Richard Blaney (Jon Finch), an ex-pilot, has been wrongly accused of committing a series of grisly necktie stranglings. But the real murderer is actually his close friend Bob Rusk (Barry Foster), a charming and seemingly harmless grocer. At one point, Rusk persuades Blaney's girlfriend Babs (Anna Massey) to accompany him home. As they enter his apartment building, the camera crosses the street, then follows them through the door and up the stairs to his room. As the two of them disappear into the apartment, the girl (we know) going to her death, the camera lingers for a moment, then pulls back, glides back down the stairs out the front door, and comes to rest once again amidst the noise and safety of the street below. Technically breathtaking, this shot conveys a feeling of absolute helplessness in the face of a growing unreason, a feeling that Hitchcock had come to share in his last years and that *Frenzy* reflects completely.

Even though Hitchcock's mood seemed to darken in his later works, he never lost his light touch or his sense of humor. His movies have always numbered among the breeziest and most entertaining ever made, a factor that worked against his being taken seriously as a film artist for many years. Even *Psycho*, one of the most effective fright films in the history of the movies, was made, he always maintained, with a good deal of humor on his part. In addition to a good laugh and a good cry, audiences have always enjoyed a good scare at the movies, and whatever its darker implications, *Psycho* certainly provided that.

Psycho was released at a time when Hitchcock had yet to be embraced by the critical establishment at large, and many prominent critics of the day dismissed the film as just another cheap entertainment that wasn't even up to Hitchcock's standard. The *New*

The screen's definitive Victorian house of horror. From *Psycho* (1960).

Yorker's review was typical in this regard: "It's all rather heavy-handed and not in any way comparable to the fine jobs he's done in the not-so-distant past." Ironically, many critics would say the same thing about Hitchcock's next film *The Birds;* that it just wasn't as good as *Psycho.*

Time was even more pointed in its criticism, writing: "At close range, the camera watches every twitch, gurgle, convulsion, and hemorrhage in the process by which a living human being becomes a corpse. Director Hitchcock bears down too heavily in this one, and the delicate illusion of reality necessary for a creak-and-shriek movie becomes, instead, a spectacle of stomach-churning horror." The magazine's comments come closer to explaining why *Psycho* had such a difficult time with contemporary critics. It was a "turning point" movie not only for Hitchcock (who would never treat murder lightly again and would from then on present it as an ugly business), but for the cinema as well, and like most such films (Sam Peckinpah's 1969 *The Wild Bunch* would be another), it was greeted with more hostility than insight. Most of this hostility was directed, of course, at the film's notorious shower-murder scene, which, while not particularly graphic (at least not in today's terms), was so *intense* that it left critics and audiences reeling. What's ironic about this is that while many of today's far more graphically bloody films have a difficult time getting even R ratings without cuts, *Psycho*'s shower murder passed censorial muster without as much as a discussion. The shot of Janet Leigh flushing a piece of paper down a toilet caused more of a flap because, at the time, the Motion Picture Production Code deemed the showing of toilets to be objectionable and in bad taste.

Imitated countless times since (though never by Hitchcock himself), *Psycho* received the inevitable sequel twenty-three years later with *Psycho II*, produced by former Hitchcock associate Hilton A. Green, who had served as assistant director on the original. The director was Australian Richard Franklin, a former film student at USC and a devotee of Hitchcock, whose previous psychofilm *Road Games*, with Stacy Keach and Jamie Lee Curtis (Janet Leigh's daughter), was a stylistic clone of *Psycho* about a maniac trucker who makes occasional pit stops to wield his bloody knife.

Psycho II took a number of years to get off the ground because it was considered imperative that Anthony Perkins reprise his role as Norman Bates, which the actor was unwilling to do unless the right script came along.[2] An original by Tom Holland (*The Beast Within*, 1982) was accepted by Perkins, and the film got the green light. Vera Miles (Leigh's sister in the earlier film) was also signed to reprise her role in the sequel, but John Gavin (*Psycho*'s Sam Loomis) was unavailable as he had given up acting to go into politics and was then the U.S. ambassador to Mexico.

Appropriately enough, *Psycho II* begins twenty-two years after the original left off. Now declared legally sane, Norman Bates is released from prison over the protests of Lila Loomis (Miles), who insists that he's still a killer and that the court's indifference to his victims by releasing him is a gross miscarriage of justice. Norman returns to his motel and the old Victorian mansion where his troubles started, and

The quintessential Hitchcock psycho: Anthony Perkins as Norman Bates.

2. Robert Bloch's own sequel to his original novel, which he titled *Psycho II* as well, was published about this same time but bore no relation to the script.

history predictably begins to repeat itself. At the film's conclusion, Norman is indeed right back where he started, having killed his real mother (the original Mrs. Bates turns out to have been his aunt) and installed her corpse in the mansion's front window, thus preparing us (groan!) for *Psycho III*.

Before *Psycho II*'s release, director Franklin insisted that he was not out to emulate Hitchcock. However, *Psycho II* is filled with unremitting references to Hitchcock and even includes re-creations of actual scenes and shots from the original film. A silhouette of Hitchcock's familiar countenance is even included at one point to recall the director's cameo appearances in his films. Franklin doesn't just contain himself to ripping off Hitchcock, though. A scene in which Mary Loomis (Meg Tilly), Lila's daughter, lies in bed in Norman's attic bedroom while Norman hovers over her with a knife is lifted straight out of *The Night of the Hunter*.

Without belaboring the point, Franklin, like many other *Psycho* sequels, is the work of another Hitchcock "aficionado" to whom being influenced by the master of suspense extends mainly to borrowing shots and plot devices from Hitchcock films. One can see why Anthony Perkins was drawn to the script, however, for unlike the original, the focus of the sequel is almost entirely on Norman, and Perkins manages to re-create and even elaborate upon his earlier performance with a wily panache.

Perkins took the director's chair himself in *Psycho III* (1986), which includes a number of nods to the master of suspense as well but stands more solidly on its own two feet than did *Psycho II*. In it, the troubled Norman makes a courageous attempt to finally throw off the shackles of "Mother" when he becomes entangled with an equally troubled ex-nun (Diana Scarwid), a character who bears a strong resemblance to Marian Crane and even has the same initials, M.C. (Maureen Coyle). He fails and heads back to the institution, but *Psycho IV: The Beginning* (1990) finds him released once more and actually settled down to a life of married bliss (Norman style) with his therapist—until he calls a radio talk show to reminisce about his past and finds his murderous ways taking hold of him again. The Bates Motel itself became the star of an ill-fated NBC television series starring Bud Cort as a fellow crazy to whom Norman, now deceased, has bequeathed the family business. *Psycho IV* and *The Bates Motel* are easily the worst installments in the *Psycho* saga.

William Castle

Compared to *Psycho II* and its like, the series of Hitchcock-inspired psychofilms turned out by

Mrs. Bates (?) makes psychofilm history as she launches her murderous assault on the showering Janet Leigh in *Psycho*.

In *Psycho III* (1986), Anthony Perkins finally directed himself as Norman Bates.

Brenda Blaney (Barbara Leigh-Hunt) becomes a victim of the psycho necktie strangler (Barry Foster) in *Frenzy* (1972), Hitchcock's last psychofilm.

B-movie master William Castle in the wake of *Psycho*'s success now seems downright clever and positively original. At the very least, they evidence little of the commercial cynicism that lay so obviously behind the making of so many *Psycho* clones. Castle entered the psychofilm field because he too felt it would be lucrative, but he came to so enjoy making this type of film and promoting it with his outrageous gimmicks that he successfully communicated his enjoyment to his audiences.

Before creating his own production company, Castle had spent years as a contract director at Columbia and other major studios, turning out one low-budget programmer after another. Like Hitchcock, his decision to make his first shocker had its origins with *Les Diaboliques*. "I wanted to work for myself," he recounted some years later. "But I had to find something sure, something that was virgin territory. I found it when my wife and I tried to get into a cinema to see the Simone Signoret picture *Les Diaboliques*. There were lines all around the block, and it

took us days to get in. I decided then and there that I had a wide-open chance at something special. If a foreign horror picture with English subtitles could draw such a huge crowd, think what an all-English-speaking picture could do!"

The property Castle chose was a mystery novel called *The Marble Forest* by Theo Durrant, a pseudonym for thirteen well-known mystery writers (including the late Anthony Boucher), who had each provided a chapter of the book in collaboration. To make it sound like *Les Diaboliques*, Castle changed the title to *Macabre* (1958) and got Robb White, a TV writer and author of a number of popular mystery and adventure novels for teenagers, to do the screenplay and put up some of the money. The film starred William Prince as a small-town doctor who gets caught up in a revenge plot when his daughter is kidnapped and buried alive and he is given a few short hours to find her before she suffocates. Like *Les Diaboliques*, the film was essentially a mystery that wrapped up with a surprise twist. To promote it,

Stacy Keach and Jamie Lee Curtis costarred as two people on the trail of a maniac trucker in Australian director Richard Franklin's *Road Games* (1981), the film that earned him the opportunity to direct *Psycho II* (1983).

William Prince and Jacqueline Scott hunt, under the concerned gaze of Philip Tonge, for Prince's missing child in William Castle's *Macabre* (1958), another film inspired by the classic *Les Diaboliques*.

The pseudonymous Jean Arless prepares to give the audience a "fright break" in William Castle's gimmicky but effective *Homicidal* (1961).

Castle secured a deal with Lloyds of London to insure each member of the audience for $1,000 against death by fright. The gimmick worked, the film (a competent, unassuming little thriller) was a success, and Castle was on his way. He followed it up quickly with two more horror-mysteries with a twist, *The House on Haunted Hill* (1959) and *The Tingler* (1959), both scripted by Robb White and starring Vincent Price. By insinuating himself into the trailers for his films and inserting into their ads the now-famous profile of himself sitting in a director's chair with a cigar stuck in his mouth, Castle soon became a familiar figure to his audiences. William Castle fan clubs began popping up all over the country, boasting 250,000 members in all by 1962, with fan letters pouring into his office on the average of five hundred a week. Then came *Psycho*, the success of which prompted Castle to veer away from the *Les Diaboliques* formula and enter the field of psychofilm with his bizarre "masterpiece" *Homicidal*, produced in 1961.

Homicidal, also .written by Robb White, takes up *Psycho*'s themes of sexual confusion and loss of identity and runs with them in outrageous style. The story centers around a murderous scheme to collect a rich inheritance—Castle had still not shrugged off the influence of *Les Diaboliques* entirely. The object of murder is Miriam Webster (Patricia Breslin), who is to share in the inheritance with her half brother

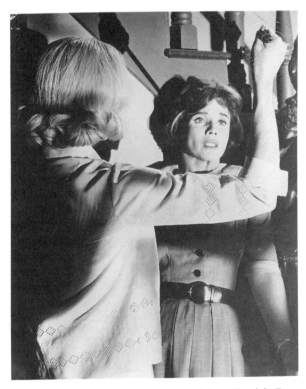

Emily (Jean Arless) prepares to cut Miriam (Patricia Breslin) out of the family inheritance in *Homicidal*.

Warren, who lives with his wife, Emily, in the soon-to-be-shared mansion where Miriam grew up. The twist is that Warren is actually a woman. Raised as a man since birth in order to collect the inheritance, she has been pretending not only to be Warren but Emily as well, the psycho of the story whose job it is to knock off anyone who stands to challenge the original birthright. The film climaxes with a beheading, at which point Castle introduced his amusing "fright break" during which there is a pause to give cowardly members of the audience a chance to flee the theater. When the film returns, the head rolls—not altogether convincingly, I might add.

Castle's "fright break" was not the only gimmick he used to promote interest in his picture. For the role of Warren-Emily, he chose an unknown young actress to whom he gave the androgynous nom-de-screen of Jean Arless for this, to my knowledge, her only film appearance to date. At the conclusion of the film, he then has Arless make a double curtain call as both Warren and Emily, leaving the audience to wonder whether Arless was, in fact, a man playing a woman or vice versa.

Critical reaction to *Homicidal* has always been mixed—although *Time* magazine's reviewer did term

John Ireland as the killer in William Castle's *Psycho*-inspired *I Saw What You Did* (1965). The film even includes a shower murder.

William Castle continued his string of psychofilms in *The Night Walker* (1964), scripted by Robert Bloch and costarring Barbara Stanwyck and Robert Taylor.

Recurring nightmares like this prompt Eleanor Ashby (Janette Scott) to believe she's going insane. From *Paranoiac* (1963), one of Hammer's numerous "mini-Hitchcocks" scripted by Jimmy Sangster.

it a better shocker than *Psycho,* a dubious assessment at best. But to me it remains Castle's premier achievement as a director, for it is the film in which he, who never intended that *any* of his films be taken seriously, pushed his Barnum-like qualities to the limit and yet still managed to craft a thriller whose shocks and twists worked. Derivative though it may be, it

somehow manages to stand on its own. And blatantly commercial though it may be, it returns the audience something for its buck. *Homicidal* may not be *Psycho,* but it's fun. Made in a spirit of total playfulness, it still imparts that spirit today.

Castle stayed with horror for the remainder of his career, though he only made a few more outright

A dysfunctional *Paranoic* family... ...een brothers Alexan... ...(...) and Oliver Reed and their sister Janette Scott with the family solicitor (Maurice Denham).

psychofilms, the best of which, *Strait-Jacket* (1964), will be dealt with in the next chapter. The high-water mark of his career, however, was his association with Roman Polanski on *Rosemary's Baby,* which Castle produced for Paramount in 1968. In Polanski's view, the huge popularity of *Rosemary's Baby* was a shock from which former B-moviemaker Castle never quite recovered. "He used to stand and stare and count up the receipts in his head," Polanski recounted.

William Castle died of a heart attack in 1977, the same year as H.-G. Clouzot, whose *Les Diaboliques* had started the whole ball rolling.

Hammer's Psychofilms

One of the reasons Hitchcock made *Psycho* was that he had become aware of the growing popularity of horror movies among the filmgoing public—particularly those that were being made on a shoestring to great success by American International Pictures. Though he had dabbled in psychofilm before, Hitchcock had never made an outright horror film. With *Psycho,* he intended to make one that would scare the pants off audiences all over the world.

When Paramount declined to back the film due to its lurid subject matter, Hitchcock chose to bankroll the film himself on a shoestring budget of $800,000—which was still ten to fifteen times the cost of one of AIP's el cheapo features. The film, of course, went on to become the biggest box-office success of Hitchcock's career.

Like AIP, England's Hammer Films had also gained a considerable reputation over the years for making inexpensive horror films that quickly turned a profit—so much so that by the early sixties the company's name had become virtually synonymous with horror. Unlike AIP's, Hammer's horrors were mostly period affairs—gothics—and though it would continue making them, the phenomenal success of *Psycho* caused the company to move in another direction as well. Thus began what Hammer president James Carreras would call its period of "mini-Hitchcocks." The irony is that while Hammer's output in this vein was undoubtedly inspired by Hitchcock, most of their plots, like the film... William Castle owed ... ...more to *Les Di-...* ...Only Jimmy Sangster, who wrote most of the mini-Hitchcocks, seemed to be aware of this, however. As a result, a majority are really psychological thrillers rather than psychofilms—in fact, as has already been noted, more of the company's gothics were actual psychofilms—but with titles such as *Maniac* (1962), *Nightmare* (1963), and *Hysteria* (1964), the difference was not readily apparent. Others such as *The Old Dark House* (1963), *Paranoiac* (1963), *Die! Die! My Darling!* (1965), and *Straight on Till Morning* (1972) did fall into the psychofilm category, however.

Hammerphiles tend to dismiss the mini-Hitchcocks as being inferior to the company's colorful gothics. Taken as a group, their formula plots tend to become somewhat evident, but individually, some of them are not bad little thrillers—unless one is expecting another *Psycho.* Hammer itself never found them to be particularly profitable, at least not in comparison to its gothics, but some of them are clever and worth noting.

Although Jimmy Sangster had already written one psychological thriller with Hitchcock overtones as early as 1958 (Hammer's *The Snorkel,* directed by Guy Green), his real flirtation with the genre did not begin until 1961 with *Taste of Fear* (released in the U.S. as *Scream of Fear*), whose script he had written for another company prior to *Psycho*'s release. When that company's option on the property lapsed, Sangster, who had grown tired of writing gothics, convinced Hammer to make it with him as producer. While there is no actual psycho in *Taste of Fear,* the hint of insanity lurks at the heart of the plot—as it does in most all of Sangster's mini-Hitchcocks. A young girl (Susan Strasberg) believes she is going crazy when she starts seeing the body of her dead father turn up in the oddest places—such as at the bottom of the family swimming pool. No one else sees him, however. The twist (á la *Les Diaboliques*) is that the poor kid is being

Mad Morgan (Danny Green) threatens to wring the hero's (Tom Poston) neck in William Castle's comedy-horror remake of *The Old Dark House* (1966), costarring Fenella Fielding.

set up for committal by her conniving stepmother (Ann Todd), who has bumped off Dad for his money and now, with the help of her lover (Ronald Lewis), is trying to get the daughter out of the way as well. Virtually all of Sangster's original scripts in this vein—up to and including what is, perhaps, his best effort in the genre, *Fear in the Night* (1972), which he also directed—chart a similar course. In *Hysteria*, an amnesia victim (Robert Webber) is manipulated into believing he is a murderer by two conniving lovers, one of whom is his psychiatrist (Anthony Newlands). And in *Fear in the Night*, the victim is once again a young girl (Judy Geeson), whose husband (Ralph Bates) and his lover (Joan Collins) are attempting to drive mad so that she will kill Collins's husband (Peter Cushing).

In the deceptively titled *Maniac*, which, though clearly made to capitalize on *Psycho*, bears an even more striking resemblance to *Les Diaboliques* than most of Sangster's other mini-Hitchcocks (perhaps due to its being set in rural France), Sangster lures the audience into thinking it is seeing a psychofilm when actually it is not. When his daughter is molested by a

neighbor, a French peasant goes berserk and kills the man with a blowtorch, after which he is captured, declared insane, and committed to a local asylum. A visiting American (Kerwin Mathews) falls in love with the maniac's wife (Nadia Gray), but the two are unable to marry unless the maniac agrees to a divorce, which he says he'll do if the two help him escape. A guard is enlisted to assist in the break, but the maniac pulls a double cross by killing the guard, leaving the couple to dispose of his body, then threatening their lives. It's all a clever scheme, however, cooked up by the guard and the wife, the real lovers, who bumped off the husband prior to the breakout with the intention of making Mathews the scapegoat.

Sangster's *Paranoiac*, based loosely (and uncredited) on the novel *Brat Farrar* by Josephine Tey, contains many of these same ingredients but adds a twist: this time around, the villain is indeed a psycho.

Simon Ashby (Oliver Reed) is trying to drive his sister, Eleanor (Janette Scott), insane as she is the only one who stands in the way of his claiming the family fortune. His plan runs amok, however, when a man (Alexander Davion) shows up insisting that he's

The definitive Mad Morgan (Boris Karloff) with Gloria Stuart (center) and Lillian Bond in James Whale's original (and vastly superior) version of *The Old Dark House* (1932).

Eleanor and Simon's elder brother, Tony, who disappeared years before and has been presumed dead. The skeptical family solicitor (Maurice Denham) subjects the man to close scrutiny and, convinced that he is the real Tony, announces him as the rightful heir. This drives Simon further round the bend, of course, for he knows that the real Tony is dead, because he was the one who killed him and walled up his corpse in the family chapel. Hired by the solicitor's son to play the role of the long-dead brother, the bogus Tony finally reveals the murderous truth about Simon, who subsequently perishes in a fire. Nicely scripted by Sangster (though directed a bit toward the obvious by Freddie Francis), *Paranoiac* is by no means a great psychofilm, but it is one of the company's best mini-Hitchcocks, boasting a strong, though anything but

Susan Strasberg in *Scream of Fear* (1961), one of the first and best of Hammer's "mini-Hitchcocks," directed by Seth Holt.

99

Frances Green and Janina Faye flirt with danger at the derelict shack where a local child molester allegedly takes his victims. From Hammer's *Never Take Sweets From a Stranger* (1960).

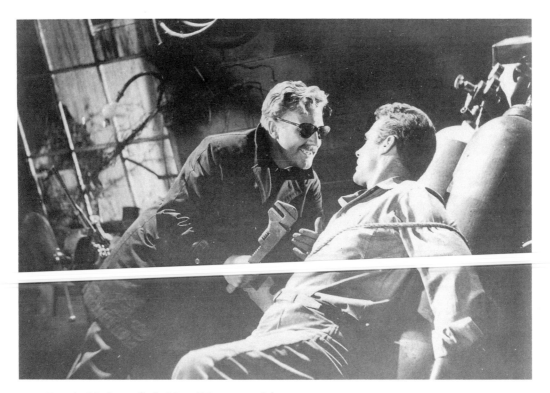

Hero Kerwin Mathews finds himself in a very tight spot
with psycho (or is he?) Donald Houston in Hammer's
Maniac (1962).

One of several bloody murders from Hammer's clever
psychofilm *Nightmare* (1963), directed by Freddie Francis.

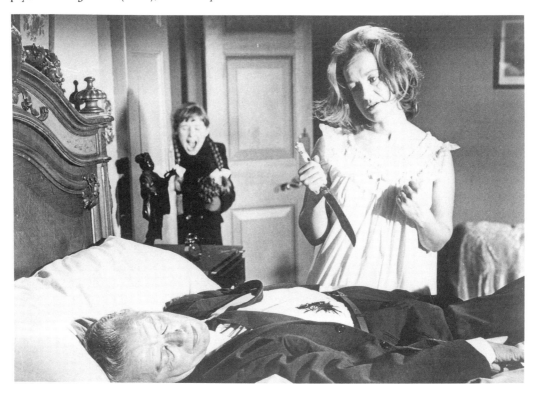

Brian De Palma. The master of suspense or the American
Jean-Luc Godard? My guess is the latter.

subtle, performance by Oliver Reed as the super-charged psychopath.

Janette Scott, the victim of a psycho in *Paranoiac*, is herself the psycho in *The Old Dark House* (1963), the 1932 James Whale classic remade by Hammer in collaboration with William Castle. Adapted by Robert Dillon from the J. B. Priestley novel *Benighted*, the plot centers once again around the inheritance of a large family fortune over which the heirs are being knocked off one by one. Like the Whale film, it is essentially a black comedy, though in Castle's hands the humor is typically played out in much broader strokes.

Tom Poston plays an American car salesman who is forced to seek shelter at forbidding Femm Hall, the ancestral home of the wealthy but eccentric Femm family, whose only apparently sane member, Cecily (Janette Scott), quickly urges Poston to leave before

As heroine Jennifer Salt watches through binoculars, private eye Charles Durning comes up with the evidence in De Palma's first and best Hitchcock-inspired psychofilm, *Sisters* (1973).

he is done in as well. The twist, of course, is that Cecily herself is the most demented of all the Femms and that it is she who is killing off her relatives. In the end, however, she gets her comeuppance when she is killed by one of her own instruments of death, an exploding clock.

"My idea was to combine two entertainment factors—thrills and laughs—into a single package," Castle said at the time of the film's release. "Looking at it from another point of view, the comedy-thriller is also easier to sell. You can sell it in three different ways—as a comedy, as a thriller, or as both." Unfortunately for both Castle and Hammer, *The Old Dark House* proved an impossible sell in any category and was a critical and box-office disaster. Though shot in color, the film was inexplicably released in black and white. To add to the mystery, prints now circulating on television are in color.

103

De Palma's homage to *Psycho's* classic shower murder sequence in *Dressed to Kill* (1980). Here it's only a dream, though.

No less of a commercial disaster was *Never Take Sweets From a Stranger* (1960), one of Hammer's few forays into the realm of the serious psychofilm, the story of an elderly child molester (Felix Aylmer) whose family's wealth and position ensure him freedom from confinement and allow him to walk about the community at large. This ultimately leads to the death of a little girl, who drowns while attempting to escape his clutches.

Based on the play *The Pony Cart* by American Roger Garis, the film was an unusual bid by the company to break away from its Hammer Horror image and be taken seriously by the critics. In keeping with this aim, producer Anthony Hinds told the press during production, "I believe this will be one of the most talked about films in years. It deals with a vital, urgent problem common to all countries—the menace of the psychopath permitted to roam at large. I think this is a film that should have been made twenty years ago." In his zeal, Mr. Hinds had obviously forgotten about both versions of *M*.

The bid failed, for instead of being applauded, the company was vilified by the press for using such a touchy subject as a vehicle for one of its typical Hammer Horrors, a criticism that was largely unfair in that it had more to do with the company's past reputation than with the film in question, which *was* atypical of the company and not at all sensational.[3] Because of this, and the inability for the producers to get a Code seal of approval, the film received only a

3. Hammer's low-budget but compelling antiwar film *Yesterday's Enemy,* released the year before, suffered a similar fate. Faithfully transcribed from a well-received BBC television play by Peter R. Newman, the film was tossed off by the critics largely because of Hammer's connection with it. The critical consensus, which is not justified by the film itself, was that Hammer had turned Newman's play into just another blood-and-thunder war epic on the order of the company's earlier *The Camp on Blood Island* (1958). The failure of both *Yesterday's Enemy* and *Never Take Sweets From a Stranger,* however, prompted Hammer to get out of the message business for good.

De Palma sends up the Hitchcock blond in his satiric *Dressed to Kill*. Here, blond Angie Dickinson is about to meet her doom at the hands of transvestite psycho Michael Caine disguised in a blond wig. [Caine's real hair is blond as well.]

spotty American release. In Britain it was quickly relegated to second-feature status on a double bill, with one of the company's more overt Hammer Horrors, where it soon vanished without fanfare.

Brian De Palma

It was a tribute to the creative stature and popularity of the late Alfred Hitchcock that even before his death, critics and filmgoers had begun to look around for a successor. The message was clear: he was simply too cherished a presence to face losing. Obviously, a giant talent such as Hitchcock's is not so easily replaced, for a suspense film by him will forever remain as distinct from that of any other as a watercolor by Homer is from an oil by Picasso. Still, each time a new suspense or psychofilm is released, we can't help but weigh it against Hitchcock's work. The loss continues to be felt. The search for a successor goes on.

Since the release of *Sisters* (1973), Brian De Palma has virtually been shouting at us from the screen, "It's me! I'm the new Hitchcock! Can't you see?" In interviews, he denies such aspirations, though he will admit to having been strongly influenced by Hitch-

cock's work ("At first, I didn't know exactly why I was so impressed," he says. "It was like suddenly finding someone who is speaking your language.") and has taken to repeating some of the late director's more well-known catch phrases such as "I'm a visual stylist!" and "I'm not interested in content!" De Palma's flow of psychofilms—*Sisters, Dressed to Kill* (1980), and *Blow Out* (1981), as well as *Body Double* (1984), which is more psychological thriller than psychofilm—would seem to dispel all doubts, however. On the surface Hitchcock pastiches all, they evidence practically an obsession on De Palma's part with imitating the master of suspense if not exactly emulating him. A more subtle reading of De Palma's work, however, reveals that while he may indeed be obsessed with Hitchcock's work—particularly *Psycho*, which De Palma has continued to pick over, as if it were an old carcass, for nearly two decades now—his real allegiance is to a vastly different director: Jean-Luc Godard, the anarchic French filmmaker who, until very recently, fashioned a career out of sending up traditional film genres and playing havoc with the formal techniques of film (it was Godard who pioneered the "jump cut" in his influential 1960 Bogart pastiche *Breathless*). Early on in his career, De Palma

105

John Lithgow plays a jack of all trades: political assassin and mad slasher psycho in De Palma's *Blow Out* (1981).

admitted to wanting to become the American Jean-Luc Godard, and his first two improvisational features, *Greetings* (1968) and *Hi, Mom!* (1970), show Godard's influence straight up.

De Palma's dilemma is that as American audiences, let alone the major studios, seem to have little interest in finding an American Godard, he has been forced to disguise himself as someone more obviously commercial: namely Alfred Hitchcock. *Sisters*, De Palma's first and best Hitchcock pastiche, shows fewer traces of the Godardian influence in that while it is certainly full of movie-buff in-jokes and technical experimentation á la Godard, it stands on its own as an effectively made psychofilm rather than as a send-up of one. As De Palma grew more bankable within the industry, he began to exercise his Godardian penchants more blatantly. *Dressed to Kill*, an obvious send-up of *Psycho*, with its two lampooning shower scenes, its parody of *Psycho*'s conclusion where shrink Simon Oakland explains away Norman's illness (—De Palma even uses some of Oakland's dialogue—) its intentionally absurd miscasting of pert Nancy Allen as a high-priced hooker, and its conceit of killing off star Angie Dickinson a quarter of the way through the film, reveals the real De Palma in full—as have most of his films since. Take *Blow Out*, for example, De Palma's playful send-up of Antonio-

ni's *Blowup* (1966), in which a movie sound-effects man (John Travolta) coincidentally records the audio of a political assassination in progress. At one point in the film, Travolta returns to his office to find that all his tapes have been erased by someone involved in the conspiracy. As he darts about in a panic, De Palma's camera suddenly and dizzyingly begins panning around the room, not once, but several times, calling attention to itself and completely rupturing the suspense that has so carefully been built up. This is De Palma at his subversive best (or worst, depending on one's point of view); it is De Palma being Godard, calling the audience's attention to the fact that it is watching a film at the precise moment when another director (such as Hitchcock) would be striving to maintain suspense in order to preserve his illusion. As a result of this, it is difficult not to take De Palma at his word; that he *is* primarily a stylist and that he is *not* particularly interested in content except as it relates to the medium of film itself. Putting it another way, *Dressed to Kill*, for example, is not so much a psychofilm as it is a film about *Psycho*, about why that film worked on audiences the way it did, as well as a send-up of the very mechanics that made it work. It is a movie about the movies that uses Hitchcock not just as a vehicle for satire but as a mask as well.

6

THE FEMALE PSYCHOS

Lizzie Borden took an ax, and
gave her mother forty whacks.
When she saw what she had done,
she gave her father forty-one.

While the male of the species has certainly played a dominant role in the history of crimes of madness, he has not had a monopoly on it, for the annals of murder are filled with true-life examples of female ax killers, poisoners, serial murderers, stranglers, child molesters, and so on. Not so in the movies, however, where the woman has more often been cast as the psycho's victim. It is easy to charge that this reflects male chauvinism—and indeed there may be some truth to that charge in that the literary convention of the female as victim (or damsel in distress) dates all the way back to the birth of the male-dominated art of storytelling itself. It does, though, reflect a certain reality in that throughout history women have more often been the victims of violent crime rather than its perpetrators. Still, the female psycho does exist, and until relatively recently, the movies have chosen to ignore her—except as a joke.

Frank Capra's *Arsenic and Old Lace* (1944) is a good example. In the film, two dotty old women (Josephine Hull and Jean Adair) kill off lonely old men with elderberry wine laced with arsenic, after which their equally dotty nephew (who thinks he's Teddy Roosevelt) disposes of the bodies in the cellar, which he believes to be the Panama Canal. Hull and Adair are not merely senile, they are mass murderers, *psychos,* who kill as a result of being trapped inside their delusions to such a point that they can no longer

separate them from reality.

Admittedly, *Arsenic and Old Lace* is not a serious psychofilm. It's a comedy that treats the escapades of the two murderous old aunts as a vehicle for macabre humor. Also, while Hull and Adair may be crazy, they are not the chief focus of the film, for many other crazies populate the screen in this classic American farce.

Gloria Swanson's faded movie queen, Norma Desmond, in Billy Wilder's biting attack on Hollywood, *Sunset Boulevard* (1950), is quite a different story, however. Norma too is trapped by her delusions—the delusion that her glamour has not yet faded, that she is loved for herself by the down-on-his-luck screenwriter (William Holden) whom she has turned into her kept man, that her fans continue to remember and write to her, and finally, that the Hollywood she helped to build is still anxiously awaiting her return. The difference here is that Norma's psychological entrapment is used not as a vehicle for comedy but for tragedy. As a result of her delusions, she becomes a monster. And that leads to the death of the screenwriter and her retreat into a madness from which—like her future male namesake, *Norman* Bates—it is doubtful that she will ever return.

With its decaying Hollywood mansion, its Grand Guignol atmosphere, and its theme of broken dreams leading to a broken mind, *Sunset Boulevard* could

Gloria Swanson as faded movie queen turned psycho Norma Desmond in Billy Wilder's grand guignol tale of the clash between the old and new Hollywood, *Sunset Boulevard* (1950).

The tormented Hudson sisters—Joan Crawford and Bette
Davis in *What Ever Happened to Baby Jane?* (1962).

almost be mistaken for a horror movie. It would be
stretching a point to call it one, of course, but there is
no question that it is a psychofilm, and that the
psycho at its core, a woman, perhaps for the first time,
is as believably and sensitively fleshed out as any of
her male counterparts in the psychofilm field. What's
more, its theme of the aging movie queen whom the
parade has passed by—and who goes bonkers because of it—would be repeated several times in a
number of outright horror/psychofilms to come. The
irony is that the theme would unfold not just before
the cameras but behind them as well.

Ax Murderesses and Other "Ladies"

Had Norma Desmond successfully made the transition to talkies and promoted herself once more into
a major star, it's a good bet that her career would have
wound up resembling that of Joan Crawford. The
epitome of the movie star, Crawford spanned both
the silent and sound eras. When her career began to
wane in the forties, she made a comeback in *Mildred
Pierce* (1945) by tossing off her glamour-queen image
to play a hard-driving working woman and mother, a
role that won her an Oscar. The early sixties found her
in a similar predicament, for by this time Crawford
was older even than Gloria Swanson was when she
played the fading Norma Desmond. Roles were not so
quickly forthcoming, but they did come. The one she
took was again a complete departure for her, and
again it succeeded in returning her name to the
spotlight—but this time with a price. In order to keep
working, Crawford would remain typecast as a queen
of Grand Guignol until the end of her days. Ironically,
it is for this role, rather than for the bulk of her career,
that the onetime glamour queen is best remembered.

Hollywood played no small part in this, of course,
for when it finally came time to turn her into a
cultural icon with her very own screen biography, the
vehicle Hollywood chose was not the typically rose-
colored, sentimental star bio that most screen legends
are treated to, but the Grand Guignol *Mommie Dearest*
(1981)—in which Faye Dunaway portrayed the late

Joan Crawford makes her debut as a scream queen in Robert Aldrich's *What Ever Happened to Baby Jane?*

Crawford not as a woman, as a movie star, nor even as a failed human being, but as a campy psycho: as someone out of *Strait-Jacket* (1964), the William Castle film in which Crawford starred as an ax murderess.[1] While other aging movie queens—Bette Davis, Olivia de Havilland, Tallulah Bankhead, et al.—launched similar comebacks by appearing in horror films, they did not become forever identified with such roles as Crawford did. Crawford should have paid closer attention to the admonitions of

Sunset Boulevard, for in many ways, it became *her* story.

Robert Aldrich's very profitable *What Ever Happened to Baby Jane?* (1962), the film that launched Crawford on her final (and ultimately downward spiraling) career, was made in the wake of *Psycho*'s huge success. While it pays its nods to *Psycho* (nosy neighbor Anna Lee, for example, is named "Mrs. Bates"), it bears more of a relationship to *Sunset Boulevard* in that it too is a psychofilm about Hollywood's periphery, that dark place where broken dreams invariably lead to broken minds.

Bette Davis plays Baby Jane Hudson, a former child star whose career began to hit the skids when she grew up and lost her curls. Crawford plays her actress-sister Blanche, whose star began to rise at about the same time, but who was forced into retirement at the height of her fame as the result of an auto accident that left her crippled. Both now live secluded

---

1. At one point in *Mommie Dearest,* Crawford goes berserk and chops down an offending tree in her backyard. As she wields her ax, Dunaway clearly recalls the image of Crawford in *Strait-Jacket,* and she is even made up to look the same. It should be noted that Christina Crawford, who did not exactly paint a glowing picture of her mother in the book upon which *Mommie Dearest* is based, thought the film to be a macabre joke as well.

A group of old pros runs through the script of *Hush . . . Hush, Sweet Charlotte* (1965). From left to right: Joseph Cotten, Bette Davis, director Robert Aldrich, and Joan Crawford (who later bowed out and was replaced by Olivia de Havilland).

from the rest of the world in a sort of mini-mansion where the slatternly Baby Jane takes care of Blanche in exchange for her paying the bills.

Baby Jane is the psycho of the film, the child star who never grew up. She lives in the past and dreams of a comeback, which (á la Norma Desmond) she tries to engineer with the help of a down-and-out musician (Victor Buono) who connives to take her money, even though it is painfully obvious to him that she has long since lost her talent. Because her sister controls the purse strings, Baby Jane schemes to separate her from her money by reducing Blanche to a prisoner in their own home. Launching a campaign of terror to weaken, and perhaps kill, her sister, Baby Jane starves her by serving her a dead rat for dinner,

brutally kicks her when she attempts to crawl to a phone and call for help, and finally ties her up in bed. When the disreputable Buono catches a glimpse of the near-dead woman, he flees the house, leaving Baby Jane's comeback plans in ruins. Reverting completely to her childhood, Baby Jane takes Blanche to the beach, where she presumably perishes in the broiling sun, and sits alone eating an ice-cream cone. The requisite twist, which occurs late in the film but not at the end, is that whereas Baby Jane is undeniably the psycho, it is really Blanche who is the film's villainess. Jealous of Baby Jane's early fame, Blanche had determined early on to eclipse that fame even if she had to kill Baby Jane to do it. However, in an attempt to run her sister down in the family limo, it

111

was Blanche who became crippled. Thinking it an accident, the guilt-ridden Baby Jane then sacrificed her life and her career to take care of her unfortunate sibling.

After securing the rights to the Henry Farrell novel on which the film is based, Robert Aldrich persevered to get Bette Davis, whom he approached first, to accept the role of Baby Jane, which she was initially reluctant to do. Though still a major star, Davis had not had a solid movie role in some time. Davis had never thought of herself as one of Hollywood's glamour queens, but the role of Baby Jane put her off at first because, even though it was a flashy part, she had never appeared on-screen before as such an offensive hag. Adventurous lady that she was, she did accept and threw herself into the part with zeal, going so far as to insist that she be made up to look even worse than originally planned. Having worked with Joan Crawford on an earlier film, Aldrich felt that she would accept the less showy role of Blanche with little persuasion, which she did. It's a well-known fact that the two stars had nothing but antipathy for one another, but contrary to legend, there were no flare-ups of temperament on the set, and production on *What Ever Happened to Baby Jane?* proceeded quite smoothly. Released to mainly negative reviews, the film went on to become an unexpected box-office smash that spawned a whole new series of psycho-films boasting aging but still name stars in films whose titles were often quite lengthy and frequently ended with a question mark.

Aldrich's own follow-up to his successful *Baby Jane* was *Hush . . . Hush, Sweet Charlotte* (1965). This too was based on a Henry Farrell novel (unpublished) and again featured Bette Davis as a mentally deranged woman (Charlotte) who turns out to be more victim than victimizer. When her married beau (Bruce Dern) is ax-murdered, presumably by Charlotte herself, she seals herself off from the world in her Southern mansion and proceeds to make time stand still for herself. Forty years later, she continues to dress out of date and live in the past. That past is catching up with her, as another ax killer is on the loose, and everything points to crazy Charlotte's being the guilty party. She isn't, of course. The wicked one is her unctuous cousin (Olivia de Havilland), who'd always been jealous of Charlotte's wealth; it was she who killed Charlotte's beau because she'd wanted him for herself. With the aid of a trusted former lover (Joseph Cotten), de Havilland has been scheming to get Charlotte committed so that she can take over the family fortune. In a turnabout of events, Cotten is murdered, de Havilland is unmasked, and Charlotte is released from the past so that she can rejoin the land of the living.

To capitalize on the successful pairing of Davis and

Writer Cecil Kellaway tries to get Bette Davis to talk about the crime that haunts her past in *Hush . . . Hush, Sweet Charlotte*.

The conspirators (Joseph Cotten and Olivia de Havilland) work their wiles on Charlotte (Bette Davis).

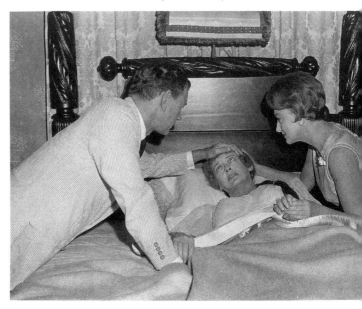

Crawford in his earlier film, Aldrich originally cast Crawford in the film, but as she was unavailable, her role went to de Havilland, whose established screen persona of Southern-belle charm and vulnerable femininity made her a deceptive villainess indeed. Perhaps to compensate for the loss of Crawford, Aldrich filled his supporting cast with equally familiar

Charlotte (Bette Davis) matches wits—what's left of them— against her evil cousin (Olivia de Havilland).

names, including Cotten, Agnes Moorehead, and Mary Astor. Moorehead, who spent most of her career playing villainesses and eccentrics, would later star in her own clone of *Charlotte* called *Dear, Dead Delilah* (1972), a low-budget shocker about—what else?—an ax murderer and an inheritance, directed by John Farris, the best-selling author of *The Fury* and other horror novels.

As a result of the combined box-office successes of *Baby Jane* and *Charlotte,* writer Henry Farrell was able to make a minor cottage industry out of such fare and turned out other scripts in a similar vein, including *How Awful About Allan* (1970 TV movie) and *What's the Matter With Helen?* (1971), both directed by Curtis Harrington. The former starred Anthony Perkins as a blind mental patient who is released from the hospital and placed in the care of his sister (Julie Harris). The plot centers around whether Perkins is cured and being driven back to insanity by some nefarious schemer or whether he was ever cured at all—sort of a lukewarm-up for *Psycho II.*

What's the Matter with Helen?, on the other hand, is a variation of *Baby Jane* set once more on the lunatic fringe of Tinseltown. Shelley Winters and Debbie Reynolds star as the mothers of two convicted murderers who flee their pasts and settle in 1930s Hollywood. To make ends meet, they open a school for talented young hoofers seeking to break into the movies. However, Winters is quite mad (her kid must have gotten his murderous instincts from somewhere), and soon corpses of all kinds—including those of rabbits and Reynolds—start piling up. Harrington's follow-up, *Whoever Slew Auntie Roo?* (1972), written not by Farrell this time but by Jimmy Sangster (among others), follows a similar path. Shelley Winters again stars as a deranged frump, who, similar to the wicked witch in *Hansel and Gretel,* is bent on fattening up her young niece and nephew for the kill.

Unable to take part in *Charlotte,* Joan Crawford nevertheless went on to appear in three more psychofilms before making her final fade-out as an anthropologist in a grade-Z apeman-on-the-loose movie

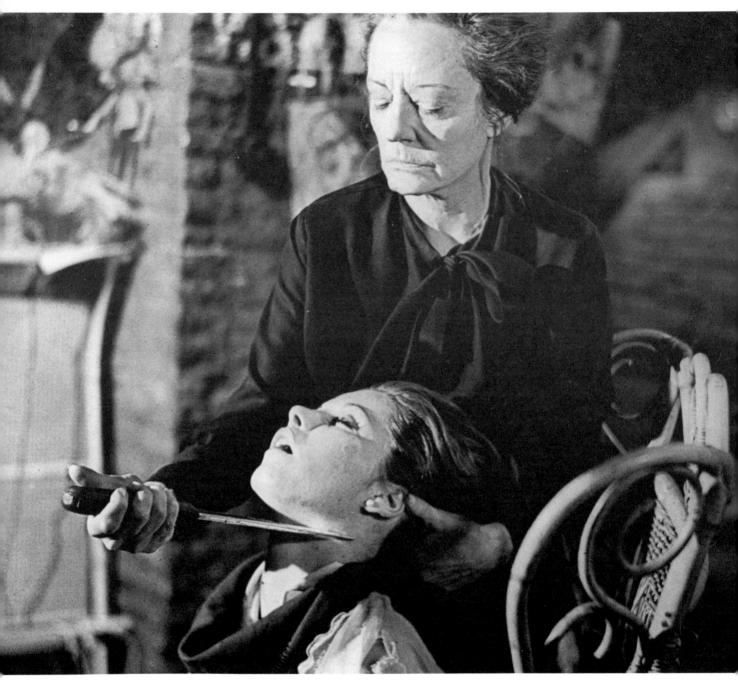

Psycho Mrs. Trefoile (Tallulah Bankhead) is determined to ensure her daughter-in-law's (Stefanie Powers) fidelity to her dead son, even if she has to kill her to do so. From Hammer's *Die! Die! My Darling!* (1965).

called *Trog* (1970). In the aforementioned *Strait-Jacket*, which was scripted by Robert Bloch, she played a jealous woman who beheads her two-timing husband and his girlfriend when she catches them together in bed. Released from an institution many years later, she returns home to rejoin her now-grown daughter (Diane Baker) only to have the nightmares of her past resume when various people start turning up dead and headless. The twist is that it is not Crawford who is wielding the ax but her

Shelley Winters with Micheal MacLiammoir in *What's the Matter With Helen?* (1971), director Curtis Harrington's variation on the *Baby Jane/Charlotte* formula.

daughter, who witnessed the original murder and has been emotionally unstable ever since.

I Saw What You Did (1965), also directed by William Castle (from a script by William McGivern), again placed Crawford in the role of a sinister victim. The psycho, however, is her lover John Ireland, who has just gone berserk and knifed his wife in the shower—a scene in which Castle copycats Hitchcock to a shameful degree. When Crawford gets too possessive, Ireland knifes her too. The main plot, however, centers around two prankish teenagers who like to pick phone numbers at random and call people up saying, "I saw what you did, and I know who you are." The suspense begins when they connect with Ireland, who takes them at their word and sets out to track them down. All in all, *I Saw What You Did* is not a bad little thriller, though it is marred significantly by an atrocious musical score (by Van Alexander) that sounds like something off the track of a 1950s sitcom. The less said about *Berserk* (1967), Crawford's last psychofilm, the better. In it, Crawford plays the head of a circus whose employees are being systematically and gruesomely pink-slipped by a sadistic killer.

Even though Crawford did manage to rejuvenate her failing career with the success of *What Ever Happened to Baby Jane?*, the clear beneficiary of that film's (and *Charlotte's*) popularity was undoubtedly Bette Davis, who not only managed to renew her fame by appearing in a host of other horror and psychofilms, but used that fame to win roles in other types of television and theatrical movies as well.

The best of Davis's post-*Charlotte* vehicles was Hammer's *The Nanny* (1965), a low-key psychofilm whose restrained style stood out in marked contrast to the high-camp excesses of *Baby Jane* and *Charlotte*. Davis plays the title role, a woman who has been taking care of other people's children all her life—to the detriment of her own illegitimate child, whom she has had little time for, and who dies before her eyes due to complications arising from an illegal abortion. Her mind reeling under the weight of this responsibility, she returns home and turns on the bathwater to give her two small charges, Susie and Joey Fane, a scrub, not realizing that while she was out, Susie had fallen into the tub to get a doll and been knocked unconscious. Inadvertently, the little girl is drowned. Unable to accept this responsibility as well, Nanny snaps and places the blame for the accident on mischievous Joey (William Dix), who is institutionalized for a time but deemed incurable and returned

Bette Davis and Jill Bennett in Hammer's *The Nanny* (1965), directed by Seth Holt.

home. Fearing that Nanny will try to kill him too, he obnoxiously insists on keeping his own room. He locks his door at night, prepares his own meals (in fear that she might try to poison him), and continually accuses her of planned treachery in front of his incredulous and frustrated parents (James Villiers and Wendy Craig). When Joey's ailing aunt (Jill Bennett) begins to suspect that the boy may be telling the truth about Nanny, the old woman finishes her off by holding back her medicine when the aunt suffers a massive coronary. Now all alone with the boy, Nanny tries to drown him in the tub as well, but his life is saved when, at the last minute, the sick woman is overcome with the reality of what she's doing and restrains herself in time, breaking down in tears.

The Nanny is not a high-tension psychofilm, though it does have its share of suspenseful moments. It is bolstered considerably by a good script (by Jimmy Sangster) and solid performances by all concerned, particularly Davis, who has a tendency to chew up the scenery in such films but here manages to keep herself in remarkable check. Her nanny is never overtly sinister because the character itself is not sinister. She is sick, and her breakdown at the film's conclusion when her reason returns, however briefly, is not only quite believable but pathetic and moving as well.

What really separates *The Nanny* from the pack, however, is its superb direction by the late Seth Holt, whose last completed film this was. He died suddenly

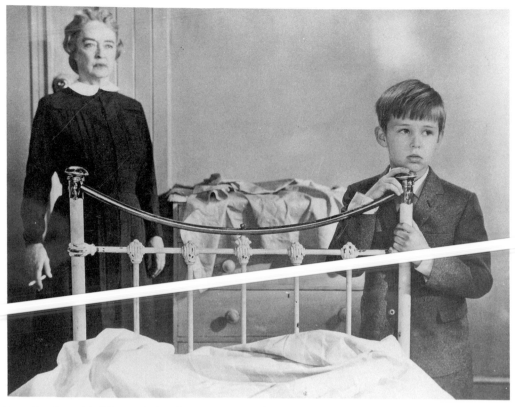

Bette Davis and William Dix in *The Nanny*, one of Hammer's best psychofilms.

at age forty-eight in 1971 shortly after beginning another Hammer Horror called *Blood From the Mummy's Tomb* (completed by Michael Carreras). Holt embarked on a film career after being blown away by seeing *Citizen Kane* (1941). Its influence stayed with him and is even apparent in *The Nanny*, the last of a small handful of films made by Holt following his transition from film cutter to director. As with his earlier thriller *Taste of Fear*, Holt never really goes for the jugular in *The Nanny*, but there is scarcely a single shot in the film that fails to arrest the eye. Even the film's dialogue scenes, which most directors tend to toss off, are framed by Holt with a compelling, painterly eye. The influence of *Kane* is most apparent in Holt's use of depth of focus for the film's frequent long shots, shots that serve to enhance the drama as well as the suspense by allowing us to clearly see what's going on in a variety of rooms at once. Holt also supervised the editing, which, like his direction, flows beautifully. While Hammer may have turned out more profitable films than *The Nanny* (though it was a box-office success), as well as those that are today more revered by the company's many fans, *The*

Nanny remains its most meticulously crafted production.

The screen's most famous ax murderess, of course, is not a fictional character but the real-life woman whose bloody crime (*if* she was guilty of it) is immortalized by the well-known children's skip-rope rhyme that heads this chapter. Her name is Lizzie Borden, and though her tale has been told quite often both in fiction and on film, it was never treated better than in Paul Wendkos's riveting 1975 television film, *The Legend of Lizzie Borden,* scripted by William Bast.

In its few short lines, the grim limerick about the sensational Lizzie Borden murder case of 1892 manages to score a number of factual inaccuracies. Perhaps because it is so famous, I expected to hear it introduced at the beginning of the film. And yet writer Bast and director Wendkos chose to conclude their film with it, a decision that, considering the irony of the title (*The "Legend" of Lizzie Borden*), nicely points up its real purpose, which was to explore the facts, not the myths, of the case. Not only was Lizzie declared innocent of murder, but her father and (step)mother died from approximately forty fewer ax

117

Bette Davis as the murderous title character in Seth Holt's low-keyed and superbly crafted *The Nanny*.

blows than the rhyme would have us believe.

Unlike many nostalgia-drenched movies about famous events in America's past, *The Legend of Lizzie Borden* is a scrupulously precise film. It is not a documentary, but its re-creation of the murder house in Fall River, Massachusetts, is exact down to the poses of the murder victims and the decor of the rooms in which their bodies were found. More astonishing yet (particularly for a television movie), the film actually uses its wealth of detail not just to

Elizabeth Montgomery as ax-murderess (or was she?) Lizzie Borden in the excellent television docudrama *The Legend of Lizzie Borden* (1975), directed by Paul Wendkos from a script by William Bast.

entertain the jaded eye of the home viewer, but to speculate on some of the most baffling aspects of the case.

An elusive figure not just to history but to her contemporaries, Lizzie is portrayed by Elizabeth Montgomery as a very private girl whose predicament aroused the sympathies of nineteenth-century women's-rights advocates of both sexes. Rightly or wrongly, her case became a political forum, and the film suggests that while Lizzie was certainly no political activist, her motive may indeed have sprung from a desire to be free of the repressive life she was suffering at the hands of her domineering and incredibly stingy father (Fritz Weaver). At any rate, the film says, that's why she was found innocent.

At one point, in a dreamlike flashback, little Lizzie is forced by her mortician father to touch one of the draining corpses in his embalming room. Terrified, the girl jumps back, accidentally ripping one of the tubes from the dead flesh and splashing blood against the wall. When she clubs her stepmother with an ax, blood splashes the wall in a similar manner, pointing up a link with her childhood that is unmistakable. Could the passive acceptance of death as just another form of human experience that was drummed into her early on by her father explain why Lizzie was able to slaughter her family so easily? Elizabeth Montgomery plays Lizzie that way—face devoid of expression, even hostility, as she wields the ax. Admittedly,

Lizzie Borden was often doped up with morphine on account of the epileptic spells from which she reportedly suffered, and that might account for her passivity. But the film soft-pedals this idea and with great validity, I think. The evidence is definitely against the possibility that an intruder could have committed the crime, which is what Lizzie herself insisted. And yet, Lizzie Borden never killed again. She used her inheritance to buy a bigger home in a better part of town, where she lived alone until she died in 1927. Did she really strip herself naked, "creepy-crawl" her parents to death like some nineteenth-century member of the Manson family, then wash up so as to be unmarked by bloodstains and get redressed in the same clothes she'd worn that morning? Like an efficient prosecuting attorney, this superior TV movie builds from established facts and says, yes—she did it to gain her independence. And she was able to live at peace with herself because deep down she truly believed that lesson her father had drummed into her: that death was simply life with the pain removed.

Bad Seeds

The 1954 publication of William March's classic crime novel *The Bad Seed* caused an immediate stir, for in it, the author voiced his outspoken opinion that heredity, not environment, was the primary cause of criminal behavior. March viewed the situation this way: As modern man is a descendant of primitive man, it is likely that he occasionally inherits a primitive gene that succeeds in taking root. March called this lingering gene "the bad seed" and insisted that if his theory was correct, it would begin to evidence itself in a person at a very young age. Just how young is what caused the stir, for in his book, March sketched his killer as a cold-blooded nine-year-old girl. It should be noted that March does not imply that primitive man was necessarily evil, just that he lived by a set of rules that today no longer apply. Primitive man simply took what he wanted, often killed to get it, and did what was necessary to survive afterward. Such behavior in modern man, however, is deemed not only antisocial but, at its most extreme, vicious and perhaps evil.

In *The Bad Seed,* little Rhoda Penmark is just such a throwback. When an elderly neighbor promises to leave her a valuable trinket after she dies, Rhoda opts to step up the process and shoves the old lady down the stairs, claiming afterward that the death was an accident, which, of course, everyone believes, as Rhoda is "just a child." When a schoolmate wins a penmanship medal that Rhoda felt she should have won, she drowns him at a school picnic and confiscates the medal for herself. And when the handyman

The face of a murderess? Rhoda's (Patty McCormack) mother (Nancy Kelly) is beginning to think so. From

Mervyn LeRoy's flawed screen version of William March's controversial novel *The Bad Seed* (1956).

in her apartment complex begins to catch on to her, she locks him in his room, sets fire to it, and burns him alive. Rhoda's mother, Christine, too catches on, but as it was she who gave birth to the child and therefore passed on "the bad seed,"[2] she accepts the blame

2. Plagued by recurring nightmares rooted to her childhood, Christine questions her father, a former crime reporter named Richard Bravo, about them and learns that she is adopted. Her real mother (and Rhoda's real grandmother) was a woman named Bessie Denker, a vicious killer who was executed for slaughtering her entire family for fun and profit.

Tuesday Weld's cute, sexy, and deadly Sue Ann Stepanek in *Pretty Poison* (1968) is a grown-up version of Rhoda. With Anthony Perkins.

herself, poisons Rhoda to keep her out of the hands of the police, then commits suicide. By a quirk of fate, however, Rhoda survives. Everyone decides Christine must have gone mad—what with that background, they conclude, it's no wonder!—and smiling Rhoda lives on to perpetrate even more crimes.

Adapted for the stage by playwright Maxwell Anderson, *The Bad Seed* enjoyed a considerable run on Broadway before being bought for the movies by director Mervyn LeRoy. When the film's script (by John Lee Mahin) was submitted for Code approval, however, the project ran into an immediate snag, because the script's ending ran counter to Section 12 of the Code's special regulations on the depiction of crime in motion pictures. The Section stated that

"pictures dealing with criminal activities, in which minors participate, or to which minors are related, shall not be approved if they incite demoralizing imitation on the part of youth." Approval of the script was therefore denied unless the ending—which allowed Rhoda to get off scot-free—was changed. Director LeRoy was outraged, although his stated reason demonstrates little understanding of his film's basic theme. "The culprit here was not some hardened criminal," he protested in his autobiography, "or even a soft criminal, but a child, and nobody could possibly take it seriously." I doubt that William March would agree.

At any rate, a compromise was reached, the ending was changed, and LeRoy got the go-ahead to make his film of *The Bad Seed* (1956)—which laughably concludes with little Rhoda's being dealt her come-uppance by a fiery deus ex machina, literally, a bolt of lightning from the hand of God. Of course, one can't help but ask of this ending why, if God were intending to intervene, He didn't do so earlier? He might have saved a number of innocent lives.

This bogus ending is not the film's only shortcoming. Little more than a photographed stage play, it suffers from a lack of tension due to its being confined, for much of its length, to a single room in the Penmark home, which characters enter to converse, then exit either stage right or stage left. Even the handyman's death is treated as it was onstage—his screams are heard off-screen. Curiously, the only time the film does come alive cinematically is at its ridiculous conclusion, when Rhoda marches through the rainy night to the pier where her mother tossed the penmanship medal into the water and gets blasted by lightning while trying to fish it out.

Some of the performances are equally stagebound, and this too detracts from the film's effectiveness. LeRoy recruited his four leads from the original Broadway production, an unusual move for a Hollywood adaptation, which, in this case, didn't work out too well. Patty McCormack is excellent as the cute but malevolent Rhoda, whose frilly dresses, devious politeness, and adorable blond bangs mask her inner monstrousness. Henry Jones is also good as the slow-witted but fatally perceptive handyman. As Rhoda's guilt-ridden mother, however, Nancy Kelly is not only excessively weepy but at times even maudlin. And as the alcoholic mother of the boy Rhoda killed for his penmanship medal, Eileen Heckart overacts outrageously. Still, Kelly and Heckart (as well as McCormack) did get Oscar nominations for their work, though the awards went to others.

Paul Wendkos's made-for-TV version of *The Bad Seed* (1985) is markedly superior to the LeRoy film in most respects. Scripted by George Eckstein from the Maxwell Anderson play and William March novel rather than from John Lee Mahin's earlier screenplay, it is not only less confined and more cinematic, it also retains the novel and play's original ending. Carrie Wells is properly angelic as the little girl whose name, for some reason, is changed to Rachel, but she lacks McCormack's mysterious ability to look like a demon even as she is behaving most sweetly. Where the new film succeeds most over the old, however, is in Blair Brown's centerpiece performance as the girl's mother. Unlike Nancy Kelly, Brown never surrenders to bathos in her portrayal of a tormented woman who comes to realize that she has lucklessly passed on "the bad seed" to her only child.

A sequel to *The Bad Seed* would seem a good bet for Hollywood, though in some respects it's already been

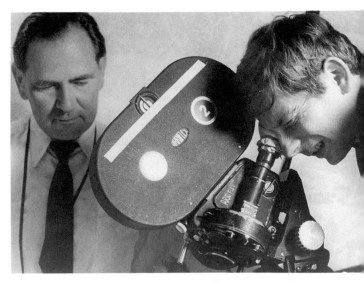

Director Roman Polanski lines up a shot for *Repulsion* (1965) as cinematographer Gil Taylor looks on.

made in the form of *Pretty Poison* (1968), a film whose theme (and title) bears a strong relationship to *The Bad Seed*. Most female psychos (not vamps or villainesses, but *psychos*) have been portrayed in the movies either as dotty old women (*Arsenic and Old Lace*) or as aging harridans (*Baby Jane*, et al.). *The Bad Seed*, however, revealed the uncomfortable truth that even a cute little girl might be capable of committing cold-blooded murder. I say "truth" because the record shows that many of history's most notorious psychos, both male and female, did indeed set out on their lives of crime before they had reached puberty. *Pretty Poison* expands upon that uncomfortable truth by showing us the female counterpart to the male psycho, whom I have dubbed the "smiler with a knife."

Tuesday Weld's Sue Ann Stepanek in *Pretty Poison* is cute, sexy, and deadly. Like Rhoda Penmark, Sue Ann seems to have been born without a conscience. This, combined with her adult craving for sensual excitement, adds up to a potentially explosive package indeed. And explode it does. When she meets up with a formerly institutionalized young man named Dennis (Anthony Perkins), who pretends to be a CIA operative in order to get her interested in him, she

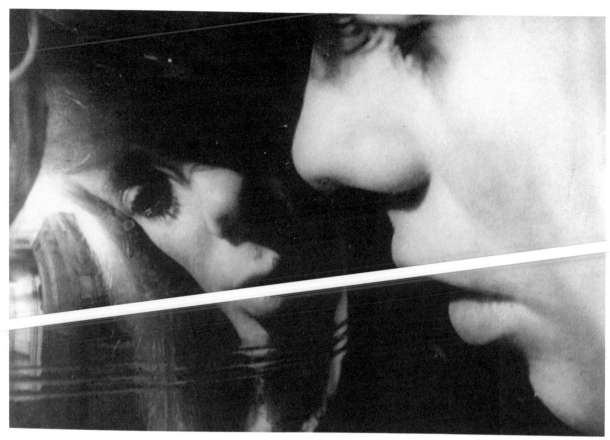

Psycho Carol Ledoux (Catherine Deneuve) fails to recognize her own distorted image, a mirror of her madness, staring back at her from a tea kettle in *Repulsion*.

responds to his fantasy all too willingly. While spying on a lumber company that Dennis insists is being manipulated by a foreign government into poisoning the local water supply, the pair is caught by a guard, whom Sue Ann zealously clubs to death with a heavy pair of pliers. She then tries to coerce Dennis into killing her overly strict mother (Beverly Garland). When he can't bring himself to do so, Sue Ann shoots the woman herself, then pins the blame for both murders on Dennis when he tries to confess everything to the police. As Dennis has a history of unstable behavior and Sue Ann strikes them as the blond, all-American high-school girl, the police believe her story and Dennis is sent to prison. His former therapist believes him, however, and sets out to bring Sue Ann to justice by watching and, perhaps, catching her in some act of violence. Which, at the film's unsettling conclusion, this bundle of pretty poison has already begun laying the groundwork for with her new "beau" (Ken Kercheval).

Less a creature of willful evil than a desperately sick young woman, whose psychosis also took root in her childhood (or earlier) and likewise leads to mur-

der, is Catherine Deneuve's beautiful but deadly Carol Ledoux in *Repulsion* (1965), whom director Roman Polanski and cowriter Gerard Brach based on a girl they had both known. Polanski wrote in his autobiography,

> Apart from her beauty, the most striking thing about her, on first acquaintance, was her air of sweet innocence and demure serenity. It was only when she started living with a friend[3] of ours that another facet of her personality emerged. He told us strange stories about her—how she was simultaneously attracted to and repelled by sex as well as prone to sudden, unpredictable bouts of violence. This tied in with our secondary but no less important theme: the lack of awareness of those who live with the mentally disturbed, familiarity having blunted their perception of the abnormal.

Repulsion's surface resemblance to Hitchcock's *Psy-*

---

3. In his lurid biography of Polanski (*The Roman Polanski Story*, Delilah Grove Press, 1980), author Thomas Kiernan suggests that this friend was actually Polanski himself.

Carol (Catherine Denueve) experiences one of her nightmarish hallucinations.

cho, released five years earlier, brought accusations from critics that it was little more than a skillfully made imitation. Like *Psycho,* Polanski's film deals with a sexually repressed person whose psychological conflict leads to two murders, after which the killer loses all touch with reality and retreats into a shell of total madness. While *Repulsion* certainly belongs to the same psychofilm school, its resemblance to *Psycho* pretty much ends there, for, among other things, Hitchcock chose to tell his story from the victims' point of view, thus making it more of a thriller, whereas Polanski forces us to see through the eyes of the psychotic, making his film more of a case study. The result is a surrealistic nightmare that has more in common with the films of Luis Buñuel, whose subsequent *Belle de Jour* (1967)—which also cast Deneuve as a woman suffering from a psychosexual conflict—appeared to return the homage. If *Repulsion* owes a debt to any film, however, it is to Michael Powell's *Peeping Tom* (1960), which Polanski has admitted is one of his favorite films. More about *Peeping Tom,* however, in Chapter 9.

The unexpected worldwide success of Polanski's debut feature *Knife in the Water* (1962), made in Poland, served to launch the director on his career in the West, though he initially had some difficulty getting that career started. His breakthrough came about when producers Michael Klinger and Tony Tenser approached him about making a low-budget horror film for their independent production company, The Compton Group. Polanski and Gerard Brach wrote the screenplay for *Repulsion* in seventeen days with, Polanski later said,

> one overriding aim in mind: to ensure that Klinger and Tenser financed it. To hook them, the screenplay had to be unmistakably horrific; they were uninterested in any other kind of film. Anything too sophisticated would have scared them off, so the plot of *Repulsion* . . . included bloodcurdling scenes that verged on horror-film clichés. Any originality we achieved would have to come through in our telling of the story, which we wanted to make as realistic and psychologically credible as we could.

Polanski achieved his goal, for few psychofilms— not even *Peeping Tom*—are as disturbingly grim and

The walls of Carol's (Catherine Deneuve) apartment begin to crack asunder in her disturbed mind.

psychologically disorienting as *Repulsion*—with the possible exception, perhaps, of Polanski's future psychofilm on a similar theme, *The Tenant* (1976). Polanski gave Klinger and Tenser exactly what they wanted and more: a horror movie that earned big bucks and critical raves and that is today considered one of the most powerful such films ever made.

Ironically, *Repulsion* opens in a beauty parlor. Carol Ledoux is manicuring the gnarled hand of an elderly woman. Carol's face is empty of expression, her eyes transfixed. Thinking her ill, the manager sends her home. On the way, she passes a group of construction workers and is only vaguely aware of their lustful glances and sexist catcalls. Later, during one of her nightmarish hallucinations that an intruder has broken into her bedroom to rape her, she imagines him as being one of the road men.

Carol lives with her sister, Hélène (Yvonne Furneaux), whose personality is quite different. Hélène seems open and stable. She has a married boyfriend Michael (Ian Hendry), who spends many a night sharing her bed. Her bedroom being next to Hélène's,

Carol can't help but overhear the moaning and groaning of the pair's nocturnal diversions. As she covers her head with her pillow, we see that she is deeply disturbed by their sexual activities. Soon it becomes obvious that she is inwardly repelled by them as well.

Attracted to her, a young man named Colin (John Fraser) tries to pick her up. Confusing her passivity for assent, he drives her home. While parked outside her apartment, he makes a casual advance, and Carol is immediately overcome by two conflicting emotions: attraction and repulsion. Colin mistakes her confusion for shyness and persists by kissing her. Reacting with alarm, she jumps from the car and dashes up to her flat, wiping her mouth, then brushing her teeth.

Her psychological state deteriorates further when she begins to imagine large cracks in the walls of her apartment. Helene and Michael decide to go on a holiday together in Italy. Despite her desperate pleadings, Carol is left alone in the gloomy apartment, where her madness begins to fester. Soon the fanta-

125

Psycho birthday girl Margot Kidder prepares to cut more than her cake in Brian De Palma's *Sisters* (1973).

sized intruder (who at first resembles one of the road men and then Michael) begins stalking the flat. She forces a dresser against her bedroom door to prevent his entering (repulsion), then permits him to break the barrier down (attraction). In the morning, she finds herself nude upon the floor, the bedroom a shambles as a result of the rape that has taken place solely in her mind but that she has physically acted out as well.

Frustrated because she won't return his calls, Colin breaks into her apartment to demand a confrontation. Apologetically, he turns to close the door on a nosy neighbor, and Carol picks up a candlestick and splits his skull. When the landlord (Patrick Wymark) arrives to collect the overdue rent and, interpreting the half-nude state she greets him in as a come-on, tries to make love to her, she symbolically castrates him by slashing him to death with Michael's straight-edged razor. Hélène returns to find Colin's corpse submerged in the bathtub, while a neighbor discovers the landlord's body in the living room. Locating the completely mad Carol under a bed, Michael picks her up and carries her out of the apartment as the camera pans to a Ledoux family photograph. Hélène is kneeling at her father's side, her head on his knee, her mother sitting in a chair close by. And Carol—she is standing behind them all, separated and alone, the same empty expression and blank stare characterizing her face even as a child. Already, madness had begun to claim her, though tragically, it went unnoticed until too late.

To immerse the audience in Carol's nightmare world, Polanski creates an almost overpowering atmosphere of madness and decay. His visualization of the apartment that Carol's psychosis has let deteriorate into filth is so well-wrought that one can almost smell it. The corpse of an uncooked rabbit lies rotting in the living room while unseen flies buzz voraciously about it. The passage of time is expressed by showing the day-by-day growth of the eyes on some spoiling potatoes in the kitchen. Rooms grow visually distorted, their walls turning to clay at Carol's touch. A gauntlet of disembodied hands appears in the hallway to grope her as she tries to make it from room to room. Realistic and credible to the extreme, the spectacle of her hellish descent into irrevocable madness is a frightening sight to behold, though perhaps one of the film's most chilling scenes is also one of its most deceptively serene. As Carol sits quietly in a chair, a sunbeam strikes the seat of another chair opposite her. After studying it for a moment, she reaches over and pathetically tries to brush the sunlight away.

Brian De Palma's *Sisters* (1973) is another psychofilm in which the main character's derangement seems to have taken root at a very early age—due in this case to a pregnancy that resulted in a freak accident of birth.

Danielle Breton (Margot Kidder), a French Canadian model, and Philip Woods (Lisle Wilson) meet on a TV quiz show where she wins a cutlery set. They spend the night together in her apartment. The following morning Philip awakens to the sound of quarreling in the next room—Danielle's twin sister, Dominique, has arrived to celebrate their birthday and, outraged to find a man present, storms off. Danielle returns to find Philip dressed and about to leave, but she persuades him to spend the day, requesting that he go to the drugstore and pick up some pills to help ease her growing distress. As Danielle has a habit of leaving her drapes open, these activities are being observed off and on by a neighbor Grace Collier (Jennifer Salt), a reporter whose frequent stories about "Why We Call Them Pigs!" (shown to us via split screen) have not endeared her to the local police.

Nola (Samantha Eggar) feels her tension rising. Her unchecked emotions will unleash the deadly force of *The Brood* (1979).

Philip returns with the pills and a birthday cake for both Dominique and Danielle. He lights the candles and, carving knife in hand, presents the cake to the sleeping Danielle in the next room. Suddenly, the knife is snatched up by a mad woman—Dominique, who plunges it into his groin, then into his mouth. Dying, he manages to crawl to the window and write *help* in his own blood on the glass. Grace sees all this and calls the police. But by the time they arrive, the confused Danielle and her creepy ex-husband Dr. Breton (played to the hilt by William Finley) have cleared up Dominique's mess and stashed the corpse in a fold-a-bed. Believing her to have imagined the incident, the police abandon Grace to solve the crime on her own, which she does when she learns that Danielle and Dominique were Canada's first pair of Siamese twins. She discovers that they were surgically separated in a unique experiment performed by Breton himself, following which Dominique died and Danielle developed a deadly dual-personality disorder.

Sisters remains De Palma's most self-sufficient chiller to date in that his penchant for "quoting" Hitchcock had not yet reached the level of parody that

127

Candy (Cindy Hinds) huddles in her room after a terrifying encounter with *The Brood*.

it would attain in his future films. Nor does he send his story up à la Godard. The ironic result is a film that is at once less characteristic of the future De Palma and a more effective psychofilm because of it. The plot of *Sisters* is tightly constructed and full of clever red herrings—though one of them is an unforgivable cheat involving *two* shadows where there could only be one. De Palma's imaginative use of split screen (a definitely *un*-Hitchcockian technique) is also quite effective. No small part of the film's overall scariness, however, is due to Bernard Herrmann's brilliant score, which is as visceral and unsettling a piece as any he composed for the late great master of suspense himself.

The Brood (1979) by director David Cronenberg, Canada's answer to Robin Cook as a "master of medical horror," is a psychofilm that suggests that its main character's "bad seed" behavior may have sprung from yet another source: child abuse.

Institutionalized psycho Nola Corvath (Samantha Eggar) is being kept in strict isolation by her therapist, Dr. Hal Raglan (Oliver Reed), because of her unique ability to manifest in physical form the demons of her inner rage. Whenever aroused to anger or any other strong emotion, Nola wills her malevolent creatures of the id—her brood—to come alive and act out her vengeful fantasies. She sends the brood out to kill her mother, who abused her as a child, then her father, who had stood by watching the abuse without intervening—though the couple did divorce sometime later. Separated from her own husband, Frank (Art Hindle), Nola sets her deranged sights on their daughter, Candy (Cindy Hinds), whom Nola herself had abused prior to being institutionalized. She commissions the brood to kidnap the girl and hold her captive at the institute. The repentant Raglan intervenes on Frank's behalf, agreeing to rescue Candy from the clutches of the brood provided Frank keeps Nola emotionally placated throughout the dangerous mission. Frank is revolted, however, by the sight of Nola

128

Director Clint Eastwood shows psycho groupie Jessica Walter how to go on the attack with a knife in *Play Misty for Me* (1971).

giving "birth" to yet another of her brood. Her temper flares, the brood comes awake, and Raglan is killed. The creatures turn on Candy, but Frank manages to save her by strangling his wife and silencing them. Spiriting Candy away from the hellish place, Frank fails to notice, however, that the disturbed child's arm has begun to sprout small, fleshy sacs—the ominous sign of another brood yet to come.

Though critically drubbed upon release, as well as chastised for its repulsive gore, *The Brood* was the first Cronenberg film in which the writer-director succeeded in fully integrating his penchant for splattery special effects with his theme. The gore, though quite graphic, never dominates—as it does, for example, in Cronenberg's *Videodrome* (1983), a film whose serious theme is all but drowned out by an overwhelming emphasis on grotesque effects. This never happens in *The Brood*, not even at the film's stomach-churning conclusion where Nola reveals how she gives birth to her id creatures by showing Frank the

amniotic sac in which they develop clinging to her thigh. Unquestionably this scene is repulsive, but it cannot be considered an effects-for-the-sake-of-effects sequence, because by this time the audience is *demanding* an answer to how she does it. And Cronenberg's response, a perversion of the act of giving birth, ties in fully with his theme. Abused as a child, the disturbed Nola vents her rage by spawning an unnatural brood—to which, because of Nola's past mistreatment of her, Candy now sadly belongs as well. The vicious circle draws closed. The sickness and the violence go on.

Angels of Vengeance

For my money, the scariest portrait of a female psycho the screen has yet given us is Jessica Walter's neurotically obsessive and insanely possessive groupie in *Play Misty for Me* (1971), the film that

Ruth Roman already knows the proper way to wield her bloody blade in *Knife for the Ladies* (1973).

marked Clint Eastwood's directorial debut. I say the "scariest" not because the role itself is especially unique or frightening, but because Walter's nerve-racking performance is. As the psycho fan whose spurned ardor leads to wrathful vengeance, she is astonishing. Her quicksilver changes of mood terrifyingly unpredictable, she literally makes the hairs bristle on the back of one's neck.

Director Eastwood stars as a low-key disc jockey on a Carmel, California, radio station that specializes in jazz and old standards. Taking requests from his audience, he is asked repeatedly by a sultry-voiced caller (Walter) to "Play 'Misty' for me." After hours, she tracks him down at his local hangout Murphy's Bar and strikes up a conversation, goading him on at first by playing hard to get. They subsequently become lovers, but Eastwood grows increasingly uncomfortable with the relationship when she reveals

signs of a jealous, possessive streak that borders on sickness. When her possessiveness reaches the point where he is no longer able to breathe, he dumps her for Donna Mills. Walter won't let go and launches a campaign to win him back by abruptly showing up to cook his meals and clean his apartment as if their relationship hasn't changed. She even strips on occasion so as to arouse his lust. But Eastwood puts his foot down and gives her the gate for good. For a time, all is quiet, but then all hell breaks loose as Walter mounts an assault on Eastwood's nerves and even his life. She ransacks his apartment, slashes his furniture and paintings, and even attacks him with a knife as he lies sleeping alone in bed, after which she flees into the night like some phantom Jill the Ripper. Not knowing when, where, or whom (him or Mills) she will strike next, Eastwood turns to the police, but the cop (John Larch) assigned to the case is killed in his

Betsy Palmer plays a mass murderess in Sean S. Cunningham's *Friday the 13th* (1980).

stead. Eventually, Walter is subdued, but not before subjecting both Eastwood and the audience to a few more hair-raising frissons.

Play Misty for Me remains one of Eastwood's best films to date as a director, a fact due mostly to Walter's virtuoso performance. A likable actor with virtually no range (his superstar status continues to elude me), Eastwood fares slightly better as a director because he tends to stick with what he knows best: action. Still,

despite their frequent flare-ups of enervating mayhem, most of his films are overlong and rather ponderous. But in *Misty*, he manages to strike a right balance in that he makes the viewer (like the character Eastwood portrays) come to realize how crazy Walter is in a gradual manner. The first half of the film may indeed strike some as slow, but for Walter's character to emerge as scary as it does, such leisurely treatment is required. In fact, while the second half

131

contains most of the film's action and shocks, it is the leisurely first half that proves more fascinating (particularly upon second viewing) because of the many subtle clues to Walter's madness that the actress and director Eastwood drop for us along the way.

Not so subtle was Eastwood's second excursion into psychofilm, *Sudden Impact* (1983), a plodding action film in which the director-star reprised his role as Dirty Harry Callahan in order to ferret out a female psycho (Sondra Locke) who is killing men seemingly at random. *Sudden Impact*, unlike *Play Misty for Me*, offers no suspenseful buildup to its psycho's vengeful eruptions into violence. In the film's very first scene, Locke reveals her character in full in a colorful flash when she empties a .45 into the groin of her first victim inside a parked car.

As we come to find out, Locke's male victims are not as innocent as they appear, for, years before, they (as well as a lesbian member of their group) had raped both Locke and her sister, the latter having died. Determined to settle the score, the physically recovered but emotionally scarred Locke returns to the town where they all live and tracks them down one by one. The vacationing Harry stumbles into the case, meets the girl coincidentally, and falls for her. Despite (or perhaps because of) her predisposition toward violence, Locke strikes him as just his type, for, as it turns out, in addition to being rapists, her victims are dregs of society in other ways as well. To old eye-for-an-eye Harry, this angel of vengeance is some kind of chick. While protecting her from the remaining bad guys, who have grown wise to her by now, he not only helps her finish settling her score, he even lets her go at the end, knowing that the grateful girl can never be his due to her pathological mistrust of men. Even in psychofilms, it seems, the course of true love doesn't always run smooth. Especially those made by Clint Eastwood.

Zoë Tamerlis plays another rape victim who seeks murderous revenge in Abel Ferrara's *Ms. 45* (1980), a Polanski-inspired psychofilm alternately titled *Angel of Vengeance*. Then-sixteen-year-old Tamerlis plays Thana, a mute garment worker who is raped twice in a single afternoon. She manages to kill her second assailant, chops up his body, puts the pieces in bags, and starts disposing of them in various spots around town. Having armed herself with the dead man's gun, she blows away another potential assailant who tries to return one of the bags to her, then mounts an all-out war on the city's seeming wealth of hustlers, prostitute-beating pimps, street gangs preying on women, and other male miscreants. Invited to a costume party by her superchauvinistic boss (Albert Sinkys), who repeatedly badgers her at work because he secretly wants to get into her pants, Thana dresses up as a nun, and when her boss puts the moves on her at the party, she shoots him down, then starts blasting away at every other male in the room. She is finally brought down by her hysterical friend Laurie (Darlene Stuto), who stabs her in the back in order to bring the massacre to a halt. For the first time in the film, the mute girl utters a sound—a primeval scream of pain.

Ms. 45 has gained a considerable cult following over the years due to its kinetic direction by then-newcomer Abel Ferrara and its strong lead performance by the mysteriously alluring Tamerlis, who made her screen debut in the film but has done little else since. NYU film-school graduate Ferrara had dabbled with psychofilm previously in his own debut film *Driller Killer* (1979), a low-budget splatter movie loosely based on a Los Angeles skid-row-slasher case, in which the director himself (using the pseudonym Jimmy Laine) played the title role of a deranged painter who goes about murdering derelicts with a high-powered drill. By Ferrara's own admission, that film was little more than a primitive warm-up for the more sophisticated *Ms. 45*, which, while containing all the right exploitation-flick ingredients (namely sex and violence), is not just an average one. For one thing, it offers a potent political message that Tamerlis herself was instrumental in bringing to the film and that she has continued to expound and expand on in interviews since. A self-styled sixties-ish revolutionary on the order of the early Jane Fonda, the youthful Tamerlis is perhaps a bit out of step with most members of her seemingly conservative and pro-Reagan generation in that she is genuinely committed to a radical viewpoint that she is determined to express through her films. To her, *Ms. 45* is not just about Thana's physical exploitation but her—or anyone's—*social* exploitation as well. "It's truly, in my more elaborate view, about anyone who's been raped or screwed in any way," she says. "The real villain is Thana's boss, who wants to keep his women for forty years in his service. He's the one person she sets out to kill."

Apparently not all members of the predominantly male (and misogynistic) Times Square audience that saw the film during its initial New York City run caught on to the subtleties of Ms. Tamerlis's more elaborate view. Tamerlis admits that after the film's release, she often dressed up as Thana while appearing in public. On one such occasion, a sniper made an attempt on her life, and she suffered a bullet wound in her hip. Though the case went unsolved, she remains convinced that the attack was perpetrated by some deranged male who was prompted to act by her unsettling performance in *Ms. 45*. Either Ms. Tamerlis suffers from masochistic delusions of grandeur, or she is right. Both alternatives are scary indeed.

7

THE REAL-LIFE PSYCHOS

I thought Mr. Clutter was a very nice gentleman.
Right up to the time I cut his throat.

—Perry Smith (Robert Blake)
in Richard Brooks's *In Cold Blood* (1967)

Early in 1980, at the height of England's infamous and then unsolved Yorkshire Ripper murder case, a top Hollywood studio took out an ad in *Variety* announcing plans to produce a "major theatrical motion picture" about the case. At the time, the murders were still capturing headlines all over the world, for despite an increasing number of victims—roughly fourteen in all by the time the Ripper was apprehended—the police still had no clues, and what was termed the largest manhunt in England's history was fast coming to nothing. Worse still, the Ripper had even taunted the police by sending them an audiotape with his voice on it.

Because the murders were still going on, a hue and cry arose both in England and in America about the studio's plans, which were deemed a gross exploitation of a sensational and tragic event for the purpose of making money. Very quickly, the studio backed off and the film was never made—even though the case was solved a year later and a book about it (by David Yallop) has since been written.

This story poses some interesting questions. For example, at what point does a psychofilm that purports to explore the facts surrounding a real-life case cease being valid as drama and cross over into mere exploitation? If the Yorkshire Ripper film had been made when originally announced—namely, before the killer had been caught and his motives revealed—

what would the film really have been about? What cautionary messages about and insights into the phenomenon of random and apparently motiveless murder would it have offered? The answer, of course, is none—or, at best, not many.

A problem arises, however, when all such films start getting lumped into the same category. A good case in point is Edward Dmytryk's 1952 film *The Sniper*, in which Arthur Franz plays Eddie Miller, a rather passive and nondescript young man who, in his darker moments, turns out to be a woman-hating monster. Set in San Francisco, it chronicles the tense manhunt for Miller, a sexual psychopath who has taken to shooting down unsuspecting and defenseless women at random with a high-powered rifle. Seeing the film on television allegedly prompted a Florida youth, also a sexual psychopath whose gun served as a surrogate penis, to go around shooting women at random through the windows of their homes. Captured and convicted of murder, the deranged youth was sent to prison for life. The boy's grieving parents, who never realized their son was so disturbed (even their neighbors viewed him as the archetypal "boy next door"), avoided seeing the offending film for years, but finally watched it when it again popped up on television. Screenwriter Harry Brown recounted that he received a letter from them. Realizing who they were and expecting some kind of denunciation

133

Eddie Miller (Arthur Franz) takes deadly aim in Edward Dmytryk's *The Sniper* (1952).

of his film's incitement to violence, he was surprised when they unexpectedly thanked him for making the picture—because, they revealed, as uncomfortable as it made them to watch it, it had given them an insight into the tortured mind of their son that they had never had. Perhaps, they concluded emotionally, if they had recognized the signposts of his illness earlier, they might have been able to avert the tragedy, and his victims would still be alive. The irony is that most contemporary critics dismissed *The Sniper* as a good thriller that ultimately failed as a serious psychofilm because it just didn't provide any insights into the nature of Franz's behavior.

So, who's right? The boy's parents? Or the critics? The answer, as usual, probably lies in the eye of the beholder. And his proximity to the event itself.

The Psycho Loners

A film that may have been suggested by an actual case, but does not purport to be about that case, is not a docudrama but rather a psychofilm à clef. Its aim is to explore certain psychological truths about a specific type of killer rather than recount the day-by-day events of a specific case. Insight, not straight reportage, is the primary goal. Because of this, many film-makers find the docudrama format, with its avalanche of facts that must somehow be dealt with, too confining and prefer to get at the heart of the matter by dealing with the subject as a psychofilm à clef instead. Perhaps the most famous example of this is Alfred Hitchcock's *Psycho*, which novelist Robert Bloch based on the real-life 1957 case of Wisconsin

134

In *The Texas Chain Saw Massacre* (1974), another psychofilm à clef based on the Ed Gein case, there's terror . . .

... and many more moments of terror (above and opposite).

mass murderer Ed Gein.

A quiet but well-liked middle-aged farmer who was often called on by his neighbors to baby-sit for them, Gein was also a mom-fixated sexual psychopath who indulged in necrophilia, cannibalism, and finally murder—usually at the time of the full moon. His crimes were eventually uncovered by a local deputy sheriff who came upon the headless corpse of Gein's own mother hanging on a hook in his squalid farmhouse, which was littered with the bones and flesh of Gein's victims as well as parts of other bodies Gein had recently disinterred. *Psycho's* taxidermy angle was drawn from the fact that Gein often made waistcoats from the skin of his victims and wore them about the house. Sentenced to life in prison without parole, Gein died in 1984.

Bloch's Norman Bates is a lot closer to the real Gein than is Hitchcock's. Nevertheless, the film does paint an accurate psychological portrait of the type of killer Gein was and makes some compelling suggestions as to what may drive a guy like that to lunacy. Norman's nightmare world in the film may be an old mansion rather than a farmhouse, but its overpowering atmosphere of suffocation, decay, and arrested development is just as telling. Like Norman, Gein had been disturbed for many years, but it was not until after his dominating mother died and he was left alone to brood on his sick fantasies in seclusion and complete freedom that those fantasies staked their final deadly claim and led him to murder.

Tobe Hooper's terrifyingly effective *The Texas Chain Saw Massacre* (1974) is another psychofilm à clef based on the Gein case. Again, some liberties have been taken. For example, the film offers not one killer but three, all of them brothers, as well as a bloodsucking grandpa who lives upstairs in a state of virtual mummification. The film draws more closely on the psychological truths of the Gein case, however, in its

depiction of the ghoulish farmhouse where the brothers play out their bloody fantasies. Like Gein's den of iniquity, it is a barbaric hellhole littered with the bones and flesh of both animal and human victims. *Chain Saw* is also upfront about the cannibalism aspect of Gein's pathology, which *Psycho* didn't go into at all. Gein did, in fact, eat parts of his victims as well as parts of the corpses he dug up. In *Chainsaw,* the murderous brothers, like Gein, kill not just for perverted sexual reasons but because of their equally perverted hunger for human flesh.

Chain Saw has been subjected to much criticism over the years that it is little more than a "repulsive gore film," a criticism not justified by the film itself, which, unlike many films of its type, is remarkably free of bloody effects. Like *Psycho,* the film's primary aim is to scare audiences half to death. And it succeeds. Despite a cripplingly low budget, it is even somewhat sophisticated, one of the few spawns of *Psycho,* in fact, whose makers actually seem to have learned something from the master of suspense. Apart from being loosely based on the same real-life

Leatherface (R. A. Mihailoff) and his new meat-loving family in the terrible *Leatherface: The Texas Chainsaw Massacre 3* (1989).

Roberts Blossom plays the Ed Gein character in *Deranged* (1974). The film renamed the character Ezra Cobb.

cement this, Hooper and coscreenwriter-producer Kim Henkel then begin with an opening screen crawl and accompanying narration aimed at making the audience believe that the film it is about to see is frighteningly based on fact—which, of course, it is, but only in part. Throughout, Hooper employs similar tricks, not the least of them being the sound of the chain saw itself. Only once—and very briefly—do we actually see the chain-saw blade make contact with human flesh. But the recurring sound of the machine, combined with our mental image of its potentially ghastly capabilities, is what really makes our hair stand on end.

Hooper's sequel *The Texas Chainsaw Massacre Part 2* (1986) is, if anything, even more of a study in derangement than the original—and a lot bloodier as well, for which it was roundly criticized. Hooper wisely avoided participation in the lame third installment in the series, *Leatherface: The Texas Chainsaw Massacre III* (1990), which was little more than a rehash of elements from the first two, and every other mad-slasher film ever made.

The only psychofilm that lays claim to being a docudrama about the Gein case is *Deranged* (1974), though even here the names and some of the facts have been changed to protect the guilty. Produced by Tom Karr and codirected by Jeff Gillen and Alan Ormsby (who also cowrote the script), the film carries the subtitle *The Confessions of a Necrophile*. Roberts Blossom plays Gein, here renamed Ezra Cobb, a middle-aged madman who kills women for their pelts, which he wears around the house. He also stuffs some of his victims in order to keep the mummified corpse of his mother company at mealtimes. Blossom is closer to the real Gein in age if not actual physical appearance—though even here there is some resemblance. He acquits himself in the gloomy part well, although the film's emphasis overall is more on black humor than it is on probing his demented character.

In setting out to chronicle the gruesome exploits of another true-life sex killer, the Moonlight Murderer of Texarkana, producer-director Charles B. Pierce found himself in the same situation faced by the producers of that announced Yorkshire Ripper film— namely, that his story was without an ending. Although the Ripper was finally caught, the moonlight murderer of Texarkana wasn't, and so Pierce's film about the case, *The Town That Dreaded Sundown* (1977), fails to shed any light either on the killer's possible identity or the motives that drove him to rape and murder.

The Texarkana killer, like Ed Gein, was another "full-moon" murderer who claimed five victims in the spring of 1946, after which he simply disappeared. The consensus was that he committed suicide after failing in an attempt to assault and murder a

case as *Psycho*, *Chain Saw* doesn't attempt to duplicate the earlier film in any way other than the manner in which it tries to get under the audience's skin. Hitchcock often stated that the reason audiences found his film so frightening was because he succeeded in making them imagine more horrors than they, in fact, saw. After the jolting shower murder of Janet Leigh, the violence in *Psycho* actually decreases, yet the film grows more intense because the audience, now no longer knowing what to expect, begins to expect the worst and starts playing on its own fears. The horrific title of Hooper's film—*The Texas Chain Saw Massacre*—operates on the same level in that it makes the viewer cringe before he has even sat down. To further

Middle-aged madman Ezra Cobb (Roberts Blossom) stuffs his victims to keep his mummified mama company at mealtimes. From *Deranged* (1974).

sixth victim whom he then feared would identify him to police. A few days after the attempted assault, an unidentified man hurled himself beneath the wheels of a passing train. Abruptly, the murders ceased. Though the murders remained unsolved, the case was marked closed.

Pierce gets around the identity problem by cover-

ing the face of his killer (Bud Davis) with a hood. He then introduces a hotshot Texas Ranger (Ben Johnson), who has been specially called in to solve the case due to the failure of the hick locals to come up with a single clue. Johnson finally picks up the scent and almost nails his quarry after a speedy pursuit, but is foiled when a passing train blocks his

140

"A completely uncontrolled vegetable walking around in a human body": Tony Curtis in the title role of Richard Fleischer's *The Boston Strangler* (1968).

Tony Curtis as *The Boston Strangler* finds himself throttling
his wife (Carolyn Conwell) as he relives his crimes.

way, and the killer simply vanishes into the archives
of local myth.

Apart from some nice photography (by Jim Rob-
erson) of the colorful Texarkana locales where the
incident took place, *The Town That Dreaded Sundown*
is not much of a psychofilm, or even much of a thriller
for that matter. Without much of a story to tell, Pierce
opts for the familiar and turns his film into a laughable "good ole boy" car-crash picture that might
better have been called *Smokey and the Psycho*.

Screenwriter Edward Anhalt and director Richard
Fleischer faced a very different dilemma with their
film about *The Boston Strangler* (1968). Albert De-
Salvo, the alleged strangler, had confessed to the
thirteen hideous crimes that had turned Boston into a
city of panic from June 1962 to March 1963, but due
to a lack of corroborating physical evidence, he was
not charged with being the strangler and was tried
instead for a series of earlier offenses, including rape
and armed robbery. Remanded to Bridgewater State
Hospital for treatment pending trial, DeSalvo escaped
on the night of February 24, 1967. Recaptured, tried,
and eventually convicted of those earlier crimes, he

was sentenced to life imprisonment at Walpole State
Prison. Six years later, he was found murdered in his
cell, but his killer was never caught.

The dilemma Anhalt and Fleischer faced was this.
Although DeSalvo had confessed to being the Boston
Strangler, providing the police with numerous details
about the victims, their surroundings, and their
deaths that only the actual killer could have known,
he had never been tried and convicted as such. By
portraying him as the strangler in their docudrama
about the case, Anhalt and Fleischer were leaving
their backers, Twentieth Century-Fox, open to criticism for libeling DeSalvo, not to mention a possible
lawsuit—despite the fact that their film was to be an
adaptation of Gerold Frank's award-winning nonfiction book about the case, which had been at the top of
the *New York Times* best-seller list for over five
months. Frank's book, *The Boston Strangler* (NAL,
1966), provided an exhaustive, day-by-day history of
the case, concluding with DeSalvo's detailed descrip-
tions of the murders to Massachusetts assistant attorney general John S. Bottomley (played in the film by
Henry Fonda). It left no doubt as to who the killer was

Richard Attenborough as necrophile and strangler John Reginald Christie in Richard Fleischer's subdued but gripping *10 Rillington Place* (1971).

Director Richard Fleischer (in light coat) on location at *10 Rillington Place*. Richard Attenborough (Christie) is standing to his left.

because DeSalvo himself left no doubt, and yet neither Frank nor his publisher were criticized or sued. Perhaps because more people go to movies than read books, Fleischer's film may have seemed fairer game, for upon its release, the expected criticisms came in in waves. Writing in the *Los Angeles Times,* Kevin Thomas asked, "Should a film label a man a mass murderer, even though he has confessed to the crimes, when he has yet to stand trial?" *Esquire*'s Wilfrid Sheed was even more pointed. He wrote that *"The Boston Strangler* is dirty pool . . . movies should not bring in convictions before courts do, and . . . a man with a living wife and children should be left to molder quietly in his asylum. I would not care to have been in their particular playground the day the film hit Boston."

Claiming that the film was a distorted portrayal of

his life (in fact, Anhalt's screenplay followed Frank's scrupulously researched book very closely), DeSalvo sued to halt the film's release, but a federal court judge refused to issue an injunction on the grounds that the film was "a responsible treatment of a theme much broader than the fate of its central character." Director Fleischer confirmed this intention. "The film," he said, "is the story of a fragmented personality. If anything, [it] would help DeSalvo if he ever came to trial."

Fleischer's right. If his film errs at all, it is on the side of DeSalvo, not against him, for it portrays him not as some willfully evil creature stalking the streets of Boston but as a hopelessly insane schizophrenic, a man whom DeSalvo's own attorney F. Lee Bailey once described as "a completely uncontrolled vegetable walking around in a human body." And Tony

144

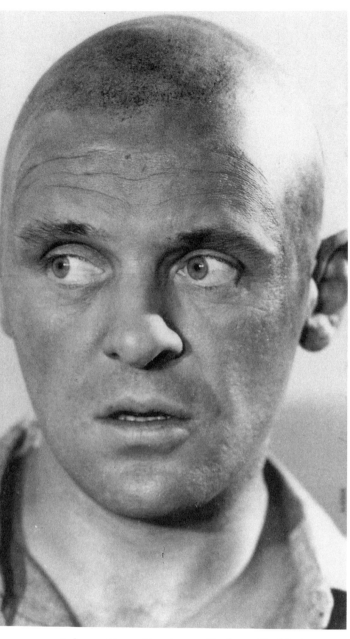

A shaven Bruno Hauptmann (Anthony Hopkins) prepares to walk the last mile in *The Lindbergh Kidnapping Case* (1976).

(1958) and *Sweet Smell of Success* (1957), campaigned long and hard to win the role, knowing it was a long shot because he would have to be cast against type. Anticipating Robert De Niro's physical sacrifices for the role of Jake LaMotta in *Raging Bull* twelve years later, he gained between twenty-five and thirty pounds and had his face rebuilt with a false nose to make himself look like DeSalvo; he even perfected a convincing Boston accent. His efforts earned him the role, and had the film not received such negative publicity, he might have received an Oscar nomination as well, for his performance was certainly unexpected and quite potent indeed. In the end, however, he had to content himself with his reviews, which were mostly quite positive.

Using a variety of techniques such as split screen and "jump cutting," Fleischer attempted to show the great mass of details the Boston police had to sift through before finally cracking the case, as well as the panic the city went through during DeSalvo's nine-month reign of terror. "It is a story of a city in confusion," Fleischer said. And living in fear as well. A freshman at Boston University during this time, I can attest to that. The strangler was on the minds of virtually everyone, but particularly women, who had come to feel so vulnerable that many of them—including some of my classmates—had taken to stashing long-needled hat pins in their purses just in case the strangler knocked at their door. Female enrollment in karate classes also skyrocketed at this time. One girl I knew, a fencing enthusiast, told me that she slept at night with her foil under her bed—until one evening she heard a prowler in the alley. After that, she said, she slept *with* her foil. An absorbing study of a murderer's mind and of the manhunt it took to uncover it, *The Boston Strangler* paints a vivid picture of this kind of panic as well.

Perhaps in response to the unfair criticism that he had sensationalized his film on the Boston Strangler case by using razzle-dazzle techniques to communicate its many complexities and overall unwieldiness, Fleischer chose a very different style for his next psychofilm docudrama, despite the fact that it was based on a case that, in England, was so sensational it contributed to that country's abolition of the death penalty.

Ten Rillington Place (1971) is about mass murderer John Reginald Christie (Richard Attenborough), who drugged, raped, and strangled eight women (one of whom was his wife) between 1940 and 1953, secreting their bodies in his garden as well as in a large cupboard, which he then covered over with wallpaper, inside his rented home. The bodies were discovered by the landlord after Christie had flown the coop. Arrested and tried for multiple murder, he was hanged in 1953. But that's only part of the story.

Curtis's performance as DeSalvo—certainly the best of his career—bestows upon the character every nuance of this description.

His career foundering at the time, Curtis, who felt that Hollywood had never taken him seriously as an actor despite his fine performances in *The Defiant Ones*

Eric Roberts as murder Paul Snider in Bob Fosse's *Star '80* (1983).

Accused of murdering his wife and two daughters, Green Beret Captain Jeffrey MacDonald (Gary Cole) testifies before an Army hearing. He will finally be brought to justice ten years later. From *Fatal Vision* (1984).

Kurt Russell as Texas Tower killer Charles Whitman in *The Deadly Tower* (1976), a television docudrama about the case.

A shy and sickly man (he was gassed during World War I), Christie could also be quite persuasive, which explains how he was able to lure many of his victims to his murderous lair at 10 Rillington Place, an address that eventually became as well-known to Britishers as 10 Downing Street. Under the pretext of being a skilled amateur doctor or chemist, he convinced them that he had a special cure for their asthma and other lung ailments. While his wife was out, he invited them over for treatment. Making them inhale gas, he rendered them unconscious, raped, then strangled them to avoid detection. After subletting his upstairs flat to a mentally deficient young man named Timothy Evans (John Hurt) and his pregnant wife Beryl (Judy Geeson), Christie announces to the impoverished Evans that he is an accomplished abortionist and agrees to perform the illegal operation on Beryl in order to help them out of their jam. Aroused at the sight of her naked and unconscious form, however, Christie rapes and strangles her instead, then convinces the half-witted Evans that although she died from the surgery, the police will probably believe Evans guilty of foul play and charge him with murder. Evans flees but is caught, tried, convicted of murder, and hanged. After Christie himself is hanged, however, Evans's case is reviewed, and he is posthumously declared innocent of the crime for which he was executed. As a result of this legal blunder, which Christie, having provided the most damning evidence against Evans, had coldly manipulated, Britain officially ended the death penalty so that such a mistake could never happen again.

As sensational as the ingredients of its story (based on a book by Ludovic Kennedy) are, *10 Rillington Place* is a strikingly low-keyed and subdued psycho-film. Although there are two manhunts in the film—first for Evans, then for Christie, both of whom are quite easily found, it is not a complex police procedural about a city in terror. In fact, most people, including the police, didn't even know about the murders (except for Beryl Evans's) until after Christie's cupboard was discovered and the bodies were found. Unlike DeSalvo, Christie was a shy and reclusive madman—more an Ed Gein type—and Richard Attenborough plays him exactly that way. Attenborough's major deficiency in the role is that while he succeeds in conveying the Milquetoast and manipulative aspects of Christie's character, he fails to communicate Christie's alternate air of superiority. As Christie was sexually insecure since youth, most psychologists agree that it was his inability to reconcile his feelings of sexual inadequacy and shyness with his feelings of dominance that led to his bursts of murderous (read vengeful) rage. As the pathetically dim Evans and his luckless bride, John Hurt and Judy Geeson register much more strongly overall.

Apart from its riveting story, what makes the film so effective is its realistic and creepy atmosphere. And the reason it's so realistic and creepy is that Fleischer chose to shoot the film on location at 10 Rillington Place. He made his decision and his film just in time. A year later, the notorious murder house was torn down to make way for a parking garage.

Bruno Richard Hauptmann was allegedly another inconspicuous type with delusions of superiority that perhaps drove him to murder. His victim was the

Psycho gun freak Bobby Thompson (Tim O'Kelly) in Peter Bogdanovich's *Targets* (1968), also based on the Whitman case.

Lindbergh baby, though there remains some doubt as to whether he intentionally killed the child. (Indeed, there is much doubt that he was involved in the kidnapping at all.) The body was found buried in the woods not far from the Lindbergh home. It is doubtful that, with the area crawling with federal, state, and local cops during the months following the kidnapping, Hauptmann would have risked exposure by returning to bury the body so close to the crime scene. The speculation is that as he was making off with the baby, a rung on his makeshift ladder broke, and he dropped the child accidentally. Finding the child dead from injuries suffered in the fall, he then buried its body along his escape route through the woods. Finally captured, he was charged with kidnapping and murder. Though he pleaded innocent, the evidence against him was so overwhelming that he was convicted and sentenced to death in the electric chair.

In Buzz Kulik's absorbing 1976 television film *The Lindbergh Kidnapping Case*, Anthony Hopkins paints a vivid portrait of Hauptmann. A petty criminal in his native Germany, he emigrated to the U.S. illegally following World War I (during which, like Christie, he too was gassed) to make his fortune—just like America's Lone Eagle hero, Charles A. Lindbergh. Arrogant but not bright enough to win fame and fortune honestly (according to the film), he chose the

149

Heroes or losers? Desperados or psychos? Clyde Barrow (Warren Beatty) and Bonnie Parker (Faye Dunaway) take on the law in Arthur Penn's controversial *Bonnie and Clyde* (1967).

route of crime instead and kidnapped the firstborn child of a man who was looked up to in a way Hauptmann felt he should be as well. The $50,000 ransom he received was issued in easily traced gold certificates. Knowing this (it was reported in the media), he made no attempt to move and even challenged the police to find him by spending some of the cash in and around his home. The bills were traced to him and he was caught. Additional evidence proved equally damaging. For example, the phone number of Lindbergh's go-between in the ransom negotiations was found written on a wall in Hauptmann's home. Like a shifty-eyed little boy who simply will not own up to the truth, Hopkins arrogantly professes his innocence. He even makes jokes in court about the prosecutor's case. Pointing up the poor

workmanship of the kidnapper's ladder (whose wood proves an identical match to some lumber found in Hauptmann's garage), he quips that he, a skilled carpenter, wouldn't have botched such a job. The brilliance of Hopkins's performance lies in his subtle conveyance of Hauptmann's wily sense of accomplishment at having succeeded at his goal, which was to become as well-known a figure as Lindbergh, and even linked with such a man, for all time. By pleading innocent of any wrongdoing right to his grave, he also assures that his case will remain controversial, which it has, for some still insist that Hauptmann was but a scapegoat, a martyr-victim to postwar anti-German feeling. In fact, there is mounting evidence that he was altogether innocent.

DeSalvo and Christie were killers whose psychoses

150

Bullets and reality come crashing home for Arthur Penn's *Bonnie and Clyde*.

derived from sexual appetites that became violently twisted, whereas Hauptmann's alleged motivation stemmed more from a desire for recognition that had zoomed completely out of control. His was more a crime of self-esteem than passion, spawned by a compulsion to achieve notoriety even through crime as a way of bolstering his inwardly low self-image. Evidence put forth by the prosecution in Abby

Mann's controversial television docudrama *The Atlanta Child Murders* (1985), directed by John Erman, portrays convicted killer Wayne Williams (Calvin Levels) as this kind of psycho as well.

The Atlanta Child Murders tells the story of the intense manhunt for the slayer of twenty-eight children, mostly black, that turned Atlanta into a city of panic from 1979 until 1981. The case was declared

Martin Sheen and Sissy Spacek in Terrence Malick's *Bad-lands* (1973), a film loosely based on the Charles Stark-weather-Caril Fugate murder spree of the 1950s.

officially closed with the conviction of twenty-six-year-old Wayne Williams, a self-styled music pro-moter, who was tied by fiber and other circumstantial evidence to two of the victims. As the murders ap-peared to cease following his capture, officials were convinced that Williams had committed the other murders as well but, due to a lack of real evidence, couldn't try him for them.

Preceding, and especially following, its initial broadcast, Abby Mann's film (which he executive-produced in addition to writing) was subjected to a great deal of criticism for implying that Williams was actually railroaded by Atlanta's predominantly black officials, because the murders were giving them and their city a bad reputation and they desperately needed a suspect, *any* suspect, to pacify the hounding mob. Mann insists that his script was fair and scrupu-lously researched, its facts drawn from detailed inter-views with all concerned that he had personally conducted as well as from the trial transcripts them-selves. Nevertheless, Atlanta mayor Andrew Young,

District Attorney Lewis Slaton (played in the film by Rip Torn), and others denounced the film as inaccu-rate and misleading. *Time* magazine even editorial-ized against the film in an article that took issue with the docudrama format itself, claiming that, because viewers tend to lump such programming into the same category as news and information, the historical record is irrevocably damaged when writers and directors take liberties with the facts of a given case for the purpose of enhancing its drama.

Did Abby Mann do this? CBS, which aired the film, and Mann insist otherwise. There is no question, however, but that Mann's script does raise some disturbing questions about the handling of the case as well as suggest that there may have been a rush to judgment. But, and this is a very large but, the film also paints a convincing portrait of Williams as some-one who could very well have committed the crimes as a means of drawing attention to himself.

Although he was the recipient of a great deal of publicity at age fourteen for building his own radio

Upstanding young students and psycho killers. Bradford Dillman and Dean Stockwell at home, on campus, and alone as thrill killers Artie Straus and Judd Steiner in Richard Fleischer's *Compulsion* (1959), based on the Leopold and Loeb murder case.

station, Williams's fame had substantially dwindled since then, but he remained a brag-and-boast type convinced of his innate superiority, particularly over his fellow Atlanta blacks, many of whom, like some white supremacist, he viewed as underachieving and even deficient. The murders could therefore have been his way of getting even, his deranged method of striking out against what he felt to be his Achilles' heel, the blackness he shared with his victims. The prosecution believed this to be true, and Mann suggests as much himself. Like the promoter he sees himself as, Williams calls an immediate press conference following his interrogation, even handing out printed statements to reporters as if they were press kits. Even more telling, however, is a subtle exchange that occurs in a video arcade at the beginning of the film where the off-camera killer attempts to lure one of his victims. The exchange suggests how the killer was able to win the confidence of his randomly selected and mostly poor victims and points to his being self-styled entrepreneur Williams. When the child remarks that he doesn't have enough money to play the video game, the killer offers to stake him. Later in the film, Williams is shown making similar offers to other nonvictims. It may be a subtle clue, like fiber evidence, but it is no less compelling.

Like the juror who leaves the courtroom at the end of the film saying that she believed Williams to be guilty but felt the state had failed to prove it, my feeling is that Mann believes Williams is guilty too but couldn't conclusively say so. The film was made to express his, if perhaps no one else's, reasonable doubt.

Another self-styled entrepreneur whose delusions lead him to murder is Eric Roberts's Paul Snider in Bob Fosse's cautionary show-biz tale *Star 80* (1983), which tells of the events that led up to the brutal shooting of starlet Dorothy Stratten (Mariel Hemingway).[1] The focal point of the film is not Stratten but her husband and mentor, Snider, a cheap hustler through whose drive to become a big shot like Hugh Hefner (Cliff Robertson), the gorgeous girl becomes a playmate of the month for *Playboy,* then captures the playmate-of-the-year spot and a film contract as well. Feeling himself being squeezed out of the picture and

1. Fosse's film was beaten to the punch by an exploitative TV movie called *Death of a Centerfold: The Dorothy Stratten Story* (1981) in which Jamie Lee Curtis was miscast as the doomed starlet. Bruce Weitz took the role of Snider, and while he is good, he is no match for Roberts. The movie is vastly inferior to Fosse's in every way.

Reporter Sid Brooks (Martin Milner), attorney Tom Daly (Edward Binns), and psychopath Artie Straus (Bradford Dillman) discuss the killing with police lieutenant Johnson (Robert Simon) in *Compulsion*.

robbed of the success for which he has so longed, Snider flips out, shoots the girl in his apartment, then turns the gun on himself. The case made headlines everywhere.

Star 80 is a disturbing film to watch not only because of its inevitable outcome but because of Roberts's skin-crawling performance as the fatally self-deluded Snider, a man who, despite his boyish charm on the outside, is nothing more on the inside than a sleazeball with stars in his eyes. His derangement lies in the fact that he is unable to see himself as others see him. The ultimate victim of the *Playboy* philosophy, Snider suffers a fatal blow to his expansive self-image when Stratten, who is inexorably

154

bound up with that image, attempts to exit his life once and for all. Her decision takes a deadly turn, but its outcome was inevitable given the nature of Snider's fatal vision.

Arguably the screen's definitive portrait of the type of psycho who goes on the rampage because of his innate feelings of superiority is *Fatal Vision,* a 1984 NBC docudrama based on the best-selling book of the same name by reporter Joe McGinniss. The film tells the true story of high-school honor student, Princeton graduate, and Green Beret doctor Jeffrey MacDonald, who, following a ten-year struggle by his father-in-law, Freddy Kassab (Karl Malden), to bring him to justice, was convicted of murdering his wife and two small children.

The genesis of McGinniss's book, one of the most exhaustive accounts of a real-life murder case ever written, is interesting in itself, for McGinniss came to write the book on the invitation of MacDonald himself. McGinniss approached the case with an open mind, but as the damning evidence unfolded at MacDonald's trial, he began to fear that MacDonald might, in fact, be guilty after all. "When it came, the jury's verdict was very upsetting to me—as it was to all who had come to know, and to like, Jeffrey MacDonald," McGinniss wrote in an article for *TV Guide* prior to the film's broadcast. "During the months and years that followed, however, as I probed deeper into the case and into the nature of the man, I gradually found myself forced to accept—to my sorrow—that this charming, intelligent, and thoroughly likable human being had committed what is perhaps the worst crime a man can commit: the murder of his own children." MacDonald's subsequent lawsuits against McGinniss, his publisher, and now NBC are still pending as of this writing. So as not to be included, let me state right off that what follows is a review of the film and a description of Jeffrey MacDonald as a character in it, not a comment on the merits of the case itself.

The fascinating thing about *Fatal Vision* is that on surface viewing one finds it difficult to believe that MacDonald—one of those archetypal overachieving, all-American boys—could be capable of battering and butchering his family in such a savage manner, or any manner for that matter. And yet the physical evidence presented against him in the film is not only compelling, it's impossible to refute. The jury, hand-picked by MacDonald's attorney, Bernie Siegel (Barry Newman), thinks so too and brings in its guilty verdict in just over six hours. The film, challenged with telescoping McGinniss's six-hundred-plus page book into a three-hour running time, amazingly succeeds in presenting all this evidence clearly, plus many of the subtleties of the case as well. Chief among these subtleties is the character of MacDonald, whom a psychiatrist in the film diagnoses as suffering from a paranoid psychosis—a fatal vision that his view of things, and *only* his view, is the correct one. When confronted with the irrefutable fact that his account of what happened on the night of the murder simply doesn't conform to the extensive physical evidence found at the crime scene, MacDonald, like Bruno Hauptmann, suggests no alternative explanation other than that the evidence, certainly not he, must be wrong—and not just wrong but laughable and absurd. This demonstrates not only a contempt for the evidence but a contempt for anyone "stupid enough" to accept it over his account, which has more holes in it than a slab of Swiss cheese. Even Siegel tries to caution him about his arrogance ("You don't have to be Laurence Olivier, just be a little humble") but to little avail, for this is like asking a leopard to change its spots. MacDonald's will to dominance is as much a part of him as his nose. It's what drove him to become an honor student, a doctor, and a Green Beret—all positions of respect and authority—and may even be what drove him to murder when, it is speculated, his wife came to challenge the way he was handling their daughter's bed-wetting problem. Gaining much notoriety due to the case, MacDonald, quite consistently, does little to shirk it and even encourages more by appearing on TV talk shows and agreeing to other interviews—plus a book about his case—all of which finally work against him. McGinniss writes:

> Such blind optimism in the face of reality has always been a part of MacDonald's character; some would say part of his charm. Psychiatrists who have examined him over the years call it "denial." Viewers of *Fatal Vision* should bear it in mind, for it is a clue to the disorder that lurks beneath his sunny surface and helps explain how a man who had committed such crimes could have acted for so many years as if he hadn't.

Director David Greene, writer John Gay, and everyone else connected with *Fatal Vision* deserve high marks for the sensitivity of their work on the film, but the highest marks must go to Gary Cole. In Joe McGinniss's words, he "brings the character of Jeffrey MacDonald to life with such power and precision that I got goose bumps from watching him."

Perhaps the most terrifying type of psycho loner is the random sniper—such as Arthur Franz's Eddie Miller in the film mentioned at the beginning of this chapter—for he is motivated to kill not by a desire to make a name for himself necessarily, or even a need to bolster his feelings of superiority, but because he longs for his own death, which he engineers by taking a lot of innocent people with him.

Compulsion's thrill killers: sullen Judd Steiner (Dean Stockwell) and cool Artie Straus (Bradford Dillman).

The most notorious example of this type of psycho loner is Charles Whitman, who, after murdering his mother and his wife, armed himself with a number of rifles and handguns, climbed to the top of the clock tower at the University of Texas at Austin, and on a sunny 1966 morning began sniping at passersby below. By the time police got within shooting range of him, he had killed or wounded forty-six people. Whitman was another "nice boy next door." After killing his wife, he left a note saying "Life is not worth living" and went on his suicidal rampage. The irony is that doctors found in autopsy that Whitman had a malignant brain tumor that would have killed him eventually.

The Whitman case has been dealt with twice on film. One, *The Deadly Tower* (1975 TV movie), directed by Jerry Jameson, is not so much about Whitman (Kurt Russell), who remains a cipher, a remote killing machine, for most of the film's length, as it is about the Mexican-American police officer (Richard Yniguez) who courageously jeopardized his life to break in on Whitman and fatally bring him down. Ned Beatty plays the nervy but nervous civilian who assists Yniguez in his perilous climb to the top of the tower.

Peter Bogdanovich's debut feature, *Targets* (1968), is also about the Whitman case, though in thinly disguised form. It tells two stories concurrently, one about an aging horror-film star (Boris Karloff) who feels that his type of movie monster has become passé, and the other about a father-hating gun freak who goes on a rampage to get even with his dad by shooting at people from the top of a water tower and then from behind a drive-in movie screen. Both stories finally merge when the outraged Karloff character, who is attending the premiere of his latest film at the drive-in, confronts the youth and slaps him silly. As the boy is being led away, he remarks, "I hardly ever missed, did I?"

The project started out as a straight horror vehicle in which Karloff was to play a strangler, but Bogdanovich and his then-wife and collaborator Polly Platt reconsidered, feeling, as their film openly states, that the Karloff type of bogeyman was no longer scary and that their psycho had to be more contemporary. Says Bogdanovich, "We both decided that the most modern, terrifying murderer—*modern horror*—was the sniper in Texas." And so Karloff became the hero instead.

Targets doesn't go into much more detail about its

Whitman character, here called Bobby Thompson (Tim O'Kelly), than *The Deadly Tower* does, but it does adhere to most of the facts in the Whitman case. Thompson hates his domineering father, as did Whitman, yet kills his wife and mother out of some twisted logic. Like Whitman, Thompson is also an aficionado of guns and a skilled marksman, who manages to stockpile his arsenal of weapons with little difficulty due to an absence of strict gun-control laws—though, to be fair about the issue, it is likely that the outwardly normal and likable Thompson, like Whitman, would probably have gotten around such scrutiny anyway.

Releasing the movie at the height of the clamor for more gun control that followed the assassinations of Martin Luther King, Jr., and especially presidential aspirant Robert F. Kennedy, Paramount felt it wise to accent the film's implicit, though not stated, pro-gun-control message and included a prologue to the film lobbying for tighter gun-control laws. Bogdanovich didn't agree with this decision, as his film was not intended to be a political tract, only a taut thriller, which it is.

> Paramount thought the gun-control notion would be a respectable way of selling the picture. I felt that it wouldn't be good for the picture financially because message pictures are usually box-office poison. But frankly, if they hadn't put that on, I don't think the picture would have been released [that] year. Everybody was scared. The gun-control angle helped us with some critics. It also hurt us with several critics who started to look for a message or statement about Why He Did It. We didn't tell why he did it. We never wanted to. The ad said 'This picture sheds a little light on a dark topic.' I don't think we shed much light on it. I wasn't trying to shed light on it. I just wanted to *show* the thing. In fact, the most horrifying thing about these murders is that there doesn't seem to be any reason commensurate with the size of the crime. So I didn't have any socially conscious motivations at all. By the way, that prologue has now been taken off the picture.

Actually, on most prints I've seen, it still remains.

Killer Couples

The story of Bonnie Parker and Clyde Barrow is a good place to begin this section on the screen's deadliest duos. One could argue, I suppose, that this true-life pair really belongs in a book on desperadoes rather than a book on psychos. But as portrayed in Arthur Penn's controversial *Bonnie and Clyde* (1967), each of these characters, like the psycho loners who precede them, is seen as having little grasp on reality.

Clyde (Warren Beatty) suffers from feelings of inadequacy, a need to "be somebody" coupled with doubts about his masculinity. Bonnie (Faye Dunaway) is a bored backwater Texas waitress with a thirst for excitement and sexual adventure. While seemingly mismatched, they share one thing in common: a view of what their lives could and should be that is pure romantic fantasy. And it is because of this shared fantasy that, in combination, the two become one, a deadly and nearly unstoppable force.

Penn's film has been accused of being heavily romantic as well, an attempt to turn these two historical losers into mythical figures, even heroes. But this is hardly the case. It's true that the real Bonnie and Clyde were not at all glamorous. Rather toady in appearance, they scarcely looked like movie stars Dunaway and Beatty. Yet this is precisely how they viewed themselves—not as movie stars, perhaps, but as "stars" most certainly. As in the film, they always had the Kodak close at hand so that they could take pictures of each other posing with their guns.

Bonnie and Clyde is a romanticized view of the exploits of the notorious pair, but the reason for this is that, from first frame to last, the film is told from the self-deluded perspective of the pair itself. A good example of the film's subtlety in this regard is its use of graphic violence. Only when this violence gets close to the pair or when it strikes the pair's own ranks does it turn ugly, does the blood spurt and pain and suffering follow. The reason for this is not that Penn is trying to make martyrs of the pair but that Bonnie and Clyde see things only as they relate to them. A cop blown away by them at a distance is merely a bloodless doll. But when they or someone near them take a bullet, reality suddenly comes crashing in. Over and over again, Penn strives to make this point, as, for example, when Bonnie goes to visit her mother for the last time, and the film takes on a nostalgic hue. This is how Bonnie—and Clyde, for their fantasies are inseparable—sees the get-together. As if he were nothing more than a traveling salesman, Clyde makes Bonnie beam when he says, "Bonnie and I were just talking the other day, Mother Parker, about how she wants to live no more than three miles from you." Mama's grasp on reality is a lot firmer, however. "I don't know, Clyde Barrow," she answers. "She lives three miles from me, and she won't live very long." Reacting as if they'd been doused with ice water—particularly Bonnie, whose face pales as if she'd also just glimpsed her own ghost—the two quickly escape back into their world of fantasy, where, self-absorbed, self-deluded, and self-destructive to the end, they meet their inevitable doom. Typically, Bonnie romanticizes that doom—which turns out to be not just ugly but grotesque, as their spastic bodies are literally shot to pieces—in a poem called "The Story of Bonnie and Clyde" that she sends to the newspapers to immortalize the preordained event. "Someday they'll go down together," she writes prophetically. "They'll bury them side by side. To a few it'll be grief—to the law a relief—but it's death to Bonnie and Clyde."

Like Bonnie, Sissy Spacek's Holly in Terence Malick's *Badlands* (1973) also lives in a fantasy world. Not popular in school and without much personality, she is a loner who conveys her loneliness and romanticized longings via a voice-over diary that sounds like the worst schoolgirl fiction. When she meets Kit (Martin Sheen), who will become her lover, she narrates, "He was handsomer than anybody I'd ever met. He looked just like James Dean." Later, after Kit has killed her father (Warren Oates) and they embark on a murder spree, she describes their desperate situation as if it were a production of *Romeo and Juliet:* "He wanted to die with me, and I dreamed of being lost forever in his arms."

Kit is no less a victim of his delusions. A loner as well, who never had a girl before Holly, he is glib but not bright, dominant but aimless. His sense of himself, like Holly's, is pure fiction, and he is continually given to marking various moments in his life as if to ensure their importance. After making love to Holly for the first time, an act that seems to hold no real joy for either of them, he nevertheless takes home a stone from the site of their lovemaking to act as a souvenir of the occasion. Another time, he sends a balloon aloft full of their trinkets. And at the conclusion of the film, when he is caught by the police, he quickly marks the spot with rocks.

Badlands is loosely based on the Charles Starkweather–Caril Fugate mass-murder case of 1958. Like Kit, Starkweather was a nobody with longings to be a somebody. Fugate, like Holly, was a drab girl who became his accomplice, not in the murders themselves, for she never killed anyone, but in the support she gave to the fantasies that eventually drove him to murder. She was his other half, the missing piece that resulted in a deadly duo's taking shape.

Not all screen-killer couples are male and female, of course. Some are exclusively male. But they evolve in much the same way and are no less deadly. One of the partners is usually dominant while the other is more malleable. Individually, they might never turn to murder, but, in feeding off each other's ego, they become a dangerous third person, a unified force bent on destruction. Such a pair were Chicago's Leopold and Loeb, two high-IQ college boys who, in 1924, killed and mutilated a distant cousin of Loeb's (Bobby Franks) to prove their intellectual superiority by getting away with the perfect crime. They failed, however. Arrested and convicted, they were saved from the death penalty by their defense attorney, Clarence Darrow, who gave an impassioned three-day speech against the barbarity of capital punishment that earned them life imprisonment instead. Loeb was killed in a dispute with a fellow prisoner a decade or so later, but Leopold, a model prisoner throughout his incarceration, was finally deemed rehabilitated and paroled in 1958. He died in Puerto Rico in 1971.

Alfred Hitchcock's *Rope* (1948), based on a play by Patrick Hamilton, was the first psychofilm to deal with the case. John Dall played Brandon, the more calm, cool, and collected of the duo, while Farley Granger played the hyperactive Philip, who commits the actual murder while Brandon prevents the victim, a schoolmate, from putting up a struggle. James Stewart, making his debut for Hitchcock, plays their former college professor, Rupert Cadell, whose intellectual game-playing about the "art of murder" and seeming espousal of the philosophy of the superman have fired the boys' murderous imaginations. Leopold and Loeb were similarly inspired by the philosophy of the superman, but their crime in its name predated the onslaught of Hitler's "master race" by almost two decades. At the conclusion of *Rope,* however, Cadell, distraught at discovering the crime and feeling guilty for the part he has unwittingly played in it, associates the boys' paranoid delusions with Nazism and hands the now shamefaced pair over to the police.

Richard Fleischer's *Compulsion* (1959), another psychofilm à clef about the case, keeps the story in period and is therefore free of such preachy references. The focus is on the specifics of the crime, the psychotic coupling that drove the boys to it, and the trial that ensued.

Compulsion is also based on a play, as well as a novel, written by Meyer Levin, a contemporary of the real-life killers who attended the University of Chicago with them and even shared some of their classes. In the film, Levin disguises himself as Sid Brooks (Martin Milner), an aspiring journalist covering the trial of his former classmates for his school newspaper. Dean Stockwell plays Judd Steiner and Bradford Dillman is his more dominant buddy Artie Straus. Together, they attempt the perfect crime, the murder of a randomly selected child, but are caught when a pair of glasses found near the crime scene is linked by their special design to Steiner. When the Clarence Darrow character, here called Jonathan Wilk (Orson Welles), is brought in to defend them, their guilt has been established beyond all doubt, and they have even confessed to the crime. Wilk's only remaining defense therefore is to save them from the death penalty, which he achieves via a brilliant fifteen-minute summation speech to the judge that concludes with the swaying line, "Life! Any more goes back to the hyena!"

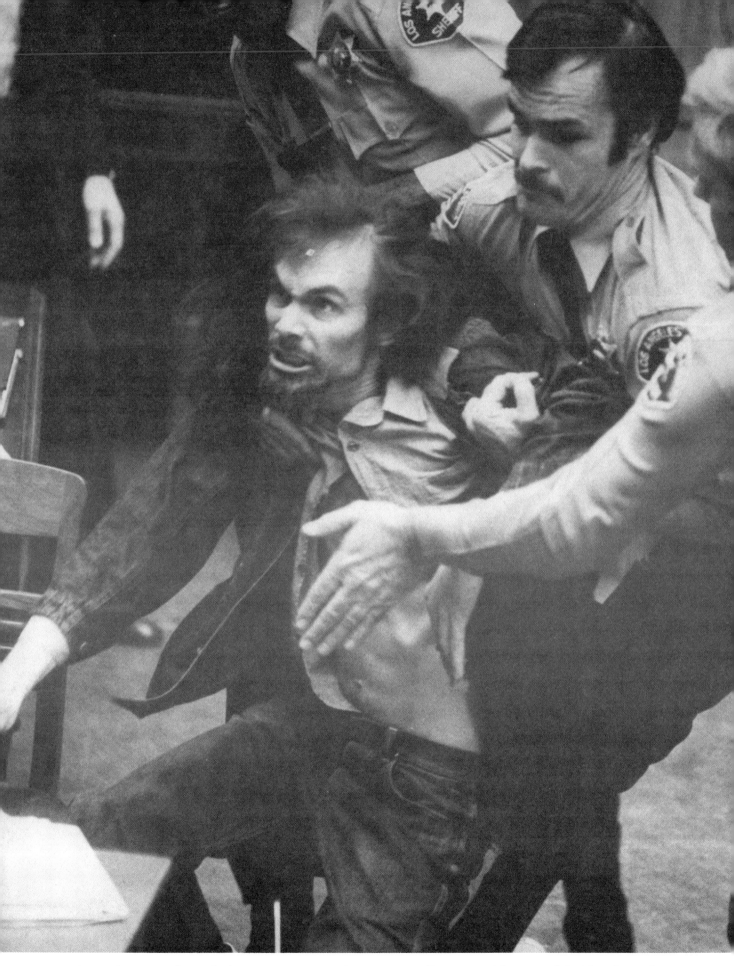

Cultist and mass murderer Charles Manson (Steve Railsback) goes berserk in the courtroom. From *Helter Skelter*
(1976), director Tom Gries's powerful TV docudrama about
the Tate-LaBianca murders.

Michael Berryman as one of the desert degenerates in *The Hills Have Eyes* (1977), writer-director Wes Craven's tense updating of the Sawney Bean case.

Unlike *Rope,* which was a veiled reworking of the details of the case, *Compulsion* altered little but the characters' names. Everyone knew it was about Leopold and Loeb, particularly the just-released Leopold, who sued author Levin for over a million dollars, claiming that he had "appropriated his name [which Levin hadn't], his likeness, and personality [which Levin certainly had] for profit." The suit was thrown out of court, but its resultant publicity helped the film, a sober if long-winded essay on the artlessness of murder, achieve a modest box-office success.

Truman Capote's *In Cold Blood,* filmed in 1967 by Richard Brooks, is perhaps the most famous examination of this type of lethal psychological interrelationship. Although he often boasted to accomplice Dick Hickock that he had killed before, runty, aspirin-popping loser Perry Smith was all talk until the fateful night of November 15, 1959, when his fantasy turned to reality and he cold-bloodedly murdered four members of a respected Kansas family, the Clutters, during the course of a robbery. Hickock himself killed no one, but even though his finger wasn't on the trigger, his complicity in the massacre was profound. It was he who earmarked the Clutters for robbery, and it was he who engineered the heist by passing bad checks to buy the materials needed for the job. More important, it was Hickock who was the dominant half of the pair. Smith looked up to him and slaughtered the defenseless Clutters, toward whom Smith admitted later he never felt any anger, as a way of proving himself to his more glib, brash, and manipulative buddy. "You're good. You're *really* good!" the impressed Smith remarks of Hickock's ease at conning various store owners into accepting his bad checks. Hickock is no less impressed later on by the ease with which Smith dispatches each of the Clutters.

Capote, who got to know the two death-row inmates quite well while researching *In Cold Blood,* firmly believed that individually Smith and Hickock were not the mass-murdering type. But by linking together, by feeding off each other's ego and inadequacies, by constantly arousing and bolstering certain expectations of one another, they evolved into a potentially violent third party that was more than capable of murder. One doesn't know until the end of the book, or the film, just who committed the actual killings. My own not atypical suspicion was that they both did, or, if only one of them was responsible, that it was the more aggressive Hickock. It seemed unlikely that the less dominant Smith could have been the primary executioner, despite all his braggadocio. And yet, as with Leopold and Loeb, that's precisely what happened. The less dominant did the killing while the partner lent immoral support. Smith was no longer just Smith at the time of the murders, but rather a two-headed Hydra that had at last sprouted claws. Both Smith and Hickock were subsequently executed for their decidedly mutual crime.

Capote's absorbing book about the case—which he called a "nonfiction novel" (the literary equivalent, perhaps, of the TV docudrama)—became an immediate best-seller in the U.S. though it fared less well abroad. In bringing it to the screen, writer-director Richard Brooks sought to retain the book's docudrama flavor by shooting on location in black and white without the use of name stars. The studio, however, insisted on color—so as to ensure a lucrative sale to television—and wanted Paul Newman and Steve McQueen to play the murderous duo. Brooks put up a fight—possibly with the author's backing, as the celebrated and quite vocal Capote could and would have denounced the film if Brooks had been forced to "go Hollywood." Capote had no say in the matter, but Brooks very much wanted his endorsement of the film because, as the director said later, "if he had disliked it, he could have murdered us." Brooks's insistence paid off. The roles of Smith and Hickock went to look-alikes Robert Blake and Scott Wilson, respectively, both of whom earned Oscar nominations for their superb characterizations—although, in my view, it was newcomer Wilson who truly stole the show.

Shot in black and white as Brooks wanted, *In Cold Blood* has a grimy, downbeat feel that's quite apropos to the subject. The film seldom goes wrong while focusing on the unhealthy symbiotic relationship that develops between the two men and climaxes in murder. Brooks's surrealistic flashbacks explaining Smith's troubled family life are less successful and at times even trite—as are his preachy pronouncements against capital punishment, an issue that Capote, in his book, urged the reader to ponder for himself. These two nits aside, *In Cold Blood* remains a quite powerful movie and one of the most insightful portraits of the evolution of a killer couple ever put on film.

Killer Cults

One of the earliest recorded murder cases in the history of crime involved a degenerate family of cannibal-killers who robbed travelers to the town of Galloway, Scotland, then killed and ate their victims to survive. This occurred in the fifteenth century. The head of the demented family, or cult, of approximately forty members was a wild beast of a man named Sawney Bean, who had abandoned civilization a quarter of a century earlier to live in a cave with his common-law wife. Together, they spawned a number of sons and daughters, who then mated with each other and sired even more offspring. Finally

161

captured, the Bean men were mutilated and allowed to bleed to death while the Bean women were burned alive.

This true tale of a cultish family that chose to live as a sort of "opposite" to society, governed by its own atavistic rules of behavior and morality, was used by writer-director Wes Craven as the basis for his much underrated *The Hills Have Eyes* (1977). Craven updated the case and relocated it to the deserts of California. While en route to L.A., a vacationing family suffers an accident in their camper and is left stranded. It soon becomes evident that they are not alone. Years before, a murderous local, who now calls himself Jupiter (James Whitworth), had fled into the hills with his prostitute wife and spawned a number of sons and a daughter. Like Bean and family, they have completely degenerated over the years into wild beasts that now revel in their opposition to society. The marooned travelers run into them, and the film becomes a tense tale of survival. The vacationers' ranks are all but decimated, but they ultimately prevail over their grotesque foes. In the film's final, unsettling scene, the last of the hill men is horrifically butchered—just as the Bean males had been—by one of the enraged travelers (Martin Speer), whose ferociously contorted face, as he wields his knife, suggests that he and his victim have ultimately reached a common level of barbarity. Slowly, the scene freezes and the screen turns bloodred.

It's easy to view this conclusion as just another "beast in man" statement, a message about how our civilization is only skin-deep. But Craven's point is much sharper than that. Speer's cumulative savagery, like the Scots' excessively brutal retribution on the Bean family, is not so much a primitive indulgence as it is a vengeful reaction to the *existence* of such creatures, who dare to share our likeness but nothing else that is human, flaunting our laws and threatening our concept of civilization and of ourselves. As such, it is not enough just to punish them. They must be *expunged*.

The idea that such a primitive band of murderous outsiders as the Sawney Bean family could have sprung up even five hundred years ago is disturbing enough, but the possibility that their antisocial kind might still be with us today is even more unsettling. That's the subject of *Helter Skelter* (1976), director Tom Gries's exceptional telefilm based on Vincent T. Bugliosi's inside account of his prosecution of the Tate-LaBianca murderers in 1970.

The murderers, headed by the messianic Charles Manson (aka Jesus Christ and the devil), shared much in common with the savage Bean family. Manson's followers procreated among themselves, lived off what they could beg or steal, and early in August 1969 proved that they could wantonly slaughter seven of their fellow human beings without mercy as well. In keeping with the cannibalistic proclivities of the Bean family, murderess Susan Atkins (played chillingly in the film by Nancy Wolfe) recounted later that she had even tasted the dead Sharon Tate's blood.

Unlike the Beans, Manson and his followers were not an actual family, but it is significant that that's what they called themselves. They were a strongly bonded cult, but for such a bond to exist, the cult leader must instill in his members a deep feeling of community—of *family*—and Manson had that power. Deeply alienated himself (having spent over half of his life in prison), he was able to spot that crippling malaise in others and feed it by promoting in them an ever more paranoid sense of isolation from regular society. By the time he got through with these losers, they all felt as he did about the Establishment, that "you people ain't got no authority over me." Of course, the hippie phenomenon of the sixties expressed many of these same feelings, and this added to the hysteria of the subsequent trial when some began to confuse the scruffy Manson band with actual "hippiedom" and insisted that they were being persecuted. Naturally, con man Manson did his utmost to enhance this confusion by spouting such rhetoric as "I am not you, nor do I condone your unjust attitude."

A nomadic band that lived in the hills and deserts of California, the Manson family eventually became what the Bean family became: deadly misfits that acted in complete defiance of society's rules of behavior and morality, rules for which they had little but contempt. That was not enough for the messianic Manson, however, whose delusions of grandeur eventually grew so paranoid that he determined to bring down existing society and replace it with his own. By leaving the words *Death to Pigs* (a familiar Black Panther slogan) written on the walls of his victims' homes, he hoped to set off a race war that would result in the white man's death at the hands of the blacks, followed by the surviving Manson family's usurpation of power from the blacks because of that race's "innate inferiority." Manson called his war to end all wars "Helter Skelter" (the title of a popular Beatles song about an English playground ride) and, according to Bugliosi, ordered the randomly chosen Tate-LaBianca murders as its opening salvo. Convicted and found guilty following one of the most notorious murder trials in California history, he and his four coconspirators received life in prison.

In addition to being one of the most sensational murder cases in our country's history, the Manson affair was also one of the most complex. In telescoping its myriad details into a coherent script for a four-hour telefilm, writer JP Miller (who also wrote

Powers Boothe as cult leader par excellence Jim Jones in
William A. Graham's *Guyana Tragedy: The Story of Jim Jones*
(1980).

The Lindbergh Kidnapping Case) achieved a small miracle, a clearheaded dramatization of an extremely bizarre crime that is not just scrupulously authentic but charged with psychological truth. Director-producer Tom Gries's insistence on shooting as much of the film as possible on the very sites where the events occurred also adds to the film's sense of realism, not to mention its eeriness—as do the performers, most of whom are dead ringers for the real-life characters they portray. Naturally, the most showy part is that of Charles Manson—which actor Steve Railsback brings off in a manner that is nothing short of electric. But he is matched every step of the way by George DiCenzo (as prosecutor Bugliosi), Nancy Wolfe, Marilyn Burns, Christina Hart, Cathey Paine (as Manson family members Susan Atkins, Linda Kasabian, Patricia Krenwinkle, and Leslie Van Houten, respectively), and a host of others. One of the highest-rated TV movies ever, *Helter Skelter* is easily one of the best docudramas television has yet produced, as well as one of its most chilling psychofilms. Yet it curiously failed to earn a single Emmy or any other major television award for any of its outstanding contributors.

If *Helter Skelter* is one of the best docudramas about cult madness ever made, Rene Cardona, Jr.'s *Guyana, Cult of the Damned* (1980) is certainly one of the worst—though admittedly, it is not strictly speaking a docudrama but rather a psychofilm à clef in which, for some reason, the lead characters' names have been changed even though the film is blatantly about the Reverend Jim Jones and the mass suicide he orchestrated among his followers in Guyana in November 1978. Shortly after the tragedy occurred, exploitation filmmaker Cardona quickly threw together a script and went into production in Mexico with Stuart Whitman cast as the messianic Reverend Jim Johnson, Bradford Dillman as his Kool-Aid dispensing aide-de-camp Dr. Gary Straw, and Gene Barry as the curious California congressman who goes to Guyana to investigate the cult and is murdered. Although the film does have its proponents among exploitation-film aficionados, it is spurious as fact and just plain dull as drama, a remarkable achievement considering the sensational aspects of its story.

Infinitely superior and far more insightful is writer-producer Ernest Tidyman's riveting telefilm *Guyana Tragedy: the Story of Jim Jones* (1980), directed by William A. Graham and starring Powers Boothe as Jones, a performance that deservedly won him an Emmy. Here, none of the names have been changed. Brad Dourif plays the Jonestown doctor, a former drug addict whom Jones binds to himself both spiritually and physically, who laces the nine hundred cups of Kool-Aid with poison, and Ned Beatty plays the at-first reluctant, but then concerned, Congressman Leo Ryan, who goes to his death trying to lead some of the cult members to freedom. It's an awesome and almost incomprehensible story, but Tidyman brings it sharply into focus by placing the core character of Jones virtually under a microscope.

Seeing the film recently, I was struck by how much the character of Jones reminded me of Jeff MacDonald in *Fatal Vision,* for both seem to have been guided by an almost overpowering will to achieve, coupled with a destructive delusion that only *their* perceptions were valid, that only what they thought was right.

At the beginning of the film, the aspiring young evangelist is shown delivering a sermon in his parents' home to a pack of dogs, who appear to be doting slavishly on his every word. Though perhaps apocryphal, this scene nevertheless foreshadows what Jones became, a man whose goal was not just to lead but to be worshiped—in much the same way that a dog worships its master and will even die for him. Blind allegiance. As a result, Jones became the cult leader par excellence, even outstripping Charles Manson in his ability to bind lost-soul followers to himself by cementing fears of being preyed on and persecuted by outsiders. The culmination of Manson's lunatic dreams of power was to have been global mass death, a war to end all wars triggered by a series of race-baiting murders perpetrated by the Family. Manson failed, but Jones succeeded in achieving such a mass death, the willing suicide of the nine hundred members of his "family," who went to their graves solely at his behest—just like the slavish dogs he wanted and needed them to be.

Throughout the film, director Graham frequently cuts to a sign in the death camp bearing the familiar slogan "Those who do not remember the past are condemned to repeat it." At other times, the sign appears unobtrusively in the background of a shot, serving as a constant and powerful reminder that the tragedy of Jonestown could happen again, just as it's happened before, for the urges that drove Jones were not dissimilar to the urges that drove Manson . . . or for that matter, history's supreme cult leader, Adolf Hitler.

But the on-screen exploits of that particular real-life psycho would fill a book themselves.

8

HALLOWEEN AND THE EXPLOITATION PSYCHO: MAD SLASHERS, DRILLER KILLERS, AND MORE

I spent eight years trying to reach him and then another seven trying to keep him locked up, because I realized that what was behind that boy's eyes was purely and simply . . . evil.

—Dr. Sam Loomis (Donald Pleasence)
in *Halloween* (1978)

By the mid-1960s, most of the familiar movie monsters of the past had virtually been elbowed off the screen by the new king of screen terror, the psycho. In a way, this shift away from the fabled creatures that had frightened us so much in the past was but a reflection of the times, for while real-life psychos had always been with us, it clearly seemed that their unsettling breed was growing in number—judging, at least, from the nightly news.

It was no coincidence therefore that Alfred Hitchcock, the cinema's premier "artist of anxiety," focused on the psychopath as the subject of his first and only outright horror film. Nor was it purely for reasons of commerce that the highly successful film he made was imitated so often afterward. The decades since *Psycho*'s release have seen a succession of real-life psychos and a parade of psychofilms unmatched by any other period. The screen psycho, like his real-life counterpart, had terrifyingly come of age. He (or she) had firmly dethroned Frankenstein's monster and Dracula as the screen's preeminent figure of fear. The psycho had become our new bogeyman.

The Night *He* Came Home

In John Carpenter's hugely successful and very influential *Halloween* (1978), the psychopath of the film, a six-year-old boy named Michael Myers who matures into a malevolent but ambiguous figure known as the Shape, is portrayed just that way—as a bogeyman, an evil force that even knives and bullets can't stop. We never know why little Michael knifed his sister on Halloween night, 1963. Nor do we know why he escapes from his asylum and proceeds to launch a campaign of fear in his old hometown on Halloween night fifteen years later. Using what amounts to standard horror-movie shorthand, scriptwriters Carpenter and Debra Hill simply dub Michael "psychotic" and let it go at that. Why does he kill? He just *does,* that's all. And at the end of the film, after being shot several times by his psychiatrist (Donald Pleasence) and falling from a second-story window, he simply gets up and vanishes into the night. No, it doesn't make sense, but it's not supposed to, for *Halloween* is hardly a serious psychofilm. It's a thrill show, and the psycho at its core is nothing more than an old-fashioned movie monster decked out in modern dress. To accent this, he even wears a mask that gives him the pasty-faced look of a zombie.

Since its release, *Halloween* has earned back more than one hundred and fifty times its cost, making it the most financially successful independent film ever made. The virtual flood of imitations that followed in its wake have also made it the most influential

Jamie Lee Curtis's Little Red Riding Hood does battle with
The Shape's Big Bad Wolf in John Carpenter's influential
modern fairy tale, *Halloween* (1978).

psychofilm since *Psycho*. How to account for such
popularity and impact? Possibly because *Halloween,*
despite its R-rated nudity and blood, is a film that
looks back. Its makers seemed to realize that the
old-fashioned kind of movie monster no longer
worked for audiences, but they were uncomfortable
with the new kind. And so they created a hybrid.

Rather than portray their psycho as a fractured personality, a recognizably human figure who does
inhuman things, they portray him instead as a symbol
of what scares society most: random and seemingly
unmotivated violence. Michael Myers, or the Shape,
is the "new evil," and the contest that ensues between
him and virginal Jamie Lee Curtis is the archetypal

Jamie Lee Curtis thinks she's escaped the murderous clutches of The Shape. For a time, anyway. From *Halloween*.

one between good and evil, between purity and the devil. In short, *Halloween* is a modern fairy tale.

Although *Halloween* was extremely popular with audiences all over the world and was even received quite well by many critics, it also triggered a barrage of criticism against what was perceived in the film as an implied message that "pure girls don't die, but loose ones do." This same criticism has been leveled at most *Halloween* clones to follow because, being clones, they emulate the film's fairy-tale motif as well. In his defense, Carpenter has stated that the critics "completely missed the boat. The one girl who is the most sexually uptight just keeps stabbing the guy with a long knife. She's the most sexually frustrated. She's the one that's killed him. Not because she's a virgin, but because all that repressed sexual energy starts coming out." Curiously, Carpenter's defense only makes matters worse because it still connects sex with violent retribution, which is the main objection most critics have against not only this film but other slasher movies of its ilk. Carpenter might better have let things go by stating the obvious: that for all its high-tech scares, *Halloween* is nothing more than an updated fairy tale in which Jamie Lee Curtis plays Little Red Riding Hood to the Shape's Big Bad Wolf. Besides, nowhere in the film is it openly stated that Curtis *is* a virgin. One of her friends merely admonishes her for not dating, which might simply be because she's shy. Or it might just be a plot contrivance, a way of making the one-on-one confrontation between her and the Shape that concludes the film seem more credible.

This does not ignore the fact that Curtis's fun-loving girlfriends do get knocked off, or that one of them, Lynda (P. J. Soles), bites the dust following a bout of lovemaking. But to see this as some kind of a puritanical message is really a bit farfetched. *Halloween* is sheer melodramatic hokum aimed at providing its predominantly teenage audience with a few solid scares for its money. Annie (Nancy Loomis) and Lynda and their boyfriends are the formula victims whose deaths pave the way for the final, suspenseful confrontation. And that they are done in when they least expect it is a common method of building suspense that's as old as the hills, a method designed to manipulate the audience into shouting, "Watch out!" In less R-rated times, these formula victims used to get bumped off by the monster while making out in their parked cars.

People, especially critics, tend to see what they want to in films, which is, of course, their prerogative. And the more meaningless a film is, the more open it seems to interpretation.

As an example, let's take a *Halloween* clone called *Slumber Party Massacre* (1982), which was not only directed by a woman (Amy Jones) but written by one,

Another teenager (P. J. Soles) bites the dust in *Halloween*.

feminist author Rita Mae Brown. The story centers around a group of girls at a slumber party that is intruded upon by a maniac (Michael Villela), who one by one starts slaughtering the buxom, scantily clad beauties with a power drill. The girls finally get even by ganging up on him, beating him with baseball bats, then carving him up with an electric saw. It doesn't take much interpretation to view the maniac's drill as a surrogate penis—especially since his female victims are often framed between his towering spread legs, cringing in fear, and he himself is often seen fondling the drill in a suggestive manner. And despite its having all the same exploitative ingredients as most other slasher films, the fact that the girls band together in the end to kill him could be interpreted as some feminist revenge message—perhaps even an antimale message—even though director Jones herself has stated that "the movie doesn't really appeal to a feminist impulse in the audience." Still, *Slumber Party Massacre* could be interpreted that way, and if more female directors made exploitation films just

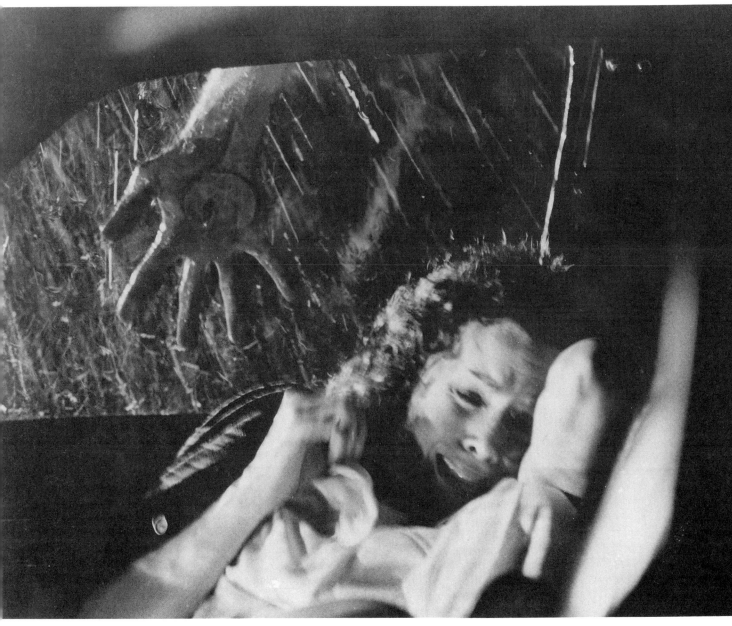

The Shape breaks into a car to make his getaway from the institution. From *Halloween*.

like it (which they are, now that there are more female directors), some critics would probably make such an interpretation—and thus another "disturbing new trend" would be born. The fact is that the recurring images of sex and violence that lace these films—the cleavages and the power drills, the cringing females at the mercy of demented male assail-ants—are not underlying messages but exploitation-film *clichés*. Unlike critics, however, audiences tend to see them exactly that way and accept such films in the proper, empty-headed spirit in which they are made.

No one is saying, of course, that exploitation filmmakers are incapable of being perverse—just that they're not necessarily perverted or conspiratorially

Donald Pleasence as Dr. Sam Loomis in *Halloween*.

puritanical. In *Silent Scream* (1980), for instance, a crazed woman (Barbara Steele), who is hidden away in a rooming house run by her mother (Yvonne De Carlo), starts slashing out at Mama's unsuspecting teenage tenants. Director Denny Harris rapidly intercuts one particular murder scene with another sequence of a couple making love—so rapidly, in fact, that it becomes difficult for the viewer to differentiate the death throes from the orgasms. I don't know Mr. Harris, but I suspect that this perverse linkage between the act of sex and the act of murder has less to do with his making some kind of statement than it does with his ability to spot a subject of growing controversy and boldly choosing to exploit it—

which, after all, is the exploitation filmmaker's stock-in-trade.

Writer-director Carpenter had already outlined his *Halloween* formula in *Someone's Watching Me!* (1978), a tense psychofilm made for television that many, including myself, consider more suspenseful than its more renowned theatrical brother. Lauren Hutton stars as Leigh Michaels, a young woman who has moved to the big city to get away from a love affair gone sour. She rents the apartment of her dreams, a multiwindowed affair that allows her a view into the other high-rise apartments that surround her. Unfortunately, everyone else can see into her glass house as well—in particular a Peeping Tom with a telescope and a tape recorder (he has bugged her apartment), who proceeds to bombard her with weird letters, mysterious, heavy-breathing phone calls, strange "gifts," and other irritants designed to intimidate her. Like the Shape, we don't really know what motivates the crazed peeper. He's simply a psycho, another Big Bad Wolf. And gorgeous Leigh, who is accustomed to being hassled by wolves, assumes the role of Little Red Riding Hood to take him on.

After discovering that her nemesis is watching her from an apartment almost directly across the way, she enlists the aid of a friend (Adrienne Barbeau), stations her at a telescope in Leigh's apartment, and armed with a walkie-talkie so that the pair can communicate, ventures across the way to investigate. After milking Leigh's ominous tour of the peeper's dark digs for as much suspense as possible, Carpenter has her look through the peeper's telescope at Barbeau and gasp helplessly when she sees her friend attacked by the madman in her very own apartment. Obviously, this scene owes a lot to a similar scene in Hitchcock's classic *Rear Window* (1954), in which Grace Kelly steals into a suspected killer's apartment and is caught by him while her laid-up boyfriend (James Stewart) watches helplessly from across the way. Carpenter's treatment not only generates a similar amount of suspense but packs a nice, surprise punch with its clever twist on the Hitchcock model.

In addition to spawning a myriad of imitations, the unexpected success of *Halloween* spawned an inevitable sequel, *Halloween II* (1981). This time around, Carpenter wrote the script (with Debra Hill) but did not direct. "I had made that film once, and I really didn't want to do it again," Carpenter said. Indeed he had—not only as *Halloween* but as *Someone's Watching Me!*

The director he and producer Hill chose was newcomer Rick Rosenthal, an American Film Institute graduate whose short suspense film *The Toyer* had impressed the pair. Since the release of the original film, of course, slasher movies had begun to proliferate, most of them far bloodier than their progenitor.

Tom Atkins and Stacey Nelkin visit the mask maker's store in *Halloween III: Season of the Witch* (1983).

Still, Hill resisted the temptation to top them for ghoulish effects. Prior to production, she announced, "What we were commended for and are setting out to do again is to give audiences an exercise in pure terror without a bloodbath." These words would come back to haunt her, for, alas, she had not learned one of the main credos of the exploitation filmmaker: Don't outwit the competition, *outdo it.*

Halloween II begins essentially where the original left off. Reprising her role as the seemingly victorious Laurie, Jamie Lee Curtis is taken to the hospital by psychiatrist Pleasence to have her wounds attended to. The indomitable Shape follows them and starts wiping out various members of the hospital staff to get at her. She finally escapes with her life, and the Shape is dispatched in a fire.

Rachel Carruthers (Ellie Cornell) barely escapes the clutches of Michael Myers (a.k.a. The Shape) in *Halloween 4: The Return of Michael Myers* (1988).

The Shape cuts yet another bloody swath through *Halloween 5: The Revenge of Michael Myers* (1989).

After the film was completed, someone came to the conclusion that while the sequel might measure up to the original, it no longer met audience expectations of the time. Terror was nice, but audiences had since come to demand something else from slasher films: grisly special effects. And *Halloween II* didn't have them. Exit Rick Rosenthal and enter John Carpenter, who went back and reshot some of the key scare sequences to insert more blood. In the film as it stands now, the Shape doesn't just kill his victims, he cuts their throats, boils their faces, and jabs them in the eye with a hypodermic needle.

Halloween II was not the monster success its predecessor had been, but it was successful enough to spawn yet another sequel, *Halloween III: Season of the Witch* (1983), a weak rehash of elements from *Invasion of the Body Snatchers*, in which the now-dead Shape was replaced by a deranged Halloween maskmaker (Dan O'Herlihy) who is bent on enslaving the world. The least successful of the three films, it finished off the series until 1988, when two sequels followed that resurrected the character of the Shape (aka Michael Myers).

Having apparently decided that he'd contributed all he wanted to psychofilm, Carpenter has since abandoned the genre and gone on to other things such as the again character-less but still compelling remake of *The Thing* (1982) and the atypically char-

Prelude to murder. From *Friday the 13th* (1980).

Psychofilm's premiere bogeyman tries to claim yet another victim (Dana Kimmell) in yet another sequel. From *Friday the 13th Part III* (in 3-D!), a 1982 release.

acter-full but otherwise banal *Christine* (1983) and *Starman* (1984). He is still a director in search of a voice, whose best film so far is probably neither *Halloween* nor *Someone's Watching Me!* but *Elvis* (1979), his superb telefilm biography of the late king of rock 'n' roll, starring Kurt Russell.

More Mad Slashers

One of the main reasons audience demands of slasher films had changed between the release of *Halloween* and *Halloween II* was the unexpected box-office success of yet another low-budget exploitation film called *Friday the 13th*. Released in seven hundred theaters nationwide during the summer of 1980, it was the second-biggest money-maker of the summer season, beaten only by producer George Lucas's *The Empire Strikes Back*. So popular was it, in fact, that it has produced a sequel almost every year since. The

intended culmination of the series, titled . . . *The Final Chapter* (1984), went on to do such brisk business that less than a year later, it was followed by yet another sequel *Friday the 13th—A New Beginning* (1985), which chalked up more than $8 million at the box office during its first weekend of release. As of this writing, there have been three more sequels, which makes the *Friday the 13th* films the longest-running and most durable series in psychofilm history.

The original *Friday the 13th* was the brainchild of independent producer-director Sean S. Cunningham, who was prompted to make the film because he desperately needed a hit. Although he had directed two movies since, he had not had a box-office winner since his debut film *Last House on the Left* (1972), which he made in collaboration with director Wes Craven. The commercial success of *Halloween* and George Romero's zombie film *Dawn of the Dead* (1979) suggested that a hybrid mixture of the pair's winning individual elements—terror in the first case,

Dana Kimmell gets even with her attacker in *Friday the 13th Part III*.

gory special effects in the latter—might do the trick for him. Following a tried-and-true method used by many successful exploitation filmmakers in the past, he dreamed up a highly promotable title and had a dramatic ad for the film composed and inserted in *Variety* to enlist backers. Once the roughly $700,000 budget had been raised, Victor Miller, who had collaborated with Cunningham in the past, wrote the script, which was shot on location in the Connecticut–New Jersey area. Distributed by Paramount, it took in over $40 million at the box office.

Friday the 13th, like *Halloween*, opens with a murder, then skips ahead a number of years and returns the killer to the scene of the crime to perpetrate even more bloody ones. The first victims are two amorous counselors at Camp Crystal Lake whose unsolved deaths result in the camp being closed down. When the camp is preparing to reopen some years later, its new counselors start getting knocked off too. The sole survivor (Adrienne King) discovers that the deranged killer (Betsy Palmer) is the mother of a boy named Jason Voorhees, who drowned due to the first victims' inattentiveness. Determined to keep the place closed, the revenge-hungry Mrs. Voorhees has been gruesomely slaughtering anyone seeking to reopen it. King is spared a similar fate when she chops off the maniacal woman's head with a machete during their climactic duel.

What made the film appealing to audiences was not just its escalating suspense but its series of ever more graphic throat-slashings, ax murders, decapitations, and other amazing special effects by Tom Savini, who'd handled the same chores with similar wizardry on *Dawn of the Dead*. These effects, which are even more flamboyantly grisly in the sequels to follow, have become the trademark of the series and have since been handled by a variety of makeup specialists, although Savini did return to help out on the ill-named *Final Chapter*.

With Mrs. Voorhees headless and dead, a new

Melanie Kinnaman defends herself against Jason in *Friday the 13th Part V: A New Beginning* (1985).

psycho was obviously needed for Part 2. That role was filled by none other than Jason himself, who, as it turns out, did not drown but has been living in the woods ever since. Part 2 takes up five years after the original left off. Again Camp Crystal Lake is about to be reopened, and as a result, its unsuspecting counselors have again started biting the dust. This time around it is Jason, who seeks revenge for the death of his mother. The film opens with his getting even with Adrienne King by tracking her to her apartment in the city and knifing her in the head. Interestingly, whereas Michael Meyers was portrayed as an indestructible bogeyman in the first *Halloween* but became a flesh and blood human capable of being killed in the sequel, *Friday the 13th* reverses the process by making Jason increasingly impervious to all manner of weapons and even capable of resurrection as the series wears on. Perhaps this is another reason why the *Friday* series remains so popular. It doesn't tamper with its rules and sustains its fairy-tale motif by keeping Jason—who, like the Shape, wears a mask—a mysterious and indomitable force right to the end. In effect, he assumes the Shape's mantle as the screen's prevailing bogeyman, not to mention its most prolific and versatile mass murderer.

In *The Final Chapter*, directed by Joseph Zito (who played the cameo part of Jason in the first *Friday the 13th*), Jason is vengefully chopped into little pieces by a monster-makeup enthusiast named Tommy (Corey Feldman), who shaves his head to look like the maniac in order to confuse him. The film ends with the implication that the emotionally disturbed Tommy, seasoned by his massacre of the real Jason, will assume the bogeyman role in the future, thereby paving the way for the next chapter, *Friday the 13th—A New Beginning*. Here is one series, it seems, that, like its star, simply refuses to die.

The big box office generated by the exploits of the Shape and especially Jason served to inaugurate a whole new subcategory of psychofilm, the commem-

Military survival team member Wallace Merck meets a gruesome fate when he encounters Jason (C. J. Graham) in *Friday the 13th Part VI: Jason Lives* (1986).

Jason (Kane Hodder) stalks Susan Blu and Terry Kiser in *Friday the 13th Part VII: The New Blood* (1988).

The most prolific serial killer in movie history travels beyond Camp Crystal Lake for the first time and arrives in New York City in *Friday the 13th Part VIII: Jason Takes Manhattan* (1989).

Another masked killer gets in on the mad slasher bandwagon. From *Terror Train* (1980).

orative-mad-slasher movie. None of the psychos in these one-shot epics would achieve anywhere near the status of their illustrious predecessors, however. The plots of these films are basically the same. A brutal murder or other traumatic incident in the past prompts someone to go mad with revenge or blood-lust and start killing people several years later, usually on the anniversary of the incident. Titles include *Prom Night* (1980), *My Bloody Valentine* (1981), *New Year's Evil* (1980), *Happy Birthday to Me* (1981), *Silent Night, Deadly Night* (1984), and so on. Others such as *Maniac* (1980), *The Prowler* (1981), *The Burning* (1982),

180

A helmeted motorcyclist responsible for a series of ritualistic murders stalks another victim in *Night School* (1980).

Another commemorative mad slasher goes on the rampage in *My Bloody Valentine* (1981).

Disturbed teenager Melissa Sue Anderson pleads with her father (Lawrence Dane) to reveal the truth of her traumatic past in *Happy Birthday to Me* (1981).

Night School (1981), *Visiting Hours* (1982), *Terror Train* (1980), *Sleepaway Camp* (1983), and many more adopted a similar formula, but sometimes had to forgo the commemorative tie-in because there just weren't enough occasions to go around, and the most exploitable ones had already been used. Very few of these films offer much in the way of interest to the serious psychofilm enthusiast. They're technology-oriented special-effects films—splatter movies. Even their bogeymen don't hold much interest—certainly not psychologically—as none of them prove indomitable enough to survive the last reel.

Somewhat more interesting, satirically at least, are Jack Sholder's *Alone in the Dark* (1982) and Charles Kaufman's *Mother's Day* (1980), the latter a ghoulishly clever psychofilm that owes more to *The Texas Chain Saw Massacre* than it does to the *Halloween–Friday the 13th* school.

Alone in the Dark is a variation on the Edgar Allan Poe story "Dr. Tarr and Professor Feather" in which some inmates take over their asylum. In *Dark,* writer-director Sholder suggests that the real asylum may be the outside world, and when four hard-core psychos break out of a state mental hospital during a power

Disfigured and deranged camp caretaker Lou David waxes sinister in *The Burning* (1981), another *Halloween/Friday the 13th* clone.

outage into this world, they find it very much to their liking but also a bit strange—even for them. The plot centers around the four's determination to get even with their new psychiatrist Dr. Potter (Dwight Schultz), who they fantasize has murdered his predecessor. After stopping off at a local shopping center to join in a looting spree, the armed band track the doctor to his home and launch a night-long reign of terror à la Peckinpah's *Straw Dogs* (1971). All are killed but the leader of the group, a deranged ex-POW played by Jack Palance, who is about to finish off the doctor and his family when the power returns and he sees Potter's predecessor being interviewed live on television. Disturbed by the death and destruction he has mistakenly caused, he spares their lives and leaves. Returning to the shopping center, he goes into a bar, where a punk band called the Sick Fucks is rocking it up with songs like "Chop Up Your Mother," and is confronted by a spaced-out teenybopper. The film ends with the two of them smiling as he presses his gun to her all-too-willing chin. Commented the director, "He's smiling because he knows that he's not alone—the whole world is crazy."

Dennis Christopher as the movie crazy mad killer in *Fade To Black* (1980).

The killer in *Prom Night* (1980).

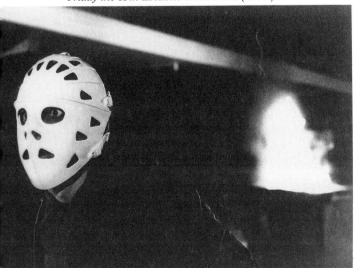

Writer-director Jack Sholder pays not so subtle homage to *Friday the 13th* in *Alone in the Dark* (1983).

The lunatics take over the asylum in *Alone in the Dark* (1983). Pictured are ax-wielding Martin Landau and earless Donald Pleasence.

Joe Spinell as the title character in the ultra-grisly *Maniac* (1981).

Heather Langenkamp struggles with her nightmare attacker, the fabulous Freddy (Robert Englund), in *A Nightmare on Elm Street* (1984).

In addition to this satirical ending, Sholder sprinkles his film throughout with in-joke references to other slasher movies. For example, the head of the hospital, who seems as crazy as his patients, is played by none other than *Halloween*'s Donald Pleasence. An apparition imagined by Potter's neurotic sister (Leigh Taylor-Allan) looks remarkably like Jason (sans mask). And when one of the psychos later disguises himself briefly in a hockey mask, he completes the reference.

More successful in its satire, yet gripping at the same time, is Charles Kaufman's unfairly maligned *Mother's Day*, a film that even Jack Sholder disparages. In it, a trio of vacationing ex-college girls are captured and tortured by two perverted hillbillies and their even more demented mother (Rose Ross). When one of the girls dies after being repeatedly raped and beaten, the other two pool their resources, strike back, and finish off murderous mama and her two sadistic siblings.

Whereas the scenes of violence and carnage are conventionally brutal and bloody (after all, this *is* an exploitation film), the film is quite unconventional in other ways. *Mother's Day*, like *Alone in the Dark*, portrays the world in which the girls live as being just as bizarre as the one they encounter in the woods.

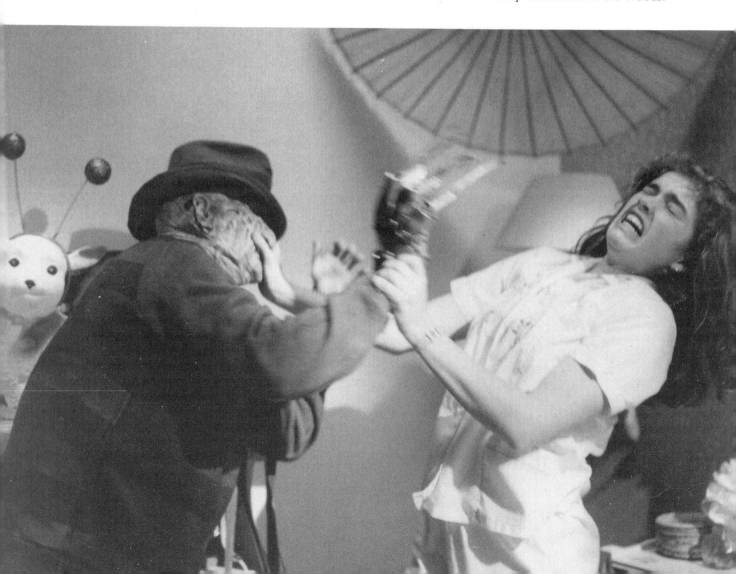

Freddy Krueger (Robert Englund) takes out his wrath on yet another victim in *A Nightmare on Elm Street 3: The Dream Warriors* (1983).

This is stressed later when one of the hillbillies defensively shouts at them that he's just as "citified" as everyone else. And just where did he get his citification? From the television. As it turns out, mad mama and her boys are consummate media junkies. Everything they think, eat, and do is a product of their exposure to the tube. Never turned off, the set crackles endlessly away at them from its place of honor in their squalid living room like some demented deity. Why do the boys rape and kill? Because it's "just like I seen on TV," one of them says. When one of the girls crowns him with an unused set at the conclusion of the film, he enters his television world for real as his head twitches and sparks fly behind the screen.

Mama and her boys are horrifically credible and just as much victims as the girls they taunt. Mama is a victim of her shortcomings because she has chosen to live in an artificial world manufactured by what she

sees on the tube. But the insidious nature of television is that it allows her (or anyone) to make such a choice so easily. At the beginning of the film, she is seen attending a final class in self-actualization—prompted, no doubt, by a program she'd seen on *Donahue* or some similar show—whose Werner Erhard–type guru cynically graduates his flock by calling them "dirt bags." The boys, in turn, are victims of mom and their own ingrained tube-itis. None of them have minds of their own.

The victimized girls, on the other hand, are not just credible as victims but believable as people. Their friendship is genuine and their loyalty to each other fierce. Not only are they the only sympathetic and likable people in the film, they are also portrayed both at the beginning of the movie and in flashback as the only together and sincere people in an otherwise neurotic and phony world. Under these circum-

It's a boy . . . Freddy Krueger (Robert Englund), the pizza-faced villain everyone loves to hate, is reborn in *A Nightmare on Elm Street 5: The Dream Child* (1989).

stances, it is difficult to take seriously the charges of "supreme misogyny" that have been leveled at the film. Unless, of course, these critics are referring to its attitude toward Mama, for *Mother's Day* is certainly no Mother's Day card. Its attack on *momism*, a word coined by the late Philip Wylie to describe the emotional subjugation of their offspring by certain smothering iron-willed matriarchs (a problem, incidentally, that one of the girls in the film suffers from too), is scarcely understated.

All of this is not to say, however, that *Mother's Day* is a masterpiece deserving of a place in the psychofilm hall of fame. It does stand tall among its exploitation-film brethren, but is finally derailed by one of those shock epilogues that makes absolute nonsense of the ending. In this case, the dead mother's even-more deranged sister leaps out of the bushes to ensnare the two girls just as they think they've emerged victorious.

This same derailment occurs in Wes Craven's

186

Guess where director Pete Walker got this idea from? From *Schizo* (1976).

One victim on ice, coming up! From *Slumber Party Massacre* (1982).

One of the more serene moments from *Blood and Black Lace* (1964), arguably the best film of director Mario Bava, father of the Italian *giallo*.

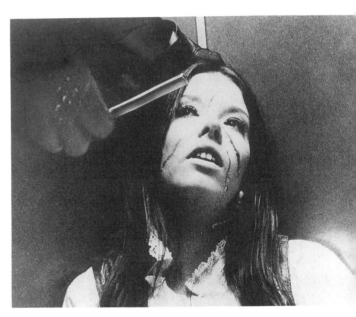

More mad slashing (literally) from *The Bird With the Crystal Plumage* (1969), Dario Argento's most coherent film.

otherwise ingenious variation on the slasher theme *A Nightmare on Elm Street* (1984). The villain of the film, a murderer and child molester named Fred Krueger, who received vigilante justice at the hands of his neighbors some years back, returns to get even by entering the dreams of their sleeping teenage sons and daughters and killing them. One courageous teen catches on to Fred's game and determines to trap him by dragging him out of the dream world and into the real one so that she can finish him off for good. Which she does, making for a very satisfactory conclusion. Unfortunately, Craven couldn't leave well enough alone and added a shock epilogue, in which Krueger miraculously returns to kill the girl's mother (and presumably the girl herself), that not only makes nonsense of the ending but sabotages the plot's carefully sustained, though precarious, sense of logic. Inevitably, a slew of sequels followed—five, in fact, which proved successful enough to turn the demented Freddy into a cultural icon.

Gialli

America, of course, doesn't have a monopoly on exploitation filmmakers or mad-slasher movies. The psycho is a universal monster, and cameras grinding away from Italy to England seem bent on recording his bloody deeds. Apart from their settings and atrociously dubbed sound tracks, these films are fairly indistinguishable from their American counterparts—except for their plots. Whereas the devious plotting and twist-ending style of *Diabolique* exerted a major influence on *Psycho* and other films around the world that were made during the first mad-slasher cycle, *Halloween* eschewed this influence, as have most other mad-slasher films made in its wake—at least in America. In European slasher films, though, the impact of *Diabolique* continues to be felt and is especially evidenced in those films made by Europe's three premier slasher directors: Italy's Mario Bava and Dario Argento, and England's Pete Walker.

Italians have dubbed these exploitation thrillers *gialli*, which translates as "yellow movies." Like their American counterparts, they are governed by certain rules, most of them stylistic, such as rapid cutting, a pounding musical score, flashy colors, and gobs of gore. Unlike their American counterparts, they, like *Diabolique*, tend more to be murder mysteries than outright supernatural horror films. Their psychos are masked but not indomitable bogeymen. By final fade-out, they and their motives are usually revealed as all too human, their identities often a surprise.

The late Mario Bava is the father of *gialli*, having made the first *giallo* in 1962. Titled *The Evil Eye*, it was the story of a sexually repressed woman (Leticia Roman) whose suspicions about men's motives in general (including those of her boyfriend, played by John Saxon) lead her to believe that she's on the hit list of a maniac preying on the women of Rome who calls himself the Alphabet Murderer. Seven years later, Bava followed up the success of *The Evil Eye* with the more exploitatively titled *Hatchet for a Honeymoon* (1971), the tale of a psycho who goes around killing brides on their wedding nights. Like *The Evil Eye*, it was relatively tame in the bloodletting department, a situation Bava corrected in his next film, *Twitch of the Death Nerve* (1971). In it, some greedy heirs graphically whittle each other down to collect a large family fortune. Bava's last film *Shock* (1977), the story of a neurotic woman (Daria Nicolodi) who suspects that her son may be psychotic, or that she herself may be going insane, was released in the U.S. under the title *Beyond the Door II*, an irrelevant and misleading title aimed at making audiences think it

was the sequel to the popular exorcism movie *Beyond the Door* (1974). Alas, it bore no relationship to that earlier film whatsoever and died at the box office. Most critics tend to agree, however, that Bava's most stylish *giallo* is *Blood and Black Lace* (1964), an intense though not overly bloody police procedural about a maniacal killer of fashion models.

The early films of Bava heir Dario Argento carried on the *gialli* tradition in spectacular fashion—beginning with Argento's very first film *Bird With the Crystal Plumage* (1969), which proved to be an unexpected worldwide smash. *Bird* is about an American painter (Tony Musante) living in Rome who sets out to unmask a black-clad psycho killer. The title is drawn from an important clue to the killer's identity that Argento subtly weaves into the fabric of the plot. *The Cat o' Nine Tails* (1971), the story of a psycho who is driven to kill due to a chromosome imbalance (shades of Roy Boulting's 1968 *Twisted Nerve*), and *Four Flies on Grey Velvet* (1972), another whodunit in which the identity of the killer is finally revealed when his image is discovered on the retina of one of his victims, follow a similar pattern. Fans tend to prefer *Deep Red* (1975), after which Argento turned to more supernatural thrillers. *Deep Red*, like *Bird With the Crystal Plumage*, is about an American expatriate (David Hemmings), in this case a writer, who sets out to trap a psycho whose identity is revealed in a surprise twist the writer might have figured out had he been able to perceive a vital clue that's been apparent all along. Eventually, Argento returned to form with his extravagant mad-slasher film *Opera* (1989).

England's Pete Walker calls his slasher movies "terror films," but they are very much like the *gialli* of his Italian colleagues. They are whodunits mixed with lots of style and graphic gore. Titles include *Die Screaming Maryanne* (1969), *The Flesh and Blood Show* (1972), *The Confessional* (1975), *Schizo* (1976), *Frightmare* (1974), and *The Comeback* (1977). In the latter, singer Jack Jones plays a has-been crooner on the verge of returning to the big time whose comeback is being sabotaged by a vengeful psycho, who turns out to be none other than his own housekeeper, played by Walker stock-company veteran Sheila Keith. Walker gets good actors for his films, and because they are not subjected to dubbing, their performances are usually quite superior to those found in most exploitation films. Not so in *The Comeback*, a confusing slasher film that is fatally done in by the somnambulistic Jones, who registers about as much anxiety throughout as a bear in hibernation.

9

LANDSCAPES OF THE MIND: THE PSYCHO CASE-STUDY FILM

> Loneliness has followed me my whole life. *Everywhere*. In bars and cars, sidewalks, stores, everywhere. There's no escape. I'm God's lonely man.
>
> —Travis Bickle (Robert De Niro)
> in *Taxi Driver* (1976)

As I wrote at the beginning of this book, the motion picture medium began flirting with psychofilm almost from its inception. The unique ability of the new medium to make real that which was unreal through special effects and other techniques had much to do with this. It comes as no surprise therefore that filmmakers have also had a long-standing fascination with exploring psychoanalytic theory on the screen—via the case study.

G. W. Pabst's *Secrets of a Soul* (1926) was one of the first such films and remains to this day one of the most famous and influential. The plot revolves around a man's (Werner Krauss) obsession with knives and his growing compulsion to murder his wife. In despair, he seeks help from a psychiatrist, who places him in therapy and finally vanquishes his inner demons. The illness turns out to have been caused by the man's deep feelings of insecurity, which reached a crisis point when he began to imagine that his wife was being unfaithful.

Striving for authenticity, Pabst employed Dr. Hanns Sachs and Dr. Karl Abraham, two disciples of Freud, to work with him on the script. The bulk of the film is taken up by the protagonist's lengthy psychoanalysis, which Pabst visualizes with superimpositions, shock cuts to the man's dream state, and other cinematic devices that have since become clichés. Even then, of course, Pabst's cinematic tricks were not new. But the use to which he put them was—namely, to reveal, layer by layer, the subconscious workings of a troubled human mind.

Dream sequences designed to express the inner thoughts and feelings of screen characters have been a staple of the Hollywood film from the beginning as well. But it was not until the forties that Hollywood moviemakers began dabbling in similar case studies. This was perhaps due to the fact that the word *psychoanalysis* had only recently become a popular term in the U.S. and that private therapy sessions were increasingly becoming quite fashionable. As might be expected, Alfred Hitchcock was a pioneer of the form. He called his film *Spellbound* (1945).

The protagonist (Gregory Peck) of the film is not a psycho but rather an amnesiac who suspects that he may also be guilty of murder. He arrives at a mental asylum calling himself Dr. Edwardes, the name of the clinic's new head chief whom no one there has met. Another doctor (Ingrid Bergman) falls in love with him. When she discovers the masquerade, for which he has no explanation, she sets out to cure him of his amnesia as well as his vague belief that he must have killed the real Dr. Edwardes and taken his place. It turns out that Edwardes was indeed murdered but not by Peck. The real killer is the previous head of the clinic (Leo G. Carroll), who'd been jealous of losing his position. Peck had simply witnessed the incident

Anatole Litvak's *The Snake Pit* (1948) resulted in legislation to improve conditions in mental institutions in twenty-six states. Shown here: patient Olivia de Havilland (seated with box of candy) and her compassionate psychiatrist, Leo Genn (in suit and tie).

and accepted the blame for it due to his subconscious guilt for having accidentally slain his own brother many years earlier.

Like Pabst, Hitchcock used all manner of cinematic devices to explore the nature of Peck's illness and reveal its root cause, including some expressionist sets designed by artist Salvador Dalí for the film's celebrated high point, a dream sequence full of surrealistically presented clues. Though more than a bit melodramatic and even pat in its resolution of Peck's inner conflict (a problem that plagues most case-study films where the patient is "cured" by final fade-out), *Spellbound* is packed with interesting visual and thematic ideas and remains even now fascinating to watch. Many years later, Hitchcock returned to the same territory with *Marnie* (1964), the story of a disturbed young woman (Tippi Hedren) suffering from kleptomania. Treated by her husband (Sean Connery), an obsessive armchair psychoanalyst who is almost as sick as she is, Marnie is not cured at the conclusion of the film but has at least come to realize some of the motivations behind her behavior. As in *Spellbound*, Hitchcock used a variety of cinematic techniques to visualize the tortured workings of Marnie's mind. Contemporary critics, however, failed to recognize that these techniques—such as dreamlike back projection and unrealistic expressionist sets—were not only integral to the film in

Behind the scenes on *Peeping Tom* (1960), the film that almost finished off the career of director Michael Powell—shown here hovering over actor Carl Boehm's shoulder.

Killer voyeur Mark Lewis (Carl Boehm) describes his hellish childhood to terrified neighbor Anna Massey in Michael Powell's controversial *Peeping Tom*.

question but evident in much of Hitchcock's past work. Instead, they dismissed *Marnie* as technically sloppy. Only now is it being recognized as the certainly problematic but quite substantial psychological detective story it is.

Director Anatole Litvak's *The Snake Pit* followed *Spellbound* by three years. It was based on a popular forties novel by Mary Jane Ward that fictionalized the author's experiences in a mental asylum where she'd been committed for treatment after suffering a nervous breakdown. The film (and the book) is as much social criticism as it is psychodrama, for conditions in the asylum where the lead character (Olivia de Havilland) is sent are portrayed as nightmarish and even inhuman. Typical of such films, however, de Havilland is fully cured at the end by a skilled and compassionate psychotherapist (Leo Genn), and she and her

husband walk off into the sunlight of restored mental health. Twentieth Century-Fox financed the project after most other studios had turned it down, and producer Darryl F. Zanuck later spoke proudly of the fact that *The Snake Pit* had resulted in legislation to improve conditions in mental hospitals in twenty-six states. Nevertheless, a similar screen case study also based on fact, called *I Never Promised You a Rose Garden* (1977), in which a young girl is institutionalized and treated for schizophrenia, suggested that even thirty years later there was still much to be done.

Though mentally ill, none of the protagonists in these case-study films are psychopaths. Nevertheless, audiences had become accustomed by these films to seeing bizarre psychological states realistically rendered on-screen. That groundwork having been laid, moviemakers entered a new sphere: the psycho case-study film.

Reclusive paranoid Trelkovsky (Roman Polanski) peers warily out his window, convinced that his neighbors are trying to drive him to suicide. From *The Tenant* (1976).

The Self-destructive Psycho

Michael Powell's *Peeping Tom* (1960) remains one of the most potent of all psycho case-study films as well as one of the sleaziest. The protagonist, Mark Lewis (Carl Boehm), works as a focus puller in a British film studio. On his off hours, he supplies a local porno shop with cheesecake photos and also dabbles in filmmaking. His ongoing project is a documentary on fear. With 16mm camera in hand, he accompanies a prostitute to her room and stabs her with a blade concealed in his tripod, all the while

Writer-director Roman Polanski as the disturbed title character in his film *The Tenant*.

photographing her contorted face in the throes of terror and death. Later in his hideaway projection room, he experiences an orgasm while watching the girl's murder unfold on-screen. More victims pile up before he is finally brought down by the police. Having planned for such a moment, he triggers a series of cameras to capture the image of his terrified face as he rushes headlong into the outstretched blade of his tripod and impales himself, thereby concluding both his nightmarish documentary and demented life.

Peeping Tom, unlike *Spellbound* or *The Snake Pit,* contains no elaborate dream sequences designed to take us inside the mind of its disturbed main character. Shot in color, it's relentlessly realistic, which, considering its subject matter and sordid milieu, makes for an unsettling filmgoing experience. The British press certainly thought so and greeted the film

as if it were the plague. Critic Derek Hill's now-famous denunciation in the London *Tribune* summed up his group's feeling best: "The only really satisfactory way to dispose of *Peeping Tom* would be to shovel it up and flush it swiftly down the sewer. Even then the stench would remain." Proving that movie critics do have some clout, the film was a resounding box-office failure, and director Powell's heretofore prestigious career was left in tatters. The creator of such esteemed British classics as *Black Narcissus* (1947) and *The Red Shoes* (1948), Powell has made only one major film since the *Peeping Tom* debacle, a costume epic called *The Queen's Guards* (1961), which itself saw box-office failure due to a spotty release. Powell remained totally confused over the outpouring of hostility that greeted his watershed psychofilm. "I couldn't believe the reaction," he said. "The press crucified me. I never discovered what the British critics found so horrendous because it's not a violent film at all. The film is a psychological study, and that's where we put our effort; there's no blood at all until the end." Curiously, Roman Polanski's British-made and even more bleak (as well as bloodier) psycho case study *Repulsion,* a film that was strongly influenced by *Peeping Tom,* received virtually unanimous praise from these same critics a scant five years later.

Originally, Powell and his screenwriter Leo Marks had planned to make a film about the work of Sigmund Freud, but when they learned that John Huston was developing a screen biography of the father of psychoanalysis to star Montgomery Clift, they scrapped the idea and began working on a script about a self-destructive young man who suffers from a psychological disorder called scopophilia, whose voyeuristic symptoms are symbolized by the film's title. The son of a distinguished behavioral psychologist (played by Powell himself), Mark Lewis frequently served as a guinea pig for his famous father's unorthodox, as well as sadistic, experiments to measure the effects of fear on the central nervous system.[1] These experiments, indeed Lewis's entire childhood, have been captured on reels of film, which the emotionally scarred and sick man continues to watch over and over again in his secret projection room. Psychologically, Lewis has had no life other than the tortured one that flickers back at him from the screen. His murderous documentary-in-progress is his way of concluding his father's experiments (and getting even with the old man), as well as the means by which he is able to furnish his life on film with a final reel. Mark knows that he's doomed, that for him there will be no

---

1. In keeping with the film's movie-within-a-movie motif, Mark Lewis is portrayed as a child by director Powell's then seven-year-old son.

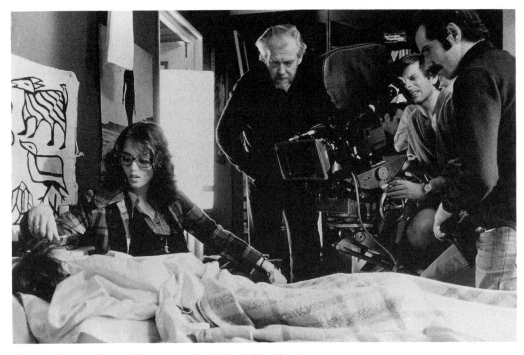

Director Roman Polanski lines up a shot of Isabelle Adjani and his double for *The Tenant* (1976). Cinematographer Sven Nykvist is standing center.

happy ending. He recognizes that he's sick and even contemplates treatment, but rejects the idea when a doctor tells him that therapy would take years. As real life offers no "jump cuts" but reel life does, he rushes instead toward the pit that has yawned for him since youth.

Released in the United States in 1962, *Peeping Tom* was shorn of almost a half hour and retitled *Face of Fear*. It played mostly on the bottom half of double bills, was largely ignored by critics as a result, and failed at the box office here as well. In 1979, however, director Martin Scorsese located the complete negative of the film (one of his favorites) while on a trip to England and urged a New York distributor, Corinth Films, to rerelease it in its heretofore unseen, full-length form. Since then, *Peeping Tom* has become a popular cult film not just here but in England where, the aroma of scandal having long since faded, it is now considered one of Michael Powell's best and most innovative efforts.

The film has also proven quite influential. Scorsese's *Taxi Driver* (1976) and *The King of Comedy* (1983) strongly echo *Peeping Tom*, as do the psychofilms of Roman Polanski, which, though more surrealistic than Powell's film, are equally grim and claustrophobic. *Repulsion*'s Carol Ledoux, in fact, is practically a

Peter O'Toole as the Jack the Ripper-like Nazi officer in Anatole Litvak's psycho case study film cum history lesson, *The Night of the Generals* (1967).

194

"Here's Johnny!" Jack Nicholson as psycho family man Jack Torrance in Stanley Kubrick's *The Shining* (1980).

Torrance breaks down the bathroom door to get at his wife (Shelley Duvall) in *The Shining*.

look-alike for *Peeping Tom*'s Mark Lewis. Both protagonists are blond and attractive, "beautiful people" almost, whom no one, especially those closest to them, suspects of suffering from a dangerous psychosis—an important subtheme of both films. Carol and Mark merely come across as shy and friendless, even vulnerable. Each speaks laconically and with an obvious foreign accent, although this is a bit difficult to explain in Lewis's case, as he's supposed to be a native Briton and was obviously due to actor Boehm's being German.[2] Still, it is another intriguing

2. On an ironic note, Carl Boehm was instrumental in breaking up director Polanski's first marriage to Polish actress Barbara Lass, whom Boehm subsequently married.

Torrance (Jack Nicholson) descends into total madness.

element that binds the two films together.

Repulsion, unlike *Peeping Tom,* was not only an important commercial hit for its director but a critical success as well. It even won a prestigious Silver Bear award at the 1965 Berlin Film Festival. Polanski's follow-up psycho case-study film *The Tenant* (1976) fared less well, though. Like *Peeping Tom,* it too was critically scorned, particularly in Europe, where reviewers called it "ugly," "self-indulgent," and "noninvolving." American critics were kinder, but the film was still a box-office flop. Polanski now sees the film as a miscalculation, a mixture of horror and Kafkaesque absurdity that just didn't work. But this is precisely what fans of the film like about it, and over the years their number has grown in size. Many, including myself, consider it one of Polanski's best films, as well as one of the most disorienting psycho-films ever made.

Polanski had originally intended to make the film on the heels of *Repulsion,* but decided to put it off because he felt critics would accuse him of repeating himself. On the surface, *The Tenant* does bear a strong resemblance to *Repulsion.* Both deal with an individual's psychological breakdown within the confines of a claustrophobic apartment. This resemblance exists, however, because it is part of Polanski's thematic territory, evident not only in these two films but in *Rosemary's Baby* (1968) and other Polanski films as well. The apartment represents a private world used by the protagonists as an escape valve from the outside world. Yet the solitude of the apartment also serves to exacerbate their illness and finally seal their doom.

The Tenant is based on a 1964 novel by French illustrator-actor Roland Topor. In it, a meek office clerk named Trelkovsky (played superbly by Polanski) rents an apartment in a run-down quarter of Paris. Trelkovsky (like Polanski) is a Pole who has become a French citizen. In his mind, though, he continues to see himself as a foreigner, an outsider. He discovers that the previous tenant, a girl whom no one seems to know very much about (another outsider), threw herself out the apartment window. As Trelkovsky takes up residence, he comes to share the girl's suicidal tendencies. Feeling spied upon by his hostile neighbors, he becomes a paranoid recluse. Eventually, he even dresses up in some old clothes that the dead girl left behind. By the end of the film,

Director Stanley Kubrick on the set of *The Shining*.

he has come to identify with her so closely that he finally throws himself out the same window—not just once, but as if attempting to reclaim his own identity, *twice!*

At the beginning of the film, Trelkovsky visits the dying ex-tenant in the hospital. Bandaged from head to toe, she lets out a piercing shriek at the sight of him, prompting another visitor (Isabelle Adjani) to remark that the delirious girl must have recognized him, a comment that baffles Trelkovsky as he doesn't even know the girl. The scream, however, is more of a warning shout, for what the bedridden former tenant really recognizes in Trelkovsky is herself. *The Tenant* ends with a reprise of this same scene, except that this time it is Trelkovsky who is lying in bed wrapped in bandages. As he looks up at his two visitors, he also screams, for what he sees is Adjani and *himself*. Like the long pan to the photograph of the already disturbed Carol Ledoux that concludes *Repulsion*, what this indicates is that Trelkovsky was potentially doomed from the beginning, that he carried within

him the seeds of his self-destruction. Alienated and already paranoid, he increasingly keeps to himself, brooding in silence within the claustrophobic apartment until his paranoia finally zooms out of all control and drives him to despair and suicide.

The same situation occurs in Stanley Kubrick's *The Shining* (1980), a psychofilm cum ghost story that owes as much to Polanski's *The Tenant* as it does to the Stephen King novel on which it is based. This is not surprising, of course, since Kubrick and Polanski are friends and admirers of each other's work. Polanski's *Tess* (1980), in fact, with its leisurely pace, photographic beauty, and meticulous re-creation of a bygone era, is virtually a homage to Kubrick's *Barry Lyndon* (1975). In *The Shining*, Kubrick returns the compliment.

Arguably, *The Tenant* could be looked at as a ghost story as well—in the sense that it is the spirit of the demented former tenant that takes over the troubled Trelkovsky and gradually drives him to doom. This is, of course, the classic ghost-story situation. But the

Deadly obsessive Terence Stamp kidnaps Samantha Eggar in William Wyler's *The Collector* (1965).

circular pattern evident in most of Polanski's work suggests a different theme. In *Chinatown* (1974), for example, private investigator Jack Nicholson, having already caused the death of one woman he was trying to protect in Chinatown, comes full circle when his efforts to help another woman he has become emotionally involved with leads to the same end in exactly the same place. Chinatown is a metaphor for Nicholson's state of mind, a state that he can't shake off even though it imperils him. The same is true of Trelkovsky and of Jack Torrance in *The Shining*. Intriguingly, Torrance is also played by Jack Nicholson.

Searching about for a supernatural subject, Kubrick came upon King's then-current best-seller and was immediately struck by its cinematic possibilities. He liked its basic story line about a family whose members come in conflict with one another when they are trapped inside a haunted Colorado mountain hotel during the winter snows. But when he came to write the screenplay with novelist Diane Johnson, he discarded most of the novel's ghost-story elements and concentrated instead on what he obviously felt was the more intriguing aspect of the story: the pathological character of Torrance, who deteriorates into an ax-wielding madman due to confinement and his inner failings. What emerged was a superb psycho case-study film, which, though a box-office success, was denounced by hard-core Stephen King fans as a travesty of the book. King himself seems to waffle on the subject by voicing approval of the film in one interview and disappointment in the next.

As played by the mercurial Jack Nicholson, Jack Torrance is one of psychofilm's premier self-deceivers, an alcoholic loser who places the blame for his shortcomings on everyone but himself. Like Trelkovsky, he is essentially a loner and a brooder in search of the right place in which to be alone and brood. The haunted hotel provides it. Charged with an unhealthy atmosphere, the hotel, like Trelkovsky's apartment, is filled with the ghostly residue of its former tenant(s). The previous caretaker (Philip

Stone) had gone mad and killed his family with an ax. Torrance hears this story at the beginning of the film, and it registers in his subconscious, resurfacing later when he loses all control and sets out to reenact the crime. He pursues his son (Danny Lloyd) outside into the hotel's sprawling hedge maze, but the boy manages to elude Nicholson, who perishes in the snow, freezing to death. The film ends, like *Repulsion,* with a slow dolly to an old photograph, which, as in the conclusion of *The Tenant,* serves as an absurdist metaphor. The photo is of the hotel's former residents circa 1921, and the youthful Torrance is standing in the foreground. Self-programmed to destruct from the very beginning, he, like Trelkovsky, has taken on the character and fate of his predecessor. As one of the hotel apparitions told him early on, "You were *always* the caretaker here." How true.

Deadly Obsessives

Everyone experiences loneliness at one time or another, but it can easily be made to go away either by calling up a friend or going out and mixing with people. The psychos in this chapter have no such outlet, however, because they are psychologically unable to relate to other people and therefore have no friends. Their futile search for human contact often leads to obsession—and that obsession often leads to the death of the object of desire.

Gerald Franklin (Terence Stamp), the protagonist of William Wyler's *The Collector* (1965), is such a deadly obsessive. A butterfly collector who has recently won £71,000 in the football pools, he buys a large house in the country, fixes up a guest room in the basement, then kidnaps a pretty art student he's had his eye on for some time to occupy it. His magical belief is that the girl Miranda Grey (Samantha Eggar), if forced to get to know him, will eventually come to love him as well. Symbolically stating his case to her in the only terms he knows, he admits that one of his pleasures in collecting is "getting to *know* the butterfly before mounting it." Obviously, this extends to her as well. She continually thwarts his efforts by trying to intimidate him (he has an obvious inferiority complex) and also by trying to escape. Overcome with frustration, he finally pleads with her in all demented seriousness, "Please, be reasonable!" In an effort to manipulate him, she tries, but to no avail, for Gerald is a psycho who loses all respect for her the minute she sits on his lap and kisses him.

The Collector is a high-gloss psychofilm that occasionally strains credulity. At one point, Miranda gets the drop on Gerald in a rainstorm and clubs him on the head with a shovel. One more blow would be enough to render him unconscious and allow her to

Alan Strang (Peter Firth) performs his bizarre private ritual in director Sidney Lumet's *Equus* (1977).

escape, but she holds back instead, and the bleeding man is able to recapture her. Considering her all-consuming desire for escape and her obvious antipathy for him, her holding back out of remorse at the sight of his bleeding forehead seems inconsistent. Locked in the dank cellar, she develops pneumonia and malnutrition while he is away for three days at the hospital having his wounds attended to. When he returns, she is dead, and he buries her in his yard under a tree. Realizing that his mistake was in having

Dr. Martin Dysart (Richard Burton) comforts the exhausted
Strang (Peter Firth) after a particularly grueling therapy
session in *Equus*.

"You talkin' to me?" Two views of Robert De Niro's disturbed Travis Bickle in Martin Scorsese's controversial *Taxi Driver* (1976).

"aimed too high," he sets his sights on another girl of his own class ("Someone I could teach," he says), and the film ends as his van follows a solitary nurse down a narrow street.

What *The Collector* lacks in believable suspense, it makes up for as a compelling psycho case-study, which is really its chief intent. Miranda seems the stronger character because, by denying Gerald the one thing he says he wants from her, she appears to hold all the cards. What she doesn't take into account, however, is the perceptiveness of her remark about his fascination with butterfly collecting—namely that he does it because he can't deal with living things. This remark not only foreshadows the conclusion of the film but eerily sums up the nature of Gerald's obsession. It's not a living pretty girl he wants at all, but a dead one.

The protagonist of Polish director Jerzy Skoli-mowski's English-language (and very Polanski-ish) psychofilm *Deep End* (1971) is a similarly deadly obsessive. Gerald Franklin may be older and wealthier than *Deep End*'s Mike (John Moulder-Brown), but they are kin in that both are shy observers who become fixated on a beautiful girl who dies as a result of their longings.

Mike, a fifteen-year-old high-school boy, takes a job in a seedy London public bath where he falls for the redheaded Susan (Jane Asher), another attendant almost ten years his senior. When he discovers that she is having an affair with one of his teachers at school, he tries to break it up. Complication piles upon complication, but in the end, he finally gets what he wants. Susan agrees to make love to him. But when he is unable to perform, he lashes out at her with a lamp. Fatally injured, she falls into the bath-house pool and drowns. He jumps in after her and caresses her dead body in the same manner that he'd caressed a poster of a nude girl in the same pool earlier in the film.

Certainly, some of Mike's shyness and sexual repression is due to his youth and inexperience, but the implication is quite strong that his development will remain arrested. Like Gerald Franklin, he cannot deal with living things, and the sexually forward Susan (like Miranda Grey) proves too much for him. The fantasy is better. All of this is tied up, of course, with the sleazy atmosphere of the bathhouse, where older customers, both male and female, come to act out their sexual fantasies, a situation that Mike learns from.

In Sidney Lumet's *Equus* (1977), based on the award-winning play by Peter Shaffer, the lonely and equally youthful Alan Strang (Peter Firth) focuses his obsessive attention not on girls but horses. Hired as a stable boy, the disturbed Strang comes to look upon the regal beasts as father confessors. Lying in bed at night, he harnesses himself up and imitates them in a private religious ceremony. When an older girl (Jenny Agutter) initiates him into sex under the watchful eyes of the priestly animals, Strang later explodes with violence and, feeling he has betrayed them, blinds each of them with a pick. "What the eye cannot see, the heart cannot grieve for" is his emotional explanation for his heinous act.

The film begins after the crime has taken place and unfolds like a psychological detective story. Shaffer based his play on an actual case but used few of its details except for the crime itself. In both the play and film, the boy's world-weary psychiatrist (Richard Burton)[3] becomes as obsessed with Strang's case as the boy is with horses. The boy's intense feelings, however mixed up, have a profound effect on the doctor. Envying Strang's passion, something he himself has never experienced, he realizes that by curing the boy, he will very likely destroy that passion and transform the youth into an emotional vegetable like himself—a theme not dissimilar to that of *A Clockwork Orange* (1971).

Unquestionably, *Equus* works better onstage than it does on film—and for one important reason. The emotional impact of the film's graphic realism gets in the way of Shaffer's heady argument. Onstage, the mutilation of the horses is powerfully but symbolically portrayed. On-screen, the gruesome images of blood gushing from the punctured eyesockets of the screaming horses are so viscerally disturbing that Shaffer's cerebral message is subverted by the audience's intense feelings that Alan Strang shouldn't be coddled or cured but drawn and quartered instead.

Faces in the Crowd

In Elia Kazan's indictment of the media's ability to

---

3. The role of the psychiatrist Dr. Martin Dysart was originated on the London stage by Alec McCowen and on Broadway by Anthony Hopkins. Anthony Perkins, reversing his *Psycho* image, also played the part on Broadway for a time—as did Burton, in preparation for his role in the film.

Vengeful psycho Max Cady (Robert Mitchum) follows Sam Bowden (Gregory Peck) and his daughter (Lori Martin) everywhere in *Cape Fear* (1962).

make instant celebrities, *A Face in the Crowd* (1957), a backwoods guitar-strummer and raconteur, Lonesome Rhodes (Andy Griffith), catches the eye of the local news media and is soon propelled into the national spotlight where he quickly becomes an Arthur Godfrey–like cultural figure. Politicians court his favor, sponsors pay him big bucks to hawk their products, his network television show gets big ratings, and the nation comes to worship him. Rhodes, however, is a taker, a manipulator with a mean streak, a small-time megalomaniac who blossoms into a big-time megalomaniac due to his growing power and influence. Capable of destroying lives and careers, he does—until, ironically, the same medium that brought him fame sends him back to obscurity. Seeing him for the blackguard he is, his media mentor (Patricia Neal) leaves his microphone open during the closing credits of his network television show, and the national audience overhears him denouncing them as a bunch of suckers and rubes. Exit Lonesome Rhodes.

A Face in the Crowd is a contemporary morality play, and a prophetic one at that. In the past forty years, all the communications media, but particularly television, have acquired a phenomenal allure, a fact that has not gone unnoticed by the esteem-hungry psychos who lurk in our midst. For them, exposure in the media has become *the* antidote to loneliness, a surefire way to achieve not just notoriety but a sense of identity. A way to become something more than just a face in the crowd. Travis Bickle and Rupert Pupkin in Martin Scorsese's *Taxi Driver* (1976) and *The King of Comedy* (1983), respectively, are two such psychos.

Scorsese and writer Paul Schrader based the character of Bickle (Robert De Niro) on Arthur Bremmer—the would-be assassin of former president Richard Nixon—who managed to achieve the notoriety for which he had so longed by gunning down presidential aspirant George Wallace instead. Naturally, television cameras were everywhere.

Bickle contemplates a similar assassination attempt on an aspiring presidential candidate (Leonard Harris), but is foiled when the Secret Service spots him in his bizarre Mohawk hairdo and rightly chases him away. Obsessed with the New York City's atmosphere of sleaze and moral decay, Bickle sets his sights instead on rescuing a child prostitute (Jodie Foster) from the degradation that surrounds her and guns down her pimp (Harvey Keitel) and other lowlifes in a final orgy of bloodletting that gains him notoriety as the avenging angel he sees himself to be.

Or does it? The ending of *Taxi Driver* shows us a series of newspaper headlines proclaiming Bickle an urban hero. After that, we see him back in his cab, as if nothing extraordinary has happened, driving away from the stunning blonde (Cybill Shepherd) who had earlier rejected him and now seeks to get back together due to his sudden fame. Like the rest of the film, which is told almost entirely from Bickle's distorted point of view, this ending is Bickle's fantasy—in fact, his ultimate fantasy of what he wants and expects his violent deeds to net him. A faceless

reject all his life, he has now become a man of stature, a man with an identity, a man able to reject others as they once rejected him.

The ending of *Taxi Driver* has often been misconstrued. The fact that it is Bickle's fantasy of how things will turn out for him and not how they do turn out is strengthened by *The King of Comedy* (1983), Scorsese's next psychofilm. The protagonist of *King* is another faceless outsider who longs for recognition. His name is Rupert Pupkin (Robert De Niro). Not an assassin but very much like one in his motives and methods of attack, he will resort to anything in order to get a ten-minute guest shot on a nationally televised and top-rated talk show hosted by his idol Jerry Langford (Jerry Lewis). Rebuffed at every turn, Rupert finally kidnaps Langford and holds him for ransom. His demand is that in exchange for Langford's life, he is to

Cady (Robert Mitchum) traps Bowden's wife (Polly Bergen) in the houseboat in the tense conclusion to *Cape Fear* (1962).

Maniacal ex-convict Max Cady (Robert De Niro) spells out his plans for revenge to his former attorney, Sam Bowden (Nick Nolte), in Martin Scorsese's excellent remake of *Cape Fear* (1991).

be given an opportunity to do his stand-up comedy routine on Langford's show that evening. Unable to do otherwise, the show's producers and the FBI agree to the terms, and Pupkin finally gets his big break even though he knows he will be headed for jail afterward. *The King of Comedy*, like *Taxi Driver*, ends with Pupkin's fantasy of his ultimate wish being fulfilled. His face plastered on the covers of newsmagazines all over the country and his life story a nationwide best-seller, he is released from prison, gets his own network television show, and dethrones the envied Langford. His dreams have come true.

It took screenwriter Paul D. Zimmerman, a former film critic for *Newsweek*, thirteen years to bring his brilliant script to the screen. The turning point was when it came to the attention of Robert De Niro, who showed it to Scorsese. What they each saw in the script were many of the same themes that ran through their previous psychofilm collaboration, the hugely and unexpectedly successful *Taxi Driver*. Scorsese and De Niro revised the script together, but, as Zimmerman later admitted to *American Film* magazine, "the script which Marty and Bobby returned to me was all mine—with maybe one new scene in it. I was absolutely gratified. [Although] the tone is tougher, darker, I think, than what I wrote."

Pupkin, like Bickle, lives within his own landscape of the mind. Though articulate and possessed of a gift of gab, he is unable to relate to others, who see him as loud, brash, and obnoxious. He, on the other hand, sees himself as "the king of comedy" and, like Bickle, takes extreme measures to achieve his identity through instant notoriety. Bickle really wants to be the presidential candidate he almost shoots. Pupkin wants to be Jerry Langford, whom he kidnaps and holds for ransom. Both men find it psychologically intolerable to be just faces in the crowd. Theirs is the new American dream, where instant celebrity has replaced wealth as the way to being seen as a winner.

No small part of the unsettling effectiveness of both films is due, of course, to De Niro himself, who earned an Oscar nomination for his performance as Travis Bickle, but was ignored by the Academy for his very different yet even more electrifying performance as Rupert Pupkin, which, I feel, is the best of his career so far. Pathetic, charming, witty, unscrupulous, insecure, and finally, creepy, his Rupert Pupkin is one of the scariest and most convincing psychopaths in screen history. Ironically, this is probably why not only his performance was ignored by the industry but why the film was too. *The King of Comedy* received many scathing reviews (because of the title and the

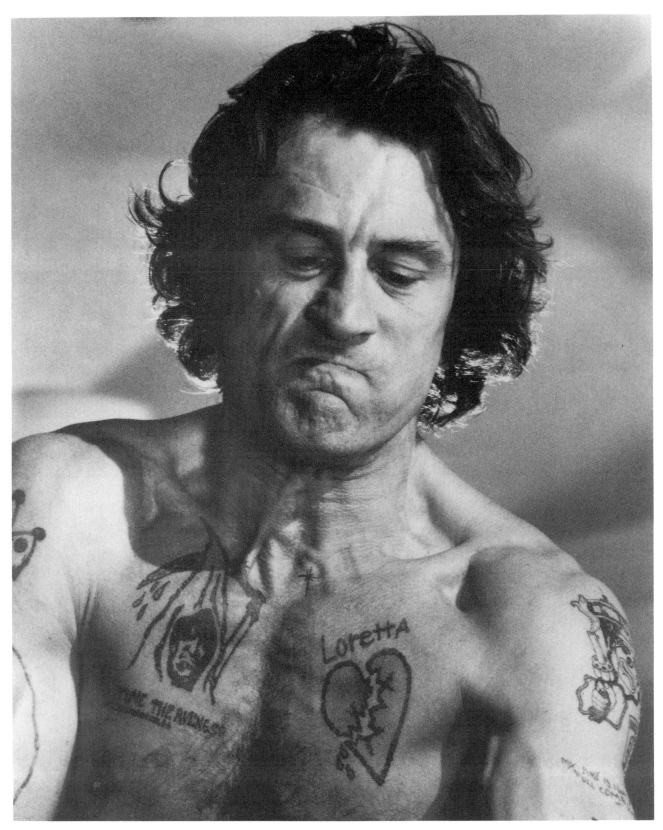

Sadistic psychopath Cady (Robert De Niro) launches his
campaign of terror against Bowden by beating up Bowden's lover in *Cape Fear*.

The final showdown between Cady (Robert De Niro) and Bowden (Nick Nolte) in *Cape Fear*.

presence of Jerry Lewis, some critics actually thought it was supposed to be a comedy!), failed at the box office—no doubt because many audiences thought the same thing—and did not fare well at Oscar time. The perception in other quarters, however, was that the film was not only socially irresponsible but even dangerous and that it should never have been made. Obviously, this adverse reaction had much to do with the revelation that real-life psycho John W. Hinckley's 1981 assassination attempt on Ronald Reagan had stemmed from his close identification with the character of Travis Bickle in *Taxi Driver,* which Hinckley had obsessively viewed fifteen times. Scorsese was summarily chastised not only for failing to learn a lesson, but for dangerously providing an even more viable modus operandi for other crazies out there with his new film. What this comes down to, of course, is the provocative question of which came first, the chicken or the egg? The movie? Or the psycho? Did Travis Bickle inspire Hinckley to play the assassination game, or was the demented Hinckley looking for inspiration? Did Hinckley's close identification with the character of Travis Bickle mold him into what he became, or did he see in Travis a reflection of his own lost soul. Did Hinckley merely emulate Travis Bickle, or did he desperately empathize with him? One must keep in mind, as this controversy about the power of the movies to influence us goes on, that the character of Travis Bickle was not made out of whole cloth but was itself a reflection—of Arthur Bremmer, a real-life assassin with a character profile very much like Hinckley's (and of whom Hinckley was surely not unaware). Many psychologists concur that assassins, political or otherwise, are inspired mainly by the deeds of other assassins. To make audiences aware of what makes these walking time bombs tick, so that their going off might someday be averted, is certainly one of the primary objectives of *Taxi Driver, The King of Comedy,* and other serious psycho case-study films.

Scorsese and De Niro continued their psychofilm collaboration in *Cape Fear* (1991), a remake of the 1962 film of the same name based on John D. MacDonald's novel *The Executioners.* The celebrated director-actor team had their work cut out for them because the original, directed by J. Lee Thompson, was a riveting psychofilm. In it, Robert Mitchum essayed his most scarifying psycho role since *The Night of the Hunter.* Max Cady, a sadistic sexual psychopath, takes up residence in a sleepy Southern town to seek revenge on the lawyer, Sam Bowden (Gregory Peck), whose eyewitness account of Cady's brutal assault on a young woman resulted in his (Cady's) being sent to prison for many years. The psychopath launches a war of nerves on Bowden and his family, but is wily enough not to commit any overtly threatening acts that might put him in jeopardy with the police. Eventually, Bowden must take matters into his own hands. Using his family as bait, Bowden lures the vicious Cady to his houseboat on a

Bowden's daughter (Juliette Lewis) and wife (Jessica Lange) fear for their lives on the houseboat in the riveting conclusion to Martin Scorsese's even more tension-filled remake of *Cape Fear*.

remote part of the Cape Fear River, where the tense final confrontation between victim and victimizer takes place and Cady is finally brought to justice.

In the remake, Nick Nolte plays Bowden and De Niro plays Cady, whose sadomasochistic character has more than a trace of Travis Bickle and, like Mitchum's Harry Powell in *The Night of the Hunter*, suffers from religious mania as well (his body is tattooed with dire religious prophecies, and his hands are scratched with ominous words). Cady's harrowing persecution of Bowden is given an intriguing twist because the ex-con has a legitimate grievance against the lawyer in this version. Bowden was Cady's public defender on the assault and battery charge, and he'd withheld evidence that might have led to his guilty client's acquittal. In other words, the lawyer had done his moral duty by getting the violent Cady off the streets, but since he was the accused's defense counsel and not the prosecutor in the case, he had committed a serious breach of legal ethics by not doing his best for his client. And it is for that breach that Cady, who has evolved into even more of a monster during his fourteen years in prison, wants legitimate redress. How he goes about seeking that redress is not only appalling but completely deranged, and his terrifying tactics almost lead to the complete disintegration of Bowden's already dysfunctional family.

The bloody final confrontation between Bowden and the murderous Cady again takes place on the Bowdens' houseboat on the Cape Fear River, where the lawyer has flown with his family not for the purpose of luring Cady out into the open but to escape from the maniac until the cops hunt him down. Cady has other plans, however. As a storm mounts and the houseboat is buffeted about and finally destroyed on the rocks, the messianic psychopath (who now takes on characteristics of Jason, Michael Myers, and Freddy Krueger as well) and the hapless Bowden engage in a spectacular, and quite grisly, duel to the death—in which Bowden and his at-odds family are spared and finally reborn.

In some respects, the remake is superior to the original. For example, Bowden's wife (Jessica Lange) and teenage daughter (played with an unnerving Lolita-ish sexiness by Juliette Lewis) are given more depth of character this time around. And De Niro's powerhouse portrayal of the sleazy, monstrous Cady succeeds in eclipsing Mitchum's earlier incarnation of the character, very fine though Mitchum's performance was. In most other respects, however, the remake merely equals the original, which was just as disturbing and suspenseful but much less flashy. The remake even makes use of the original's Bernard Herrmann score (superbly adapted and reorchestrated by Elmer Bernstein). And in a further nod to its prestigious source, the film includes original stars Gregory Peck, Robert Mitchum, and Martin Balsam in supporting roles.

10

PSYCHOMANIA

A census taker once tried to test me. I ate his liver, with some fava beans and a nice Chianti.

—Hannibal "the Cannibal" Lecter (Anthony Hopkins) in *The Silence of the Lambs* (1990)

As a look at the psychofilmography at the rear of this book will show, the eighties and nineties have exhibited no slacking off in the number of psychofilms being made here and abroad. In fact, cinema maniacs appear to be lumbering across movie screens with greater frequency than ever before—a reflection, perhaps, of real life, where the front pages of our daily newspapers and the lead stories of our nightly newscasts appear to headline one ever more ghastly psycho murder after another with frightening regularity.

As in the past, many of the recent crop of psychofilms merely exploit our fears of these disturbed and often undetected (until it's too late) individuals who lurk in our midst—the *Nightmare on Elm Street, Friday the 13th,* and *Halloween* series, for example. Others take a more serious approach by holding up a mirror to the various psycho ills plaguing our vulnerable society.

The stalking of pop-culture celebrities by psychotic fans has been dealt with several times in psychofilm—superficially in Edward Bianchi's *The Fan* (1981) and more potently in Martin Scorsese's *The King of Comedy.* Rob Reiner's *Misery* (1990), based on one of superstar novelist Stephen King's best and most personal thrillers, takes a truly scarifying look at this disturbing phenomenon—a phenomenon that many of us were only vaguely aware of until Beatle John Lennon was murdered outside his apartment

building by one of his psychotic fans.

In *Misery,* the car of best-selling novelist Paul Sheldon (James Caan) careens off a slippery Colorado mountain road in a snowstorm, and Sheldon is severely injured. His number-one fan Annie Wilkes (Kathy Bates), a nurse with a murderous past, finds him and takes him home with her. Nursing him back to health, she discovers that Sheldon has killed off Misery Chastain, her favorite literary heroine (and fantasized alter ego), in his latest novel—and that Sheldon's just-completed manuscript is a pornographic departure from the romance genre that made his name and reputation. Annie goes berserk. She burns the manuscript before the author's horrified eyes and demands that he get to work resurrecting Misery in a new romance novel while he's recuperating. Realizing his life is in jeopardy if he refuses to go along with Annie's insane request, Sheldon starts hammering out the novel under the watchful eyes of his number-one fan and keenest critic until he's strong enough to make a break for it. Annie catches on to his scheme, however, and in the film's grisliest scene, she breaks his ankles with a sledgehammer so that he can't escape and will have to finish the book. The local sheriff (Richard Farnsworth) pays a call to Annie's remote farmhouse in search of the missing author, and when he gets suspicious, Annie kills him. Knowing that she will kill him too once the book is

Literary agent Marcia Sindell (Lauren Bacall) listens raptly as best-selling romance novelist Paul Sheldon (James Caan) recounts being held captive by his "number one fan" in Rob Reiner's *Misery* (1990).

Number one fan Annie Wilkes (Kathy Bates) and the battered and bruised object of her deranged fandom, writer Paul Sheldon (James Caan), in *Misery*.

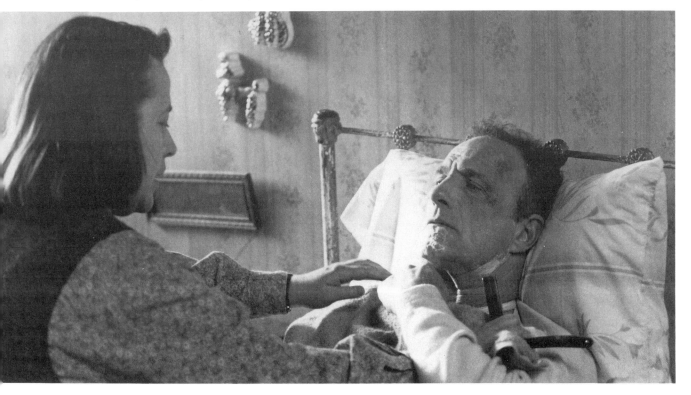

finished, Sheldon finally strikes back at his murderous admirer with the only weapon at his command—the aged typewriter she's forced him to use. At the film's suspenseful—and highly symbolic—conclusion, the beleaguered author saves himself at last by beating her to death with the very machine she's hostaged him to.

Kathy Bates deservedly won an Oscar as Best Actress for her multishaded performance as the terrifying, yet oddly pathetic, psycho fan. Caan's more subtle (and unnominated) performance as the hapless recipient of her demented devotion matches hers every step. The scenes between them are wholly credible, edge-of-your-seat stuff. Fortunately, these scenes constitute most of the film's length, for whenever *Misery* shifts away from the tense byplay between Bates and Caan, it falls apart in terms of both suspense and plausibility. Sheriff Farnsworth's manhunt, for example, seems woefully unenergetic and undersized given Sheldon's fame and the amount of publicity his disappearance has received in the media. In most countrywide searches for missing persons I've read about, practically everyone and his grandmother gets involved—even if the missing person *isn't* famous. And yet the search for Sheldon seldom consists of more than a few people at any one time. And Farnsworth's latching onto an important clue as to Sheldon's whereabouts by pouring through the author's *Misery Chastain* novels is completely ridiculous. (In King's novel, the sheriff finds his way to Annie's doorstep by much more convincing means.) For a psychofilm that otherwise strives to be chillingly realistic and psychologically probing in its scenes between the two leads, this eurekalike moment of seemingly effortless deductive reasoning stretches credibility to the limit. It's Sherlock Holmes stuff. One almost expects Farnsworth to tell his wife, "Elementary, my dear."

Family Fiends

Reflecting an even more common real-life situation, psychofilms of recent vintage have focused more and more attention on perhaps the most terrifying crazy of all—those seemingly caring yet inwardly murderous individuals who prey on those closest to them: a lover, for example, or the trusting members of their family.

In the huge box-office hit *Fatal Attraction* (1987), for example, happily married man Michael Douglas has an affair with Glenn Close while his wife (Anne Archer) is away visiting relatives. When Archer returns, Douglas terminates the affair, but the psychotically possessive Close has other ideas and refuses to be dumped so casually. At first she plays on Douglas's guilt and attempts suicide to get him back. When that ploy fails, she steps up her campaign of terror, infiltrates Douglas's happy home by befriending Archer, and ultimately threatens the life of the couple's child. As the pressure to get Close off his back mounts, Douglas's thoughts turn to murder, but Close is one step ahead of him. She attacks the couple at knifepoint in their home and is finally shot by Archer and drowned by Douglas in the family bathtub.

James Dearden's original screenplay, which he expanded from an earlier short subject of his called *Diversion*, apparently ended quite differently by having Close engineer Douglas's arrest for her murder, thereby avenging herself on the two-timing stud even in death. When that ending failed to fly with preview audiences, however, director Adrian Lyne shot the *Halloween*-style slashfest that now concludes the film, so that the deranged harpy gets *her* just desserts instead. The original, more psychologically astute and disturbing ending has since been reinstated in some video releases of the film.

Dearden returned to the domestic-malice format again in his 1991 adaptation of Ira Levin's psycho classic *A Kiss Before Dying*, a remake of the 1956 film of the same name, although the new version bears little resemblance to it—or to Levin's novel for that matter. This time around, Dearden directed as well.

A miscast Matt Dillon plays the suave psychokiller (Robert Wagner took the part in the earlier version) who carries on an affair with a vulnerable (and none-too-bright) rich girl (Sean Young—Joanne Woodward in the 1956 film) whose powerful family he has ambitious designs on. When Young's unexpected pregnancy threatens these ambitions (her tycoon father would disown her if he found out), Dillon murders her, dons a new persona, and takes up with her twin sister, also played by Sean Young (Virginia Leith played the part in the earlier film, where the sisters were not twins). Young #2 gradually finds him out and becomes targeted for death herself during the film's overwrought cat-and-mouse conclusion.

Dearden intended the film to be a twisted homage to Hitchcock's 1958 classic *Vertigo* (at one point, he even has Young watching *Vertigo* on television), but like *Fatal Attraction*, it ultimately winds up owing more to the type of psychologically empty slasher-thrill shows exemplified by *Halloween, Friday the 13th*, and their ilk.

Equally simplistic in their pursuit of little more than *Halloween*-style thrills are *Sleeping With the Enemy* (1991) and *Deceived* (1991). The former, directed by Joseph Ruben, who also made the compelling *The Stepfather* (more about which later), features Julia Roberts as a woman who finds that her young, upwardly mobile yuppie husband (Patrick Bergin) is

Michael Douglas stars as a happily married attorney and
Glenn Close as the unmarried publishing executive who
seduces him when his wife and daughter are out of town in
Fatal Attraction (1987).

Glenn Close and Michael Douglas battle it out in Adrian Lyne's *Fatal Attraction*.

a psychopathic brute with a pathological obsession for tidiness. He berates her or beats her senseless if she fails to have the bathroom towels arranged properly or is a minute late with dinner. He also gets insanely jealous if she so much as talks to another man. Knowing that divorce would only drive this creep to even greater acts of fury, Roberts fakes her death to get away from him, assumes a new identity, and takes up residence in a small town hundreds of miles away. Eventually, she falls for her next-door neighbor, a college drama teacher and all-around nice guy played by Kevin Anderson.

Bergin catches on to her charade, and when he locates her, he proves to be exactly the vengeful ogre she'd feared. Bergin clues her into the terrifying fact that he's found her by tidying up her bathroom towels and neatly arranging the canned goods in her kitchen cabinets. Then he beats Anderson within an inch of his life and comes after her with a gun. She turns the tables and shoots him instead. But he proves to be almost as unstoppable a force as Jason and Michael Myers and refuses to die until she's finally pumped enough lead in him to bring down an ele-phant.

Relentlessly predictable and cliché-ridden though much of it is, *Sleeping With the Enemy* does manage to generate a fair amount of tension whenever Bergin is on the screen. Though the film was made as a star vehicle for Roberts, it is Bergin's scary performance as the one-moment-solicitous, the next-moment-mani-acal hubby from hell that steals the show.

Deceived, directed by Damian Harris (the son of actor Richard Harris), essentially covers the same territory, with a dash of *Gaslight* (1944) tossed in for good measure. John Heard plays the manipulative, murderous husband, and Goldie Hawn plays the incessantly wide-eyed and shrieking (but ultimately resourceful, of course) heroine who discovers that the man she married isn't the man she married. In fact, she doesn't know who the hell he is—wherein lies the film's lame attempt at a twist. Determined to find out, she gradually strips away his polished veneer, then has to fight for her life when she reveals the psycho fiend that lurks beneath.

A more realistic look at the psycho husband was offered in the riveting 1991 telefilm *In a Child's Name*,

Amateur sleuth Jeffrey Hunter, victim Joanne Woodward, and psycho killer Robert Wagner in the original *A Kiss Before Dying* (1956).

the true story of a New Jersey dentist who is sent to prison for cold-bloodedly murdering his wife, then spitefully seeks to win custody of their child away from the murdered woman's caring sister and family. The film is based on a book of the same name by reporter Peter Maas, whose earlier accounts of the affair in the *New York Times* were instrumental in bringing the emotionally charged case to the public's attention and securing a just outcome.

Michael Ontkean gives a superb performance as the husband Kenneth Taylor, a woman-hating sociopath (and tidiness freak like *Sleeping With the Enemy's* Patrick Bergin) who charms the young woman Teresa into marriage with his Mr. Perfect image. In reality, image is all there is to this guy, who interacts with everyone—even his parents—by playing whatever role best suits his purposes at the time. On their honeymoon, he subjects the sleeping Teresa to a sadistic beating, then claims that burglars broke into their suite, knocked him out when he tried to stop them, and apparently assaulted her while he was lying unconscious. The severely battered woman has no memory of what happened and believes his story,

but her devoted sister, Angela (Valerie Bertinelli), is skeptical and is the first to push for an investigation when Teresa, who has since had a child with Taylor, suddenly disappears. Taylor concocts a story about his wife's drug dependency and tells Angela and the police that she left him and the child to pursue treatment at a rehabilitation center whose name and location she refused to divulge. But when Teresa's barely concealed corpse is discovered wrapped in a blanket alongside a road, Taylor is arrested and charged with her murder. The evidence against him is so overwhelming that Taylor finally comes clean and admits to the killing, claiming that it was a case of justifiable homicide, for his wife was on a cocaine binge and abusing their child at the time. Physical evidence at the crime scene gruesomely proves otherwise, however, and Taylor is handily convicted. In revenge for Angela's perseverance in bringing him to justice, he manipulates his parents (played with a telling emotional coolness by Louise Fletcher and David Huddleston) into fighting for custody of the child on his behalf. The trio uses every shoddy legal trick to block Angela and her family from even seeing

Two views of Matt Dillon as the yuppie psycho who will stop at nothing, not even murder, to rise to the top in his father-in-law's copper company. From the inferior remake of *A Kiss Before Dying* (1991).

Matt Dillon and Sean Young, who plays the twin sister-victims of the ambitious killer, in James Dearden's *A Kiss Before Dying*.

the child. But justice triumphs in the end. The imprisoned wife-killer is severed of all legal claims to the child, and custody is awarded to Angela and her husband rather than Taylor's obviously dysfunctional parents.

A tense courtroom drama as well as a gripping psychofilm, *In a Child's Name* puts most of its big-screen brethren to shame. Director Tom McLoughlin lays on the suspense—and the monstrousness of Taylor's personality and deeds—without resorting to *Halloween*-style shock tactics or buckets of blood, although there is one scene in the film guaranteed to jolt even the most jaded psychofilm fan. Teresa's murder isn't shown to us, nor do we see Taylor's Norman Bates–style cleanup of the bloody murder scene afterward—just the tail end of it as he fastidiously vacuums the carpet. With no apparent evidence that a bloody murder has been committed in the immaculately kept house, the police resort to using a forensic compound called Luminol, which renders hidden traces of blood visible by turning them a

luminous green when the lights are turned off. Shortly after Taylor's incarceration, his parents sleep over in the neat-as-a-pin bedroom where the murder actually occurred, and when Mrs. Taylor switches off the light, the entire room—walls, floor, ceiling, window blinds—radiates a greenish glow, and we get an oblique but stomach-churning idea of the magnitude of their psychotic son's hideous deed. Taylor didn't just kill his wife, he *massacred* the poor woman—as if trying, through her, to exterminate all womankind itself.

For most of its length, Joseph Ruben's *The Stepfather* (1987) unfolds the story of a somewhat different type of psycho family man with a refreshing lack of exploitative tricks as well. Terry O'Quinn delivers a strong performance as the title character, a gentle, nondescript chap who marries a series of widows and divorcées with children in search of the perfect family. As soon as his new family members show signs of being human and not robots who will march unquestioningly to his tune, his dreams of domestic bliss

The surface Jerry Blake (Terry O'Quinn) in cool repose—and what lies beneath: the obsessed psychotic. From *The Stepfather* (1987).

begin to crumble, and he kills them. Then he alters his appearance, assumes a new identity, and skips to another town to begin the deadly ritual all over again.

He marries Shelley Hack, who sees him as the ideal mate and surrogate father for her teenage daughter (Jill Schoelen), and is soon up to his old tricks when

Schoelen proves too much of a troublesome teen for him to handle. This time he fails to shed himself of his family so easily. At the film's excessively blood-splattered conclusion, his intended victims blow him away instead.

A taut, well-written (by suspense masters Brian

218

Patrick Bergin as the "hubby from Hell" in *Sleeping With the Enemy* (1991).

Billy Zane plays a shipwreck victim who relates a mysterious tale of death aboard his becalmed schooner in the psychofilm, *Dead Calm* (1989).

Garfield and Donald E. Westlake) yarn—for three-quarters of its running time anyway—*The Stepfather* was an unexpected critical and box-office favorite. As is often the case these days, its success led to the inevitable sequel, wherein O'Quinn returned to marry and murder once more despite the fact that he was obviously dead at the end of the first film. The uninspired and mostly gore-filled follow-up, *Stepfather 2: Make Room for Daddy* (1989), gets around this dilemma by simply ignoring it.

The sequel begins in an asylum where O'Quinn, having apparently survived his fatal wounds, is being held under observation. During a session with his psychiatrist, he stabs the man in the back of the neck, assumes the dead doctor's identity, and escapes to another town where he sets himself up as a family therapist. Divorced mother Meg Foster comes to one of his counseling sessions, and they start dating and soon plan to marry. Foster's close pal (Caroline Williams) sees through O'Quinn's charade, however, and he kills her. He also murders Foster's loutish ex-husband when the man attempts blackmail. Not until the wedding ceremony does Foster finally see him for the looney-tune he is—at which point director Jeff Burr pours on the ultraviolence by having the progressively more blood-soaked Foster gruesomely terminate the demented family man once and for all.

Psycho Billy Zane is held at bay by a desperate Nicole
Kidman in Philip Noyce's tense *Dead Calm*.

In *Pacific Heights* (1990), psycho Michael Keaton
becomes an unwanted member of the family when he
rents an apartment in happily married couple Melanie Griffith and Matthew Modine's renovated San
Francisco home and turns into a tenant from hell who
almost destroys their lives. Modine tries to get the
destructive creep evicted, but, because the laws of
tenancy are entirely in the wily madman's favor,
Modine winds up getting thrown out of the place
instead, and the job of getting Keaton out of their hair
and home falls to Griffith, who cleverly sets up the
psychopath so that he's nailed by the police.

Keaton is genuinely frightening as the demented
tenant, although the script never provides much
insight into the motivations behind his crazy behavior. And it's a bit hard to accept someone as crafty as
he is being felled by someone like Griffith, who, with
her wide, empty eyes and vacuous little-girl voice,
doesn't seem bright enough to challenge him, let
alone succeed. Still, what it lacks in credibility, *Pacific
Heights* more than makes up for in suspense whenever the believably dangerous Keaton is on-screen.

Billy Zane, the psycho intruder of *Dead Calm*
(1989), remains a bit of a cipher as well, but he too
commands the screen with his unnerving presence.
Following the death of their son, traumatized couple
Sam Neill and Nicole Kidman attempt to get away
from it all by taking a cruise on their yacht. They come

across Zane, the sole surviving crew member of a
crippled schooner, and rescue him from his lifeboat
while Neill goes aboard the schooner to find out what
happened to everyone else. He discovers the crew
was murdered, realizes that Zane was responsible
(although why Zane did it is never really made clear),
and hastens back to the yacht to save Kidman from
the man he now knows to be a dangerous psychopath.

Zane cuts Neill adrift, takes over the yacht with
Kidman his prisoner, and the film turns into a tense
cat-and-mouse game as Kidman uses her wiles to
keep Zane at bay while trying to slow down the
fast-moving yacht so that her husband, a skilled
seaman, can catch up with them on the jerry-rigged
schooner.

Suspensefully directed by Phillip Noyce, *Dead Calm*
is a real grabber, although it too suffers at the end
from the *Halloween* curse by having Zane turn into a
nearly unstoppable monster who returns from his
watery grave for one last try at the heroine.

Based on a 1965 novel by Charles Williams, *Dead
Calm* was also filmed in the early seventies by Orson
Welles as *Dead Reckoning* (aka *The Deep*), starring
Michael Bryant and Oja Kadar as the harried couple
and Laurence Harvey as the psycho intruder. The film
was never released, reportedly remaining unfinished
at the time of Welles's death.

Jeremy Irons plays twin doctors Beverly Mantle (left) and Elliot Mantle (right), whose strange relationship undergoes a terrifying change when they become involved with drug-gie actress Claire (Genevieve Bujold) in David Cronenberg's *Dead Ringers* (1988).

Director David Cronenberg kept the madness all in the family in his 1988 psychofilm *Dead Ringers*, the relentlessly grim story of twin gynecologists—each of them disturbed in a different way—whose twisted bond leads to psychosis and finally death. Cronenberg and coscreenwriter Norman Snider based the disturbing tale on a novel *Twins*, by Barri Wood and Jack Greasland, which was reportedly inspired by a true story.

One of the twin doctors gets mixed up with a drugged-out movie star (Genevieve Bujold) and becomes even more wigged-out. As the twins often pose as one another to share each other's girlfriends, the other twin becomes mixed up with her too, and the strange ménage à trois with sex and drugs sends both twins spiraling rapidly downhill. Ultimately, one twin kills the other to put him out of his misery, then commits suicide so that they will remain united even in death.

Cronenberg's recurring theme of loss of identity is firmly present in this perverse and fascinating drama, but unlike his previous film *The Fly* (1986), there's no emotional resonance. The twins' intertwined road to ruin is presented so clinically and with such dispassion—like one of their gynecological examinations—that we don't know what to feel about it at the end. Jeremy Irons is excellent throughout as the doomed twins. And the special effects that enable him to interact with himself in the same frame are state-of-the-art. The major element missing from the film is the point it's trying to make.

Serial Killers

Statistically, serial killers are among the rarest breed of criminal, and yet judging from the number of books written and films made about them in recent years, one would suspect that their murderous kind lurks in the shadows preying on hapless victims in every city and town from coast to coast. Because their heinous deeds are so sensational and headline-grabbing, serial killers have become the most feared criminal of our time—and thus the most prevalent (and overworked) psycho in the movies. Even filmdom's venerable mad musician, the Phantom of the Opera, has forsaken his catacombs and organ for the back alley and the knife.

Spurred by the revival of interest in Gaston Leroux's classic character wrought by Andrew Lloyd Webber's smash musical, veteran exploitation frightmeister Harry Alan Towers rushed his own version of the tale into production in 1989 starring Robert Englund (serial killer Freddy Krueger in the *Nightmare on Elm Street* series) as a different type of Phantom carved straight out of today's headlines. Shot in

Hungary to keep costs down and to make use of some elaborate period sets left standing from earlier films about the phantom's turn-of-the-century era, this retelling of *The Phantom of the Opera*, directed by Dwight Little, opens in present-day New York City where Christine (Jill Schoelen), an aspiring opera singer, is planning an audition. She comes across a century-old composition written by the Phantom and dusts it off for her use. During her performance, however, she's knocked unconscious by a falling sandbag and is transported back in time to nineteenth-century London. There she encounters and falls under the tutelage of the fiendish composer—a mystery man named Erik Destler who murders people for their faces, which he gruesomely slices off with a knife and stitches onto his more hideous face to hide (and arguably improve) his appearance. Christine finally regains consciousness and finds herself safely back in the Big Apple. But alas, she's not yet free of the phantom, for the maniac has pursued her through time. Disguised as a friend and coworker, the lunatic lothario reveals himself and chases her through her apartment for a few more less than terrifying moments before he's finally destroyed—although the open-endedness of his demise predictably leaves the way cleared for a sequel. As the Phantom, Robert Englund is quite good and surprisingly un–Freddy Krueger–ish, although he's not above dropping a Freddy–like witticism now and then. Unfortunately, the hackneyed script by Duke Sandefur provides him with little to do except kill people, and so his Phantom winds up being just one more motiveless carve-up like *Halloween*'s Michael Myers and *Friday the 13th*'s Jason Voorhees.

Phantom of the Mall: Eric's Revenge (1989) played with the classic character in serial-killer terms as well, although the updated script retains little of the original Leroux novel. In it, Eric (Derek Rydall) falls victim to a band of greedy land-developers, who burn his house down (with him in it) to make room for a money-making shopping mall. Hideously disfigured by the fire and justifiably consumed with revenge, Eric emerges now and then from his lair beneath the mall to get even with the bad guys, whom he dispatches one by one via knife, forklift, and other more gruesomely creative means. Then he blows up the mall itself. Though well-produced, *Phantom of the Mall: Eric's Revenge* is just another cliché-ridden, slice-and-dice flick.

Infinitely better is Tibor Takacs's *I, Madman* (1989), which also trades on the murderous man-in-the-mask image of the Phantom of the Opera, although its plot bears little resemblance to Leroux's novel beyond that. Jenny Wright plays a variation on the Christine character, an aspiring actress who pays the bills by working in a bookstore. She comes upon

Robert Englund as the movies' most famous muscial madman in Dwight Little's mad slasher remake of *The Phantom of the Opera* (1989).

Jenny Wright's passion for horror novels takes a bizarre twist when Malcolm Brand (Randall William Cook), the author-murderer from her favorite book, begins terrorizing her for real. From *I, Madman* (1989).

some old horror novels written by a forgotten (and presumably dead) writer named Malcolm Brand, whose bizarre, twisted plots capture her imagination. Doing some detective work to learn more about him, she finds that the author claimed his works were not fiction at all but "nonfiction confessionals," whose frightening characters were inspired by monstrous

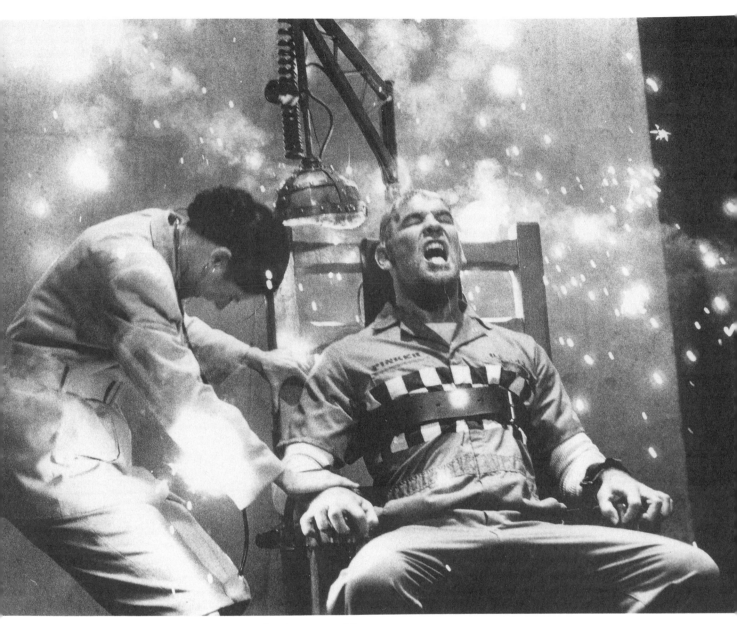

Serial killer Horace Pinker (Mitch Pileggi) goes to his well-deserved death in Wes Craven's *Shocker* (1989). Trouble is, he won't stay dead.

creatures that lived and spoke to him on another level of consciousness. When she launches into Brand's last book *I, Madman,* the Phantom of the Opera–like lead character comes horrifyingly to life and goes on a killing spree. But when she tries to convince her policeman-boyfriend (Clayton Rohner) that the fictional fiend—or possibly the still-living Brand in disguise—is responsible for the mayhem, he refuses to believe her, and the fiend soon starts stalking her.

Eventually Rohner comes around to her way of thinking, and the two of them are almost done in by the madman until Wright strikes upon the idea of unleashing another, more lethal character from one of Brand's books to destroy the masked monster. At the film's imaginative conclusion, the battling creature and Madman-Brand crash through the top-floor window of the bookstore, but instead of falling to their deaths on the street below, their bodies transform into pages from the books from whence they sprang and blow about and finally disappear on the wind. Although the plot of *I, Madman* is altogether incredible, director Takacs and his actors—particularly Wright—make it work. The film is suspenseful and, unlike most of its type, fairly unpredictable right to the end.

Perhaps hoping that lightning would strike twice and spark another successful series, director Wes Craven returned to the dreamscape of his original *Nightmare on Elm Street* with *Shocker* (1989), a semiserious, semisatiric psychofilm about a Freddy Krueger–ish TV repairman and serial killer named Horace Pinker (Mitch Pileggi). The film was a box-office failure, however, and Pinker's demented career ended with one installment.

The film costars Peter Berg as Jonathan Parker (Harker, get it?), the adopted teenage son of a cop (Michael Murphy), whose family is murdered by Pinker early on. Mysteriously connected to Pinker—it turns out he's the madman's natural son—Parker is able to identify him as the killer, and Pinker is summarily arrested and sentenced to death. But he survives the electric chair—in fact, he's renewed by the death-dealing jolt of electricity and turns into a seemingly insurmountable killing machine bent on revenge. A similar plot was used in the 1990 supernatural psychofilm *The First Power*, wherein a devil-worshiping serial killer (Jeff Kober) is also sentenced to death for his crimes. Despite the warnings of a psychic (Tracy Griffith) that the execution will only give the fiend the power to return and kill again, the execution is carried out, and the shape-shifting serial killer begins murdering anew until he's put out of business by cop Lou Diamond Phillips in a spectacular duel to the death that takes place in the Los Angeles sewer system.

Having successfully eluded the murderous clutches of serial killer Michael Myers in the first two *Halloween* films, Jamie Lee Curtis found herself up against yet another bloodthirsty killer in Kathryn Bigelow's action-filled but empty-headed *Blue Steel* (1990). Curtis plays a New York City cop who kills a robber in self-defense but is subsequently suspended from duty when investigators find no weapon on the deceased. As it happens, the gun was lifted by one of the bystanders, Ron Silver, a Wall Street trader and wild-eyed psychopath who carves Curtis's name on the unused bullets, goes on a killing spree, then seduces her into an affair.

Curtis finally realizes he's the serial-killer gunman who's terrorizing the city, but since she doesn't have any evidence that will stand up in court, she has no alternative but to put on her uniform and strap on her gun and shoot it out with the maniac on the streets of New York.

Wall Street trader and serial killer Ron Silver takes on the law in the form of Jamie Lee Curtis in *Blue Steel* (1990).

Cowriter Eric Red was no stranger to *Blue Steel*'s bizarre twist of having the serial killer manipulate the object of his deranged "affections" into a sexually underscored duel to the death. He'd used the same formula before in his script for *The Hitcher* (1986), directed by Robert Harmon. Rutger Hauer plays the serial-killer title character, and C. Thomas Howell plays the innocent lad who makes the mistake of giving the hitchhiking fiend a ride. Thereafter, the maniac won't leave his poor benefactor alone. Hauer even pins his crimes on Howell so that the guy can't turn to the police. In Hitchcock fashion, Howell becomes a hunted man on two fronts. On the run

Prince of the city? No, *Maniac Cop* (1988).

from the police *and* Hauer, he seeks help at a truck-stop diner from a pretty blond waitress (Jennifer Jason Leigh), but Hauer arrives on the scene and kills the poor girl by tying her to a pair of trucks so that she's split in two when the trucks drive off. Howell realizes that the only way to clear himself and be free of this nightmare is to take the murderous psycho on head-to-head—the same situation Jamie Lee Curtis finds herself in in *Blue Steel*. So he does what she does, and the film explodes into a lengthy, ridiculous, but admittedly exciting cross-country (rather than cross-town) chase full of screeching tires, buckets of blood, and broken glass until the twisted Hauer finally gets what he's perversely sought from the beginning—his death at Howell's hands.

Screenwriter Richard Price introduced a strong psychosexual element to *Sea of Love* (1989) as well.

The twist in this film is that the victims are all male, their bodies found nude in bed with a gunshot wound in their heads. Suspicion for the series of murders falls on a female (Ellen Barkin). As divorced, lonely, and disheveled cop Al Pacino pursues his investigation, he finds himself attracted to the woman yet obviously fearful of her at the same time. But eventually he throws caution to the wind and falls in love (and into bed) with her, even though he knows he could be her next victim. As it turns out, Barkin isn't the serial killer at all. The real murderer is her ex-husband, who, out of jealousy and revenge, has been killing each of the men she's slept with since their divorce. When Barkin discovers that Pacino had gotten close to her because she was his chief suspect, she's furious and understandably hurt and breaks off their relationship. But the love-starved, droopy-eyed, and

225

Michael Rooker plays the title character in John McNaughton's disturbing *Henry: Portrait of a Serial Killer* (1990).

Serial killer Francis Dollarhyde (Tom Noonan) prepares to claim his next victim. From *Manhunter* (1986), based on the book *Red Dragon* by Thomas Harris.

The aftermath of Dollarhyde's handiwork in *Manhunter*.

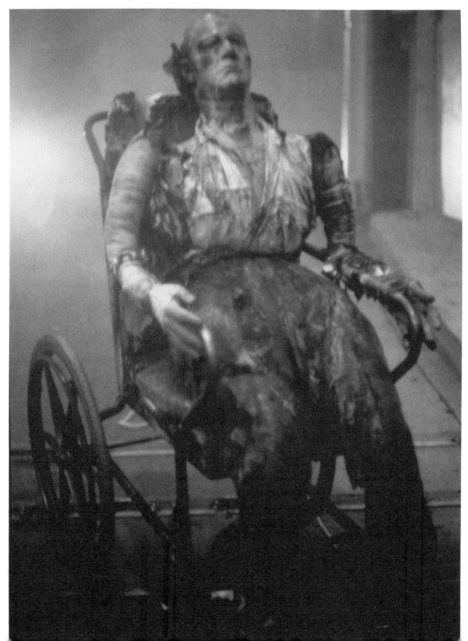

wholly pathetic-looking cop beseeches her to come back to him, and she finally gives in. Although *Sea of Love* is not without its virtues—strong characters, some genuinely scary moments—it might have been stronger and more unsettling if Barkin had actually turned out to be the killer and had the film ended the same way.

First-time writer-director John McNaughton burst onto the psychofilm scene during the late eighties with the controversial *Henry: Portrait of a Serial Killer,* one of the most potent films of its type ever made. The film was made in 1986 but not released until 1989. Slapped with an X rating by the Motion Picture Association of America, it got few playdates (most theater owners tend not to book X-rated films because many newspapers refuse to carry advertising for them). But reviews and audience word of mouth were uniformly positive enough that the film turned into a minor cause célèbre and cult hit.

Loosely based on the career of real-life serial killer Henry Lee Lucas, America's self-proclaimed body-count king, McNaughton's film isn't so much a portrait of a serial killer as a sketch of one. Like Michael Powell's *Peeping Tom,* which it resembles in its austerity and low-key style, the film casts an unflinching eye on the day-to-day behavior of its demented title character rather than wallowing in a lot of gory special effects. Unlike Powell's film, however, it doesn't try to fathom that character's behavior (McNaughton says it's unfathomable anyway) by getting inside the killer's head (would we want to even if we could?). In contrast to most other films about serial killers, McNaughton even keeps the murders themselves off-screen—at least for the bulk of the film he does. Instead, he shows us their grisly aftermath in series of slow tracking shots and overdubs the *sound* of the murders onto them. The result is like looking at a series of grotesque crime-scene photos and listening to audiotapes of what happened (many serial killers make such tapes as "mementos") and is far more powerful and disturbing than seeing a lot of stage blood fly around and skillfully contrived special effects—illusions to which audiences these days have become somewhat inured. This may be the reason why the MPAA gave the film an X (or, now, NC-17) rating rather than the R consistently bestowed upon the more exploitative type of serial-killer movie exemplified by the *Halloween, Friday the 13th,* and *Elm Street* series. McNaughton puts the sting back into such sequences by returning a disturbing sense of reality to them. When the director finally does show Henry (Michael Rooker) and his sleazeball accomplice (Tom Towles) dispatch some victims (an event the pair captures with a video camera, which tape Towles later plays over and over to Rooker's ever-increasing annoyance and disgust), he is equally

Anthony Hopkins as Dr. Hannibal "The Cannibal" Lecter in *The Silence of the Lambs* (1991).

minimalist in his use of special effects (which were beyond his low budget anyway), and the impact is equally strong. In fact, the scene is almost unbearable to watch.

The sobering, documentarylike realism of *Henry* struck a nerve with filmgoers, but the movie simply wasn't seen by enough of them to become truly influential (at least not yet) and widely imitated. Nor was its lowbrow and all-too-real title character (played with a frightening, low-key, dead-eyed intensity by Michael Rooker) the kind of bogeyman likely to spawn a sequel or spark a successful series in the manner of *Halloween*'s Michael Myers, *Friday the 13th*'s Jason, and *Nightmare on Elm Street*'s Freddy Krueger.

227

Lecter (Anthony Hopkins) wiles away the hours in his cell drawing—and planning his escape in *The Silence of the Lambs*.

Director Jonathan Demme with Anthony Hopkins on the set of *The Silence of the Lambs*.

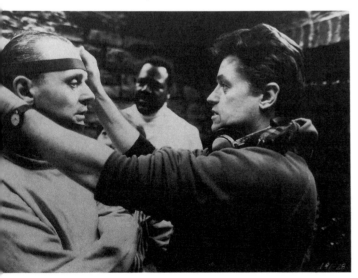

Jonathan Demme's *The Silence of the Lambs* (1991), on the other hand, accomplished both goals. A huge critical and commercial hit featuring a brilliant, charismatic, and scary-as-hell serial-killer main character, Hannibal "the Cannibal" Lecter (Anthony Hopkins), *Silence* has already spawned a number of imitations (mostly on television) and a sequel is surely to come once novelist Thomas Harris gets around to completing his next installment in the Lecter saga.

Silence itself is a sequel to the 1986 film *Manhunter*, although the latter was made by different people and featured a different actor (Brian Cox) in the Lecter role. Based on the best-seller *Red Dragon* in which author Harris first introduced the Lecter character, *Manhunter* flopped at the box office, and it took Demme's *Silence* and Hopkins's performance in it as Lecter to rescue the earlier film and the Lecter character from cinematic oblivion. Due to the latter movie's success, *Manhunter* has since found an audience on video and television (where NBC retitled it *Red Dragon: The Curse of Hannibal Lecter* for a much ballyhooed, post-*Silence* network premiere and cut it as well), and it has now become chic among many critics who originally ignored the film to praise it over *Silence*. In fact, *Manhunter* is not the better film. But much in it is very good indeed—notably Cox's performance as Lecter (who is renamed Lektor in the film) and especially Tom Noonan's genuinely frightening turn as the disfigured serial killer Francis Dollarhyde (aka "The Tooth Fairy" and "Red Dragon"), whom FBI chief Jack Crawford (Dennis Farina) and agent Will Graham (William Petersen) use the wily Lecter to hunt down. (Harris's two Lecter novels and the films made from them essentially tell the same story. In *Silence*, FBI chief Crawford [Scott Glenn] and agent Clarice Starling [Jodie Foster] use Lecter to help out on another case—the search for a serial killer dubbed Buffalo Bill [Ted Levine] who skins his victims. In both films, the wily Lecter allows himself to be used as a sort of intellectual game and to find a way to break out of jail—which he succeeds in doing at the end of *Silence*.)

The major weakness of *Manhunter* is the intrusive glitz that *Miami Vice* creator Michael Mann brings to his direction of the film. Befitting his nightmarish subject matter (which, again, is not dissimilar from *Manhunter*'s), Jonathan Demme's direction of *Silence* is darker and more subdued. And the resulting impact of the film on an audience is twice as strong. This is especially true of the several eerie confrontation scenes between the FBI-agent protagonist and the diabolically manipulative Lecter (minimized in *Manhunter* but maximized in *Silence*), which linger in the memory as the most tension-filled and chilling sequences in *The Silence of the Lambs*.

APPENDIX

A PSYCHOFILMOGRAPHY

What follows is a checklist of hundreds of psycho-films dating back to the earliest years of the cinema. The films of many countries are represented. Still, I make no pretense that this list is a definitive one.

Films that I have deemed notable because of their historic contribution to the development of psycho-film, or because they offer something extra in the way of psychological interest or aesthetic merit, I have denoted with an asterisk (*). The name that follows each title is that of the director. Titles are listed alphabetically by year.

1915

Trilby (Maurice Tourneur)

1919

Cabinet of Dr. Caligari, The (Robert Wiene)

1920

Der Januskopf (F. W. Murnau)
Dr. Jekyll and Mr. Hyde (John S. Robertson)

1922

Dr. Mabuse der Spieler (Fritz Lang)
Inferno (Fritz Lang)

1923

Trilby (James Young)

1924

Waxworks (Paul Leni)

1926

Lodger, The (Alfred Hitchcock)
Secrets of a Soul (G. W. Pabst)

1929

Pandora's Box (G. W. Pabst)

1931

M (Fritz Lang)
Svengali (Archie Mayo)

1932

Dr. Jekyll and Mr. Hyde (Rouben Mamoulian)
Mask of Fu Manchu, The (Charles Brabin)
Most Dangerous Game, The (Ernest B. Schoedsack/Irving Pichel)
Murders in the Rue Morgue (Robert Florey)
Mystery of the Wax Museum (Michael Curtiz)

Murders in the Zoo (1933).

Old Dark House, The (James Whale)
Testament of Dr. Mabuse, The (Fritz Lang)

1933

Island of Lost Souls (Erle C. Kenton)
Murders in the Zoo (Edward Sutherland)

1934

Maniac (Dwain Esper)

1935

Phantom Fiend, The (Maurice Elvey)
Raven, The (Lew Landers)

1936

Demon Barber of Fleet Street, The (George King)

1937

Love From a Stranger (Rowland V. Lee)
Night Must Fall (Richard Thorpe)

1939

Blind Alley (Charles Vidor)

1940

Chamber of Horrors (Norman Lee)
Stranger on the Third Floor (Boris Ingster)

1941

Among the Living (Stuart Heisler)
Dr. Jekyll and Mr. Hyde (Vincent Fleming)
I Wake Up Screaming (H. Bruce Humberstone)
Ladies in Retirement (Charles Vidor)
Mad Doctor, The (Tim Whelan)
Sea Wolf, The (Michael Curtiz)

1942

Fingers at the Window (Charles Lederer)

1943

Ghost Ship, The (Mark Robson)
Shadow of a Doubt (Alfred Hitchcock)

Hangover Square (1945).

1944

Arsenic and Old Lace (Frank Capra)
*Bluebeard (Edgar G. Ulmer)
*Lodger, The (John Brahm)
Man of Evil (Anthony Asquith)

1945

*Body Snatcher, The (Robert Wise)
Brighton Strangler, The (Max Nosseck)
Game of Death, A (Robert Wise)
*Hangover Square (John Brahm)
*Leave Her to Heaven (John M. Stahl)
*Spellbound (Alfred Hitchcock)

1946

Bedlam (Mark Robson)
Curse of the Wraydons, The (Victor Gover)
Locket, The (John Brahm)
Mask of Dijon, The (Lew Landers)
*Spiral Staircase, The (Robert Siodmak)

1947

Born to Kill (Robert Wise)

Crossfire (Edward Dmytryk)
*Double Life, A (George Cukor)
*Kiss of Death (Henry Hathaway)
Love From a Stranger (Richard Whorf)
Mine Own Executioner (Anthony Kimmins)
*Red House, The (Delmer Daves)

1948

Dark Past, The (Rudolph Maté)
He Walked by Night (Alfred Werker/Anthony Mann)
*Rope (Alfred Hitchcock)
Secret Beyond the Door (Fritz Lang)
Snake Pit, The (Anatole Litvak)

1949

*White Heat (Raoul Walsh)

1950

House By The River (Fritz Lang)
Room to Let (Godfrey Grayson)
*Sunset Boulevard (Billy Wilder)

1951

M (Joseph Losey)

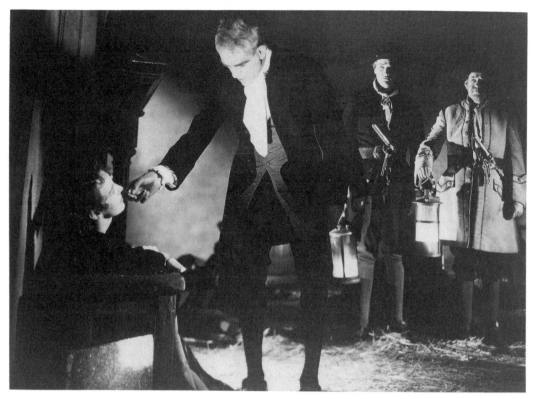

Bedlam (1946).

Son of Dr. Jekyll (Seymour Friedman)
*Strangers on a Train (Alfred Hitchcock)

1952

*Sniper, The (Edward Dmytryk)
Don't Bother to Knock (Roy Baker)

1953

Hitch-Hiker, The (Ida Lupino)
House of Wax (Andre de Toth)

1954

Mad Magician, The (John Brahm)
Man in the Attic (Hugo Fregonese)
Phantom of the Rue Morgue (Roy Del Ruth)
*Suddenly (Lewis Allen)

1955

*Night of the Hunter, The (Charles Laughton)
Svengali (Noel Langley)

1956

Alias John Preston (David MacDonald)

Bad Seed, The (Mervyn LeRoy)
Cry in the Night (Frank Tuttle)
*Forbidden Planet (Fred McLeod Wilcox)
Kiss Before Dying, A (Gerd Oswald)
Run for the Sun (Roy Boulting)
*While the City Sleeps (Fritz Lang)

1957

*Curse of Frankenstein (Terence Fisher)
Daughter of Dr. Jekyll (Edgar G. Ulmer)
*Lizzie (Hugo Haas)
Strange One, The (Jack Garfein)
*Three Faces of Eve, The (Nunnally Johnson)

1958

Cry Terror (Andrew L. Stone)
Edge of Fury (Irving Lerner/Robert Gurney, Jr.)
Fiend Who Walked the West, The (Gordon Douglas)
*Haunted Strangler, The (Robert Day)
Jack the Ripper (Robert Baker, Monty Berman)
Macabre (William Castle)
*Revenge of Frankenstein, The (Terence Fisher)
Screaming Mimi (Gerd Oswald)
Step Down to Terror (Harry Keller)
Wolf Larsen (Harmon Jones)

The Spiral Staircase (1946).

Shock Corridor (1963).

1959

Bloodlust (Ralph Brooks)
*Compulsion (Richard Fleischer)
Devil Strikes at Night, The (Robert Siodmak)
Horrors of the Black Museum (Arthur Crabtree)
Ugly Duckling, The (Lance Comfort)

1960

*Never Take Sweets From a Stranger (Cyril Frankel)
*Peeping Tom (Michael Powell)
*Psycho (Alfred Hitchcock)
1,000 Eyes of Dr. Mabuse, The (Fritz Lang)
*Two Faces of Dr. Jekyll, The (Terence Fisher)

1961

Anatomy of a Psycho (Brooke L. Peters)
Bloodlust (Ralph Brooke)
*Homicidal (William Castle)
Invisible Dr. Mabuse, The (Harald Reinl)
*Mark, The (Guy Green)
Return of Dr. Mabuse, The (Harald Reinl)
Stop Me Before I Kill! (Val Guest)
*Taste of Fear (Seth Holt)

1962

Cabinet of Caligari (Roger Kay)
Cape Fear (J. Lee Thompson)
Couch, The (Owen Crump)
Evil Eye, The (Mario Bava)
Experiment in Terror (Blake Edwards)
*Freud (John Huston)
Maniac (Michael Carreras)
*Manchurian Candidate, The (John Frankenheimer)
*Pressure Point (Hubert Cornfield)
Terrified (Lew Landers)
What Ever Happened to Baby Jane? (Robert Aldrich)

1963

Black Zoo (Robert Gordon)
Bluebeard (Claude Chabrol)
Dementia 13 (Francis Ford Coppola)
Diary of a Madman (Reginald LeBorg)
Dr. No (Terence Young)
Doll, The (Arne Mattson)
Fool Killer, The (Servando Gonzalez)
Nightmare (Freddie Francis)
Nutty Professor, The (Jerry Lewis)

Bunny Lake Is Missing (1965).

Old Dark House, The (William Castle)
Paranoiac (Freddie Francis)
Pyro (Julio Coll)
Sadist, The (James Landis)
Shock Corridor (Samuel Fuller)

1964

Blood and Black Lace (Mario Bava)
Curse of the Living Corpse (Del Tenney)
Dr. Strangelove (Stanley Kubrick)
Evil of Frankenstein, The (Freddie Francis)
Hysteria (Freddie Francis)
Lillith (Robert Rossen)
Nightmare in Chicago (Robert Altman)
Night Must Fall (Karel Reisz)
Night Walker, The (William Castle)
Secret of Dr. Mabuse, The (Hugo Fregonese)
Shock Treatment (Denis Sanders)
Strait-Jacket (William Castle)
Strangler, The (Burt Topper)

1965

Bunny Lake Is Missing (Otto Preminger)
Collector, The (William Wyler)
Die! Die! My Darling! (Silvio Narizzano)
Hush . . . Hush, Sweet Charlotte (Robert Aldrich)
I Saw What You Did (William Castle)
Life Upside Down (Alain Jessua)

My Blood Runs Cold (William Conrad)
Nanny, The (Seth Holt)
Repulsion (Roman Polanski)
Who Killed Teddy Bear? (Joseph Cates)

1966

Chamber of Horrors (Hy Averback)
Color Me Blood Red (Herschell Gordon Lewis)
Frankenstein Created Woman (Terence Fisher)
Murder Clinic, The (Elio Scardamaglia)
Psychopath, The (Freddie Francis)
Study in Terror, A (James Hill)

1967

Berserk (Jim O'Connolly)
Bonnie and Clyde (Arthur Penn)
In Cold Blood (Richard Brooks)
Night of the Generals (Anatole Litvak)
Wait Until Dark (Terence Young)

1968

Boston Strangler, The (Richard Fleischer)
Gruesome Twosome (Herschell Gordon Lewis)
No Way to Treat a Lady (Jack Smight)
Pretty Poison (Noel Black)
Targets (Peter Bogdanovich)
Twisted Nerve (Roy Boulting)

The Psychopath (1966).

Wait Until Dark (1967).

No Way to Treat a Lady (1968).

1969

Bird With the Crystal Plumage (Dario Argento)
Crescendo (Alan Gibson)
Cycle Savages, The (Bill Brame)
Daddy's Gone A-Hunting (Mark Robson)
Die Screaming Maryanne (Pete Walker)
*Frankenstein Must Be Destroyed (Terence Fisher)
Ghastly Ones, The (Andy Milligan)
House That Screamed, The (Narciso Ibañez Serrador)
Ice House, The (Stuart E. McGowan)
Mad Room, The (Bernard Girard)
That Cold Day in the Park (Robert Altman)

1970

And Soon the Darkness (Robert Fuest)
Bloodthirsty Butchers (Andy Milligan)
Countess Dracula (Peter Sasdy)
Hatchet for a Honeymoon (Mario Bava)
How Awful About Allan (Curtis Harrington)
*Le Boucher (Claude Chabrol)
Multiple Maniacs (John Waters)
Night Visitor, The (Laslo Benedek)
Playgirl Killer (Erick Santamaran)
Psycho Lover, The (Robert Vincent O'Neil)

The Mad Room (1969).

1971

Abominable Dr. Phibes, The (Robert Fuest)
Beast in the Cellar (James Kelly)
Blood and Lace (Philip Gilbert)
Carnival of Blood (Leonard Kirtman)
Cat o' Nine Tails (Dario Argento)
Crucible of Terror (Ted Hooker)
*Deep End (Jerzy Skolimowski)
**Demons of the Mind* (Peter Sykes)
*Dirty Harry (Don Siegel)
**Dr. Jekyll and Sister Hyde* (Roy Ward Baker)
Fright (Peter Collinson)
**Hands of the Ripper* (Peter Sasdy)
**I, Monster* (Stephen Weeks)
In the Devil's Garden (Sidney Hayers)
Jack el Destripador des Londres (José Luis Madrid)
Killer by Night (Bernard McEveety)
Klute (Alan J. Pakula)
Let's Scare Jessica to Death (John Hancock)
Murders in the Rue Morgue (Gordon Hessler)
**Night Digger, The* (Alastair Reid)

**Play Misty for Me* (Clint Eastwood)
Reflection of Fear (William A. Fraker)
Schizoid (Lucio Fulci)
*See No Evil (Richard Fleischer)
Someone Behind the Door (Nicolas Gessner)
**Ten Rillington Place* (Richard Fleischer)
Todd Killings, The (Barry Shear)
Twitch of the Death Nerve (Mario Bava)
**What's the Matter With Helen?* (Curtis Harrington)
What the Peeper Saw (James Kelly)

1972

Asylum (Roy Ward Baker)
Bluebeard (Edward Dmytryk)
Dear, Dead Delilah (John Farris)
Fear in the Night (Jimmy Sangster)
Female Butcher, The (Jorge Grau)
Flesh and Blood Show, The (Pete Walker)
Four Flies on Grey Velvet (Dario Argento)
*Frenzy (Alfred Hitchcock)
I Dismember Mama (Paul Leder)

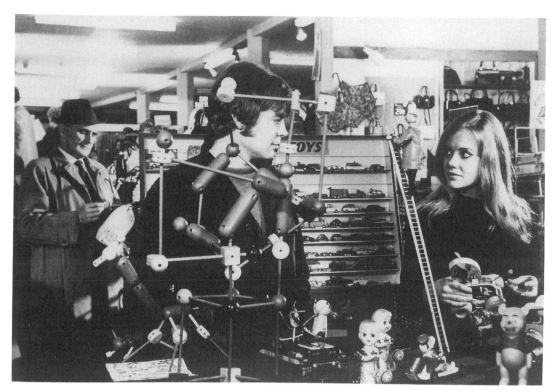

Twisted Nerve (1969).

Images (Robert Altman)
Mad Bomber, The (Bert I. Gordon)
Mad Butcher, The (John Zuri)
Man With Two Heads, The (Andy Milligan)
Other, The (Robert Mulligan)
**Ruling Class, The* (Peter Medak)
Silent Night, Bloody Night (Theodore Gershuny)
Straight on Till Morning (Peter Collinson)
To Kill a Clown (George Bloomfield)
When Michael Calls (Philip Leacock)
Who Slew Auntie Roo? (Curtis Harrington)

1973

And Millions Will Die (Leslie Martinson)
Baby, The (Ted Post)
**Badlands* (Terrence Malick)
Blade (Ernest Pintoff)
Don't Look in the Basement (S. F. Brownrigg)
**Frankenstein and the Monster From Hell* (Terence Fisher)
House of Psychotic Women (Carlòs Aured)
Isn't It Shocking? (John Badham)
Knife for the Ladies, A (Larry Spangler)
Legacy of Blood (Andy Milligan)
Run Stranger Run aka *Happy Mother's Day—Love, George*
    (Darren McGavin)
Scream, Pretty Peggy (Gordon Hessler)
**Sisters* (Brian De Palma)

So Sad About Gloria (Harry Thomason)
Terror Circus (Gerald Cormier)
**Theatre of Blood* (Douglas Hickox)
Three on a Meathook (William Girdler)
Wicked Wicked (Richard L. Bare)

1974

Apartment on the 13th Floor (Eloy De La Iglesia)
Bad Ronald (Buzz Kulik)
Deadly Strangers (Sidney Hayers)
**Deranged* (Alan Ormsby/Jeff Gillen)
Devil Times Five (Sean McGregor)
Frightmare (Pete Walker)
Groove Room, The (Vernon P. Becker)
House of Whipcord (Pete Walker)
House That Vanished, The (Joseph Larraz)
Impulse (William Grefe)
Inn of the Damned (Terry Bourke)
Madhouse (Jim Clark)
Man With the Golden Gun, The (Guy Hamilton)
Persecution (Don Chaffey)
Phantom of the Paradise (Brian De Palma)
Seizure (Oliver Stone)
Terminal Man, The (Mike Hodges)
**Texas Chain Saw Massacre, The* (Tobe Hooper)
Torso (Sergio Martino)
Twisted Brain (Larry N. Stouffer)

See No Evil (1971).

Asylum (1972).

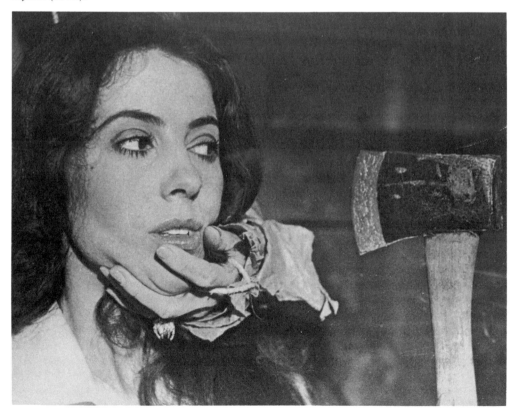

240

Fright (1971).

1975

Black Christmas (Bob Clark)
Black the Ripper (Frank R. Saletri)
Confessional, The (Pete Walker)
*Deadly Tower, The (Jerry Jameson)
Deep Red (Dario Argento)
Dr. Black and Mr. Hyde (William Crain)
*Legend of Lizzie Borden, The (Paul Wendkos)
Love Butcher, The (Mikel Angel, Don Jones)
Mahogany (Berry Gordy)
Night Caller (Henri Verneuil)
Spiral Staircase, The (Peter Collinson)
Wolf Larsen (Giuseppe Vari)

1976

Blue Sunshine (Jeff Lieberman)
Drive-In Massacre (Stuart Segall)
Eaten Alive (Tobe Hooper)
*Helter Skelter (Tom Gries)
Jack the Ripper (Jess Franco)
*Killer Inside Me, The (Burt Kennedy)
Lindbergh Kidnapping Case, The (Buzz Kulik)
*Martin (George A. Romero)
Schizo (Pete Walker)
*Sybil (Daniel Petrie)

*Taxi Driver (Martin Scorsese)
*Tenant, The (Roman Polanski)

1977

Centerfold Girls (John Peyser)
Comeback, The (Pete Walker)
Death Game (Peter S. Traynor)
*Equus (Sidney Lumet)
Haunts (Herb Reed)
*Hills Have Eyes, The (Wes Craven)
I Never Promised You a Rose Garden (Anthony Page)
Island of Dr. Moreau, The (Don Taylor)
Meatcleaver Massacre (Evan Lee)
Murder at the World Series (Andrew V. McLaglen)
New House on the Left (Evans Isle)
Shock aka *Beyond the Door II* (Mario Bava)
Strange Possession of Mrs. Oliver, The (Gordon Hessler)
Town That Dreaded Sundown, The (Charles B. Pierce)
*Twilight's Last Gleaming (Robert Aldrich)

1978

Alice Sweet Alice (Alfred Sole)
Eyes of Laura Mars, The (Irvin Kershner)
*Halloween (John Carpenter)
Magic (Richard Attenborough)

Magic (1978).

Rituals (Peter Carter)
Savage Weekend (David Paulsen)
Scalpel (John Grissmer)
*Someone's Watching Me! (John Carpenter)
Toolbox Murders, The (Dennis Donnelly)

1979

*Brood, The (David Cronenberg)
Driller Killer (Abel Ferrara)
*Murder by Decree (Bob Clark)
Natural Enemies (Jeff Kanew)
*Plumber, The (Peter Weir)
She's Dressed to Kill (Gus Trikonis)
*Time After Time (Nicholas Meyer)
Tourist Trap (David Schmoeller)
When a Stranger Calls (Fred Walton)

1980

*Altered States (Ken Russell)
Boogeyman, The (Ulli Lommel)
City in Fear (Allan Smithee)
Don't Answer the Phone (Robert Hammer)
Don't Go in the House (Joseph Ellison)
Dressed to Kill (Brian DePalma)
Dr. Heckyl and Mr. Hype (Charles B. Griffith)
Fade to Black (Vernon Zimmerman)

Fifth Floor, The (Howard Avedis)
First Deadly Sin, The (Brian G. Hutton)
*Friday the 13th (Sean S. Cunningham)
Guyana, Cult of the Damned (Rene Cardona, Jr.)
*Guyana Tragedy: The Story of Jim Jones (William A. Graham)
He Knows You're Alone (Armand Mastroianni)
Hunter, The (Buzz Kulik)
Keep My Grave Open (S. F. Brownrigg)
Maniac (William Lustig)
Motel Hell (Kevin Connor)
*Ms. 45 (Abel Ferrara)
Murder by Phone (Michael Anderson)
Phobia (John Huston)
Prom Night (Paul Lynch)
Schizoid (David Paulsen)
*Shining, The (Stanley Kubrick)
Silent Scream (Denny Harris)
Terror Train (Roger Spottiswoode)
Twinkle Twinkle Killer Kane aka The Ninth Configuration (William Peter Blatty)

1981

Amin—The Rise and Fall (Sharad Patel)
Blow Out (Brian DePalma)
Death of a Centerfold: the Dorothy Stratten Story (Gabrielle Beaumont)

The First Deadly Sin (1980).

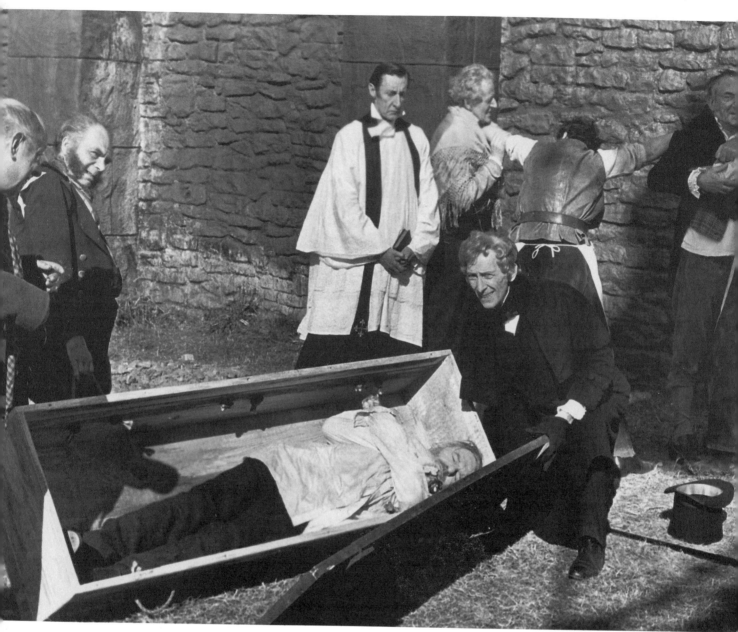

Frankenstein and the Monster From Hell (1973).

Eyes of a Stranger (Ken Wiederhorn)
Fan, The (Edward Bianchi)
Final Exam (Jimmy Huston)
Friday the 13th—Part 2 (Steve Miner)
Graduation Day (Herb Freed)
Halloween II (Rick Rosenthal)
Hand, The (Oliver Stone)
Happy Birthday to Me (J. Lee Thompson)
Hell Night (Tom DeSimone)
Midnight (John Russo)
*Mother's Day (Charles Kaufman)
My Bloody Valentine (George Mihalka)

New Year's Evil (Emmett Alston)
Nightmare (Romano Scavolini)
Night School (Ken Hughes)
Night Warning (William Asher)
Prowler, The (Joseph Zito)
Road Games (Richard Franklin)
Tattoo (Bob Brooks)

1982

Alone in the Dark (Jack Sholder)
Brainwaves (Ulli Lommel)

Dr. Heckyl and Mr. Hype (1980).

Burning, The (Tony Maylam)
Death Valley (Dick Richards)
Friday the 13th—Part 3 (Steve Miner)
Funeral Home (William Fruet)
Hospital Massacre (Boaz Davidson)
Humongous (Paul Lynch)
Jekyll and Hyde . . . Together Again (Jerry Belson)
Madman (Joe Gianonne)
Seduction, The (David Schmoeller)
Slumber Party Massacre (Amy Jones)
Still of the Night (Robert Benton)
Stranger Is Watching, A (Sean S. Cunningham)
Visiting Hours (Jean Claude Lord)

1983

Boogeyman II (Ulli Lommel)
Curtains (Jonathan Stryker)
Deadly Force (Paul Aaron)
Deadly Lessons (William Wiard)
Halloween III: Season of the Witch (Tommy Lee Wallace)
House on Sorority Row, The (Mark Rosman)
Killer In the Family, A (Richard T. Heffron)
King of Comedy, The (Martin Scorsese)
Pieces (Juan Piquer Simon)
Psycho II (Richard Franklin)
Savage Attraction (Frank Shields)

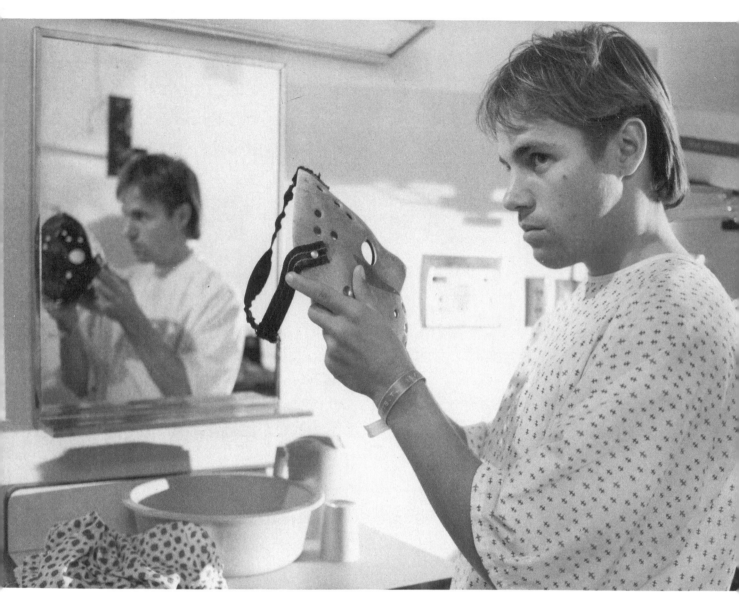

Friday the 13th Part V: A New Beginning (1985).

Sleepaway Camp (Robert Hitzik)
*Star 80 (Bob Fosse)
Sudden Impact (Clint Eastwood)
Svengali (Anthony Harvey)

1984

Angel (Robert Vincent O'Neil)
Blind Date (Nico Mastorakis)
*Fatal Vision (David Greene)
Friday the 13th—The Final Chapter (Joseph Zito)
*Nightmare on Elm Street, A (Wes Craven)

Silent Night, Deadly Night (Charles E. Sellier, Jr.)
Tightrope (Richard Tuggle)

1985

*Atlanta Child Murders, The (John Erman)
*Bad Seed, The (Paul Wendkos)
*Death in California, A (Delbert Mann)
Fear City (Abel Ferrara)
Friday the 13th—A New Beginning (Danny Steinmann)
Mean Season, The (Phillip Borsos)

246

Friday the 13th Part VI: Jason Lives (1986).

1986

Angel of Death (Jess Franco)
April Fool's Day (Fred Walton)
Backwoods (Dean Crow)
Bad Blood (Mike Newell)
Deliberate Stranger, The (Marvin J. Chomsky)
Friday the 13th Part VI: Jason Lives (Tom McLoughlin)
Hitcher, The (Robert Harmon)
Hunter's Blood (Robert C. Hughes)
Killer Party (William Fruet)
Lunch Meat (Kirk Alex)

*Manhunter (Michael Mann)
*Psycho III (Anthony Perkins)
Psychos in Love (Gorman Bechard)
Sorority House Massacre (Carol Frank)
*Texas Chainsaw Massacre Part 2, The (Tobe Hooper)

1987

Anguish (Bigas Luna)
At Mother's Request (Michael Tuchner)
Bad Taste (Peter Jackson)

Night Breed (1990).

Bates Motel (Richard Rothstein)
Blood Diner (Jackie Kong)
Blood Frenzy (Hal Freeman)
Carpenter, The (David Wellington)
*Echoes in the Darkness (Glenn Jordan)
Epitaph (Joseph Merhi)
*Fatal Attraction (Adrian Lyne)
Fatal Pulse (Anthony J. Christopher)
555 (Wally Koz)
Goodnight God Bless (John Eyres)
Grotesque (Joe Tornatore)
Hide and Go Shriek (Skip Skoolnik)
Last Slumber Party, The (Stephen Tyler)
Majorettes, The (Bill Hinzman)
Nightmare on Elm Street Part 3: The Dream Warriors (Chuck Russell)
Night Stalker, The (Max Kleven)
Open House (Jag Mundhra)
Rest in Pieces (Joseph Braunstein)
Return to Horror High (Bill Froehlich)
Shallow Grave (Richard Styles)
Silent Night, Deadly Night Part II (Lee Harry)
Sister, Sister (Bill Condon)

Slaughter High (George Dugdale, Mark Ezra, Peter Litten)
Slaughterhouse (Rick Roessler)
Slipping Into Darkness (Richard Cassidy)
Slumber Party Massacre II (Deborah Brock)
Stage Fright (Michele Soavi)
*Stepfather, The (Joseph Ruben)
Summer Camp Nightmare (Bert L. Dragin)
Swinger's Massacre (Ron Garcia)

1988

American Gothic (John Hough)
Apartment Zero (Martin Donovan)
Bad Dreams (Andrew Fleming)
Child's Play (Tom Holland)
Clownhouse (Victor Salva)
*Dead Ringers (David Cronenberg)
Edge of the Axe (Joseph Braunstein)
Fear (Robert A. Ferreti)
Freeway (Francis Delia)
Friday the 13th Part VII: The New Blood (John Buechler)
Halloween 4: The Return of Michael Myers (Dwight H. Little)
Hello Mary Lou: Prom Night II (Bruce Pittman)
Helter Skelter Murders, The (Frank Howard)

248

Jacob's Ladder (1990).

I Saw What You Did (Fred Walton)
Jack's Back (Rowdy Herrington)
Jack the Ripper (David Wickes)
Luther the Geek (Carlton J. Albright)
Maniac Cop (William Lustig)
Memorial Valley Massacre (Robert C. Hughes)
Nightmare on Elm Street Part 4: The Dream Master (Renny Harlin)
Prom Night III: Last Kiss (Ron Oliver, Peter Simpson)
Sleepaway Camp II (Michael A. Simpson)
Sleepaway Camp III (Michael A. Simpson)

1989

Amsterdamned (Dick Maas)
Case of the Hillside Stranglers, The (Steven Gethers)
*Dead Calm (Philip Noyce)
Dead Pit, The (Brett Leonard)
Edge of Sanity (Gerard Kikoine)
Friday the 13th Part VIII: Jason Takes Manhattan (Rob Hedden)
Halloween 5: The Revenge of Michael Myers (Dominique Othenin-Girard)
*Henry: Portrait of a Serial Killer (John McNaughton)

Horror Show, The (James Isaac)
*I, Madman (Tibor Takacs)
Internal Affairs (Mike Figgis)
Mind Killer (Michael Krueger)
Murder Weapon (Ellen Cabot)
Nightmare on Elm Street Part 5: The Dream Child (Stephen Hopkins)
Opera (Dario Argento)
Phantom of the Opera (Dwight H. Little)
Posed for Murder (Brian Thomas Jones)
Psycho Cop (Wallace Potts)
Sea of Love (Harold Becker)
Season of Fear (Doug Campbell)
Shocker (Wes Craven)
Silent Night, Deadly Night III—Better Watch Out (Monte Hellman)
*Small Sacrifices (David Greene)
Stepfather 2: Make Room for Daddy (Jeff Burr)
Weirdo, The (Andy Milligan)
Woodchipper Massacre (Jon McBride)

1990

Blades (Thomas R. Rondinella)
Blind Faith (Paul Wendkos)

Child's Play 2 (1990).

Blue Steel (Kathryn Bigelow)
Child's Play 2 (John Lafia)
Faceless (Jess Franco)
First Power, The (Robert Resnikoff)
Heart of Midnight (Matthew Chapman)
Jekyll and Hyde (David Wickes)
Killing Spree (Tim Ritter)
Leatherface: Texas Chainsaw Massacre 3 (Jeff Burr)
*Misery (Rob Reiner)
Night Breed (Clive Barker)
Night Visitor (Rupert Hitzig)
Offerings (Christopher Reynolds)
Pacific Heights (John Schlesinger)
Psycho IV: The Beginning (Mick Garris)
Silent Night, Deadly Night 4: Initiation (Brian Yuzna)
Slashdance (James Shyman)
Street Asylum (Gregory Brown)
Whispers (Donald Jackson)

1991

Art of Dying, The (Wings Hauser)
*Cape Fear (Martin Scorsese)
Deceived (Damian Harris)

Freddy's Dead (Rachel Talalay)
*In a Child's Name (Tom McLoughlin)
Intimate Stranger (Allan Holzman)
Jacob's Ladder (Adrian Lyne)
Kiss Before Dying, A (James Dearden)
Maniac Cop 2 (William Lustig)
Night of the Hunter (David Greene)
People Under the Stairs, The (Wes Craven)
*Pit and the Pendulum, The (Stuart Gordon)
Popcorn (Mark Herrier)
*Silence of the Lambs, The (Jonathan Demme)
Sitter, The (Edward Pei)
Sleeping With the Enemy (Joseph Ruben)
What Ever Happened to Baby Jane? (David Greene)

1992

Basic Instinct (Paul Verhoeven)
Hand That Rocks the Cradle, The (Curtis Hanson)
Prey of the Cameleon (Fleming B. Fuller)
Rampage (William Friedkin)
Raising Cain (Brian De Palma)
Single White Female (Barbet Schroeder)

Halloween (1978)

BIBLIOGRAPHY

Periodicals

Anonymous. "Robert Aldrich." *American Film* 4, no. 2: 51–62.

Anonymous. "Richard Brooks." *American Film* 3, no. 1: 33–48.

Anonymous. "Rouben Mamoulian." *American Film* 8, no. 4: 26–27, 67–69.

Burns, James H. "The Horror of Sangster." *Fangoria* 2, no. 10: 37–39.

———. "The Curse of Sangster." *Fangoria* 2, no. 11: 29–31.

Childs, Mike, and Alan Jones. "Bob Clark on 'Murder by Decree,' " *Cinefantastique* 8, nos. 2&3: 84.

Cook, G. Richardson. "Badlands." *Filmmaker's Newsletter* 7, no. 8: 30–32.

Dempsey, Michael. "Jack the Ripper in San Francisco." *American Film* 4, no. 6: 60–65.

Derry, Charles. "The Horror of Personality." *Cinefantastique* 3, no. 3: 14–27.

Everitt, David. "The Original Psycho Returns." *Fangoria* 3, no. 27: 12–15.

Irvin, Sam L. "Michael Carreras." *Bizarre* 1, no. 3: 56–58.

Kelley, Bill. "Peeping Tom." *Cinefantastique* 9, nos. 3&4: 80.

Knight, Chris. "The Amicus Empire." *Cinefantastique* 2, no. 4: 4–19.

Landis, Bill. "Curtis Harrington." *Fangoria* 3, no. 3: 51–53, 63.

Lawrence, Jodi. "Richard Fleischer." *Today's Filmmaker* 1, no. 2: 26–27, 67–69.

Lovell, Glenn. "De Palma Back in Form." *Cinefantastique* 9, nos. 3&4: 82.

Martin, Bob. "A Day for Terror." *Fangoria* 1, no. 6:14–16, 64.

———. "A Talk with John Carpenter." *Fangoria* 3, 14: 10–11, 40–41.

———. "The Real Tobe Hooper." *Fangoria* 2, no. 12: 38–40.

McCarty, John. "Legend of Lizzie Borden." *Cinefantastique* 4, no. 2: 35.

McGee, Mark Thomas. "King of the Gimmicks." *Fangoria* 2, no. 12: 34–37.

McGinnis, Joe. "*Fatal Vision:* Living With the Green Beret Murderer," *TV Guide* 32, 1984.

Montague, Ivor. "Working with Hitchcock." *Sight and Sound* 49, no. 3: 189–193.

Parish, James Robert, and Michael R. Pitts. "Christopher Lee." *Cinefantastique* 3, no. 1: 4–23.

Patterson, Patricia, and Manny Farber. "Taxi Driver." *Film Comment* 12, no. 3: 26–30.

Rickey, Carrie. "Marty." *American Film* 8, no. 2; 66–72.

Ringel, Harry. "Terence Fisher." *Cinefantastique* 4, no. 3: 5–29.

Rosen, Marjorie. "Martin Scorsese." *Film Comment* 2, no. 2: 42–46.

Seligson, Tom. "Wes Craven." *Twilight Zone* 1, no. 2: 45–50.

Thomas, Bill. "Mamoulian." *Cinefantastique* 1, no. 3: 36–38.

Books

Beck, Calvin Thomas. *Heroes of the Horrors*. New York: Collier, 1975.

Bloch, Robert. *Psycho*. Connecticut: Crest Books, 1959.

Bogdanovich, Peter. *Fritz Lang in America*. England: Studio Vista Ltd., 1967.

Brosnan, John. *The Horror People*. New York: St. Martin's Press, 1976.

Bugliosi, Vincent, and Curt Gentry. *Helter Skelter*. New York: W. W. Norton & Company, 1974.

Clarens, Carlos. *An Illustrated History of the Horror Film*. New York: G. P. Putnams, 1967.

Eames, John Douglas. *The MGM Story*. New York: Crown, 1979.

Eisner, Lotte H. *The Haunted Screen*. Berkeley: University of California Press, 1969.

———. *Murnau*. Berkeley: University of California Press, 1973.

Everson, William K. *Classics of the Horror Film*. New Jersey: Citadel Press, 1974.

Frank, Gerold. *The Boston Strangler*. New York: Signet, 1967.

Hirschhorn, Clive. *The Warner Bros. Story*. New York: Crown, 1979.

———. *The Universal Story*. New York: Crown, 1983.

Jensen, Paul M. *The Cinema of Fritz Lang*. New York: A. S. Barnes, 1969.

Jewell, Richard B., and Vernon Harbin. *The RKO Story*. New York: Arlington House, 1982.

Kass, Judith M. *Robert Altman, American Innovator*. New York: Popular Library, 1978.

Knight, Stephen. *Jack the Ripper: The Final Solution*. New York: David McKay & Company, 1976.

Kracauer, Siegfried. *From Caligari to Hitler*. New Jersey: Princeton University Press, 1969.

Lanchester, Elsa. *Elsa Lanchester Herself*. New York: St. Martin's Press, 1983.

Leaming, Barbara. *Polanski*. New York: Simon & Schuster, 1981.

Lee, Walt. *Reference Guide to Fantastic Films*. California: Chelsea-Lee Books, 1972.

LeRoy, Mervyn. *Mervyn LeRoy: Take One*. New York: Hawthorn, 1974.

London, Jack. *The Sea Wolf*. New York: Bantam, 1976.

March, William. *The Bad Seed*. New York: Dell, 1975.

McCarthy, Todd, and Charles Flynn. *Kings of the Bs*. New York: E. P. Dutton, 1975.

McCarty, John. *Splatter Movies*. New York: St. Martin's Press, 1984.

McCarty, John, and Brian Kelleher. *Alfred Hitchcock Presents*. New York: St. Martin's Press, 1985.

Peary, Danny. *Cult Movies*. New York: Delta, 1981.

———. *Cult Movies 2*. New York: Delta, 1983.

Polanski, Roman. *Roman by Polanski*. New York: William Morrow & Co., 1984.

Pratley, Gerald. *The Cinema of John Frankenheimer*. New York: A. S. Barnes, 1969.

Quinlan, David. *An Illustrated Guide to Film Directors*. New Jersey: Barnes and Noble, 1983.

Sherman, Eric, and Martin Rubin. *The Director's Event*. New York: New American Library, 1969.

Siegel, Joel E. *Val Lewton, the Reality of Terror*. New York: Viking Press, 1973.

Spoto, Donald. *The Dark Side of Genius*. Boston: Little, Brown & Company, 1983.

Symons, Julian. *Mortal Consequences*. New York: Schocken, 1972.

Topor, Roland. *The Tenant*. New York: Bantam, 1976.

Vizzard, Jack. *See No Evil*. New York: Pocket, 1971.

Warren, Doug. *James Cagney*. London: Book Club Associates, 1983.

Weldon, Michael. *The Psychotronic Encyclopedia of Film*. New York: Ballantine, 1983.

Williams, Emlyn. *Beyond Belief*. New York: Avon, 1967.

Wilson, Colin. *Order of Assassins*. London: Panther, 1975.

ABOUT THE AUTHOR

A graduate of Boston University with a degree in broadcasting and film, John McCarty is a lifelong aficionado of films of horror, terror, and the supernatural. Over the years, he has contributed articles and reviews to magazines as diverse as *Mystery Scene*, *Crime Beat*, *TV Guide*, *Cinefantastique*, *Fangoria*, and *Video Times*. He is also the author of numerous books covering various aspects of the film and broadcast media, and one novel, the psychological horror-thriller *Deadly Resurrection*. He is married and lives in upstate New York.

ORDER NOW!
More Citadel Film Books

If you like this book, you'll love the other titles in the award-winning Citadel Film Series. From James Stewart to Moe Howard and The Three Stooges, Woody Allen to John Wayne, The Citadel Film Series is America's largest and oldest film book library.

With more than 150 titles--and more on the way!--Citadel Film Books make perfect gifts for a loved one, a friend, or best of all, yourself!

**A complete listing of the Citadel Film Series appears below.
If you know what books you want, why not order now!
It's easy! Just call 1-800-447-BOOK and have your MasterCard or Visa ready.**

STARS
Alan Ladd
Barbra Streisand: First Decade
Barbra Streisand: Second
  Decade
Bela Lugosi
Bette Davis
Boris Karloff
The Bowery Boys
Buster Keaton
Carole Lombard
Cary Grant
Charles Bronson
Charlie Chaplin
Clark Gable
Clint Eastwood
Curly
Dustin Hoffman
Edward G. Robinson
Elizabeth Taylor
Elvis Presley
Errol Flynn
Frank Sinatra
Gary Cooper
Gene Kelly
Gina Lollobrigida
Gloria Swanson
Gregory Peck
Greta Garbo
Henry Fonda
Humphrey Bogart
Ingrid Bergman
Jack Lemmon
Jack Nicholson
James Cagney
James Dean: Behind the Scene
Jane Fonda
Jeanette MacDonald & Nelson
  Eddy
Joan Crawford

John Wayne Films
John Wayne Reference Book
John Wayne Scrapbook
Judy Garland
Katharine Hepburn
Kirk Douglas
Laurel & Hardy
Lauren Bacall
Laurence Olivier
Mae West
Marilyn Monroe
Marlene Dietrich
Marlon Brando
Marx Brothers
Moe Howard & the Three
  Stooges
Norma Shearer
Olivia de Havilland
Orson Welles
Paul Newman
Peter Lorre
Rita Hayworth
Robert De Niro
Robert Redford
Sean Connery
Sexbomb: Jayne Mansfield
Shirley MacLaine
Shirley Temple
The Sinatra Scrapbook
Spencer Tracy
Steve McQueen
Three Stooges Scrapbook
Warren Beatty
W.C. Fields
William Holden
William Powell
A Wonderful Life: James Stewart
DIRECTORS
Alfred Hitchcock
Cecil B. DeMille

Federico Fellini
Frank Capra
John Ford
John Huston
Woody Allen
GENRE
Bad Guys
Black Hollywood
Black Hollywood: From 1970 to
  Today
Classics of the Gangster Film
Classics of the Horror Film
Divine Images: Jesus on Screen
Early Classics of Foreign Film
Great French Films
Great German Films
Great Romantic Films
Great Science Fiction Films
Harry Warren & the Hollywood
  Musical
Hispanic Hollywood: The Latins
  in Motion Pictures
The Hollywood Western
The Incredible World of 007
The Jewish Image in American
  Film
The Lavender Screen: The Gay
  and Lesbian Films
Martial Arts Movies
The Modern Horror Film
More Classics of the Horror Film
Movie Psychos & Madmen
Our Huckleberry Friend: Johnny
  Mercer
Second Feature: "B" Films
They Sang! They Danced! They
  Romanced!: Hollywood
  Musicals
Thrillers
The West That Never Was

Words and Shadows: Literature
  on the Screen
DECADE
Classics of the Silent Screen
Films of the Twenties
Films of the Thirties
More Films of the 30's
Films of the Forties
Films of the Fifties
Lost Films of the 50's
Films of the Sixties
Films of the Seventies
Films of the Eighties
SPECIAL INTEREST
America on the Rerun
Bugsy (Illustrated screenplay)
Comic Support
Dick Tracy
Favorite Families of TV
Film Flubs
Film Flubs: The Sequel
First Films
Forgotten Films to Remember
Hollywood Cheesecake
Hollywood's Hollywood
Howard Hughes in Hollywood
More Character People
The Nightmare Never Ends:
  Freddy Krueger & "A Night
  mare on Elm Street"
The "Northern Exposure" Boo
The "Quantum Leap" Book
Sex In the Movies
Sherlock Holmes
Son of Film Flubs
Those Glorious Glamour Yea
Who Is That?: Familiar Faces
  Forgotten Names
"You Ain't Heard Nothin' Yet

For a free full-color brochure describing the Citadel Film Series in depth, call 1-800-447-BOOK; or send yo
name and address to Citadel Film Books, Dept. 1392, 120 Enterprise Ave., Secaucus, NJ 07094.